S0-DLR-921

The ABC's of
Quattro Pro for Windows

The ABC's of Quattro® Pro for Windows™

ALAN SIMPSON

DOUGLAS J. WOLF

toExcel

San Jose New York Lincoln shanghai

The ABC's of Quattro Pro® for Windows™

All Rights Reserved. Copyright©1998 by
Alan Simpson and Douglas J. Wolf

No part of this book may be reproduced or transmitted in
any form or by any means, graphic, electronic or mechanical,
including photocopying, recording, taping, or by any information
storage or retrieval system, without the permission in
writing from the publisher.

SYBEX is a registered trademark of SYBEX Inc.
TRADEMARKS: SYBEX has attempted throughout this book to distinguish
proprietary trademarks from descriptive terms by following the capitalization
style used by the manufacturer.
SYBEX is not affiliated with any manufacturer.

For information address:
toExcel
165 West 95th Street, Suite B-N
New York, NY 10025
www.toExcel.com

Published by toExcel, a division of Kaleidoscope Software, Inc.
Marca registrada
toExcel
New York, NY

ISBN: 1-58348-015-3

Library of Congress Catalog Card Number: 98-88986

Printed in the United States of America

0 9 8 7 6 5 4 3 2 1

To Joseph Jay Wheeler, **Nec Pluribus Impar** *and* **Top Gun** *at Latham and Watkins of San Diego, and his family: wife Ann, children Amanda, Christopher, and Savannah*
D.J.W.

To Susan, Ashley, and Alec
A.C.S.

Table of Contents

Chapter 4

Chapter 5

Chapter 10

Chapter 11

Chapter 12

Chapter 13

CUSTOMIZING QUATTRO PRO FOR WINDOWS 291

Chapter 14

LINKING NOTEBOOKS 309

Chapter 15

USING FORMULAS AND FUNCTIONS 319

xii	

Appendix

INTRODUCTION

This book is about Quattro Pro for Windows, the electronic spreadsheet package from Borland International Inc. It is a sophisticated tool that pushes the edge of spreadsheet technology in the Windows environment. Quattro Pro for Windows' spreadsheet replaces the ledger book, pencil, and hand-held calculator as a means of analyzing and calculating data. With the help of built-in mathematical and statistical functions, you can develop budgets, annual reports, portfolio analyses, invoices, tax statements, etc., with ease.

Quattro Pro also features a startlingly powerful and flexible full-color graphing capability that gives you many quick, creative ways to present data visually, either on paper or on-screen, even *sequentially* on-screen, like a slide show.

This software is also a database, allowing you to store large volumes of information, sort them any way you wish and extract specific entries as the need arises—such as invoices that are past due or addresses in the 92112 zip-code area.

If you have used Quattro Pro in its DOS incarnations, you will find much that is familiar. The graph annotator is now seamlessly integrated in the graph module. The pull-down menus are very close to the DOS menus.

The new paradigms of Quattro Pro include aspects that are directly linked to the Windows environment.

- **Notebooks.** Every major spreadsheet program on the market has attempted to elegantly handle multiple spreadsheets that have linked values. Quattro Pro for Windows advances the idea of a notebook: a collection of 256 individual spreadsheet pages, all fully sized—256 columns by 8192 rows. The final page of the notebook is a graphs page, holding icons of each graph created in that notebook.

- **Windows.** The salient improvement is being able to use multiple files simultaneously. DOS is highly restricted in its ability to use memory over 640K. Windows is not restricted in its memory usage, allowing you to open multiple large notebooks and work with all of them concurrently.

- **Object inspectors.** Every portion of a spreadsheet is considered by Quattro Pro to be an "object." Each object has its own unique attributes. For example, data entered into a spreadsheet cell can be formatted in a multitude of ways. Clicking the mouse pointer on the cell and opening the Object Inspector makes it a snap to enlarge the typestyle, add coloring, or change the number of zeros after the decimal point—all in a single step!

- **Expanded use of SpeedBars.** Now the SpeedBar includes a programmable macro button and the ability to create an entire SpeedBar yourself.

- **More graph types.** Quattro Pro now has 5 graph categories: Two-dimensional, three-dimensional, rotated, combination and text. You can also create graphs that "float" above the spreadsheet page and are linked to data in the notebook.

- **The graph annotator**. Introduced in the DOS version, this is now seamlessly integrated into the notebook. After you create a graph, it can be enhanced in a multitude of ways.

WHO IS THIS BOOK FOR?

This book is written for people who are not familiar with computer terminology, other spreadsheets, or even computers in general. Quattro Pro for Windows is sophisticated, but not difficult to learn. For that reason, we have designed this book so that you can start using Quattro Pro *now*, without having to wade through a 700 page manual of details and technical information. Moreover, this book is written in scenario style, bringing in the diverse elements of the program as you would normally seek to use them. For example, we begin with the concept of spreadsheets, so that you have the idea behind the process, before we tell you how to enter a mortgage calculation formula.

WHAT THIS BOOK COVERS

Before you can start running Quattro Pro, you will have to install it on your computer. Because it runs in Windows, you must first have Windows 3.0 or greater running on your hardware. The Appendix to this book covers the short steps to installing Quattro Pro.

Once you have installed Quattro Pro, start at the beginning. The first four chapters offer a step-by-step approach, in plain English, that introduces you to Quattro Pro's capabilities quickly and easily. Notebooks that you create in one chapter will be modified and built upon in the next. Later chapters discuss ways to edit entries, manipulate data, and handle blocks of data elegantly and easily—as well as how to graph and print data and use them in a database.

STYLISTIC AND TYPOGRAPHICAL CONVENTIONS

One key you will use very often is the Enter key (also labeled "Return" on some keyboards. When you read "enter such-and-such," it means to type the text on-screen and then hit the Enter key. "Type such-and-such" means simply to type the word or number on-screen and *not* press Enter.

Since this book concentrates on using the mouse rather than the keyboard, most of the instructions are for the mouse. We give you commands in two ways: "Click on the File menu, then click on Save" or, more simply, "select File ➤ Save," which means the same. (Don't worry—there's no magic ➤ character you have to find!)

There are some keystroke combinations that you will want to know how to use. These involve holding down one or more keys while you press another. For example, "press Control-Shift-D" means that you should hold down the Control and Shift keys, then hit the letter *D*.

We should mention briefly here that most of the mouse commands can also be performed with the keyboard by holding down the Alt key while you type the underlined letter in the menu you want, then typing the underlined letter in the command. For example, to select File ➤ Save with the keyboard, hold down Alt while you type *F*, then hit *S*. Usually it is easier and faster to use the mouse, but there may be times when you want to use the keyboard instead.

Besides the stylistic conventions above, this book features two typefaces aside from the regular text that you should be aware of. Any data or keystrokes that we ask you to key in appear in **boldface**. For example, we might instruct you to "type in the label **TOTALS**."

Words, data, or instructions that you read directly from the screen, on the other hand, appear in **program font**. For instance, you might read, "displays the message **File already exists**."

These conventions will become clear as you read on.

Introduction to Windows and Using the Mouse

If you are new to Windows, the next section gives you a good intro-duction to using the mouse to manipulate Windows applications and documents. Every program that runs in Windows, runs in a window. A window is a box with a border on the computer screen. Quattro Pro runs in an application window, while the notebooks you create run in a window contained by the application window, called the document window.

When you start Windows, the default Window is the Program Manager. In it are the Main window and Accessories window and the windows of any application that you have installed. You start an ap-plication (like Quattro Pro) by double-clicking on the icon that rep-resents the program. After that, the program appears in its application window. The exercises that follow are general in that they apply to any Windows application.

Exercise 1: Maximizing and Minimizing a Document Window

The document Maximize and Minimize buttons are located in the upper-right corner of the document window. They appear as an up-ward-and a downward-pointing triangle respectively.

1. Move the mouse pointer to the upward-pointing arrow in the document window and click on it. The document win-dow fills the entire screen. In place of the up and down tri-angles, a single button appears to the far right of the menu names. This is the Restore button.

2. Click on the Restore button. The document window resizes to less than full screen.

3. Click on the Minimize button. Now the document window is reduced to an icon in the lower-left corner of the screen.

4. Click on the document icon. The document-control menu appears.

5. Click on Restore. The document is restored to the size it was before you minimized it.

Keyboard Steps   You can also effect the same steps with your keyboard.

1. Hold down the Alt key and press the minus key (−). This opens the document-control menu in the upper-left corner of the screen.

2. Type N (the underlined letter in the word). The document window is minimized.

3. Press Alt-minus again. The document-control menu reappears.

4. Because Restore is the highlighted command, press Enter.

Exercise 2: Moving the Document Window Border

1. Move the mouse pointer to the left edge of the window, directly on the border. The pointer should change shape to a two-headed arrow, pointing left and right.

2. Click and hold the left mouse button.

3. Move the mouse pointer to the right. As you do, a translucent gray line moves with the pointer. The original border remains in place.

4. Release the mouse button.

Immediately, the left border of the window is shifted to the right. You can also move the other three window borders in this way.

Resizing the Document Window

One other manipulation of the window size is possible.

1. Move the mouse pointer to the bottom-right corner of the window. The pointer should assume the shape of a two-headed arrow pointing diagonally, northwest to southeast.

2. Click and hold the left mouse button.

3. Move the mouse in any direction. The upper-left corner of the notebook window remains anchored, allowing you to move the translucent gray lines representing the right side and bottom borders to any position you choose.

4. Release the mouse button. The window assumes the new size and shape.

THE TASK MANAGER

The Task Manager in Windows is the fastest way to switch from one application to another. Unlike DOS, where you had to close one application before opening another, with, Windows you can open several applications in their respective windows and access them at any time. The Task Manager keeps track of which Application windows are opened, listing them for your choosing.

To open the Task Manager and select an application:

1. Click on the Application-control button in the upper-left corner of the corner of the Window.

2. Click on Switch To. The Task List dialog box appears with a list of all open Applications.

3. Double-click on the one you wish to switch to, or click on the application name and then click on the Switch To button.

You can also use this dialog box to close an application (Quattro Pro will not let you close it unless you have saved any changes to a notebook.)

Now you're all set to start learning to use Quattro Pro for Windows. Read the Appendix if you haven't already installed Quattro Pro on your computer. Then hit Chapter 1 to get to know your spreadsheet!

Getting to Know Your Spreadsheet

This chapter introduces you to some of the basic elements of Quattro Pro for Windows: spreadsheets and notebooks, the mouse, how to start the program, and the different elements that appear on the screen. We also touch on getting help from the program, how to move about the spreadsheet, and how to leave it.

What Is a Spreadsheet?

If you've ever worked with invoices, budgets, loan analyses, tax statements, production schedules, and so forth, then you're familiar with a ledger, which is simply a sheet of paper with rows and columns. Figure 1.1 shows such a ledger with some calculations for a home mortgage worked out.

A spreadsheet program such as Quattro Pro for Windows is basically an electronic ledger sheet. It too contains rows and columns and allows you to place numbers, text, and formulas (for doing calculations) into individual *cells*. Figure 1.2 shows the information from the paper ledger as it would appear on the Quattro Pro for Windows spreadsheet.

Now you may be thinking, "Big deal, so I type on a TV screen rather than on paper." But there is quite a bit more to it than that. For example, if you were to change the interest rate on the paper ledger

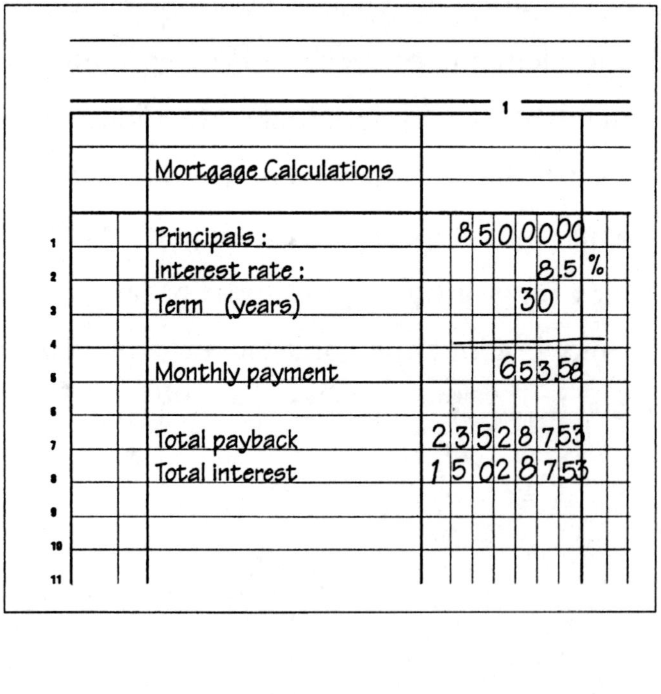

FIGURE 1.1:

A sample paper ledger sheet

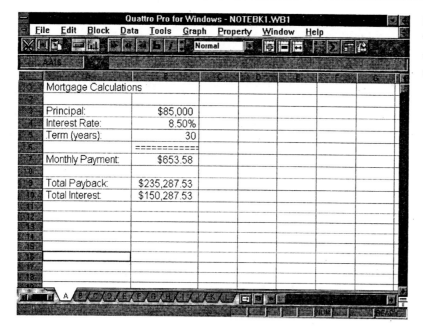

FIGURE 1.2:

The spreadsheet version of a ledger sheet

sheet, you'd need to recalculate all the different results, such as the payment on the loan, total payback, and total interest paid. (On a ledger sheet with 1000 calculations this would indeed be a laborious task!)

On an electronic spreadsheet, by contrast, you can change any number, or group of numbers, and Quattro Pro for Windows will instantly recalculate all of the formulas affected by the change. You'll never need to use a calculator or eraser for this kind of work again. For example, Figure 1.3 shows the results of changing the interest rate of the loan from 8.5% to 10%. As soon as the new interest rate was entered, all the other calculations were updated immediately.

This instant recalculation feature alone makes Quattro Pro for Windows an invaluable tool, allowing you to experiment with options and create what-if scenarios. But Quattro Pro offers much more. You can display (and print) business graphs and replot them whenever you change your assumptions. You can also store and retrieve various types

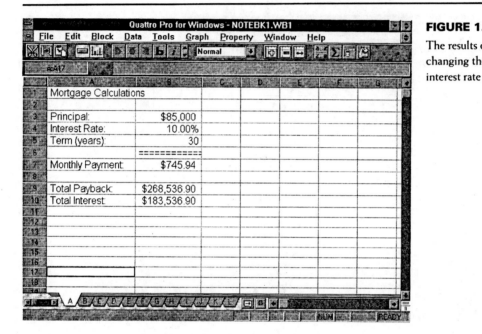

of information such as names and addresses, financial transactions, and inventory data.

As you read through this book, you'll learn a great deal about the many capabilities of Quattro Pro for Windows. Of course, the first thing you need to learn is how to get Quattro Pro for Windows up and running on your computer, so let's start with that—after a quick word about using the mouse.

USING THE MOUSE

Throughout this book you will find instructions for using the mouse. You can use Quattro Pro for Windows without a mouse, but it is highly inefficient to do so. Windows and Quattro Pro for Windows were both designed with a mouse in mind.

The mouse pointer initially appears on the computer screen as an arrow. The mouse pointer changes shape depending upon where on the spreadsheet it is located.

When an instruction says to point to something on the screen, move the mouse along your desk, or on its special mouse pad, until the arrow points to the object on the screen.

An instruction to click the mouse means to quickly press and release the mouse button. If an instruction says to

Click on the box

it means to point to the box referred to in the text and click the mouse button.

You will also be asked to "double-click" on an object. This means to quickly press and release the mouse button twice.

The instruction to drag means to point to an object, such as a cell, and hold down the mouse button, and then move the mouse on your desk or mouse pad. Instructions to drag will always tell you where to drag to, as in

Drag the mouse pointer to the bottom of the screen

When you reach the destination, release the mouse button—do not release the button until you have completed the action.

In some cases, you must select several menu options to perform a task. For instance, to open a notebook file, you must select File to display the pull-down menu and then select the Open command.

Select File ➤ Open

In instructions such as this, the ➤ is used to separate the items you must select. It means "select File from the menu bar, and then select Open from the pull-down menu that appears." You do not have to select a ➤ character on the screen or press any other key.

Your mouse may have two or three buttons. Quattro Pro for Windows uses both the left and right mouse buttons. Most of the time the left button is called for because most people are right-handed and use the right index finger to click; we'll specify when you should click the right button. If you happen to be left-handed, you can designate the right mouse button as your dominant button. (We'll cover this in the Appendix.)

Starting Quattro Pro for Windows

First off, Quattro Pro for Windows comes with a couple of tools that can make learning and using the software a bit easier.

THE KEYBOARD TEMPLATE

The booklet, "Getting Started with Quattro Pro for Windows," which comes with your spreadsheet, includes a cardboard *template* that you can place over your keyboard to help identify the uses of various function keys (those labeled F1 through F10 or F12 on your keyboard). The template is for IBM ATs and their clones, on which the function keys appear horizontally across the top.

You should remove the template from the booklet and place it on your keyboard whenever you use Quattro Pro for Windows.

THE MENU MAPS

The user's guide that comes with your Quattro Pro for Windows package includes a series of maps of the spreadsheet's menu structure. After you are a bit more familiar with Quattro Pro and its menus, you may wish to refer to the maps once in a while to review the various menu options. The endpapers to this SYBEX book also include a menu map.

INSTALLING THE SOFTWARE

Quattro Pro for Windows must be installed on your computer before you can use it. It will only work on an IBM PC or 100-percent compatible computer with a *hard-disk drive*. Quattro Pro for Windows version 1.0 needs 8 MB. Remember, Quattro Pro for Windows need only be installed once. Installation instructions are provided in the Appendix; read it first before proceeding.

After you have installed Quattro Pro for Windows, follow the instructions below to run it:

1. Enter or log onto the hard disk, if necessary, by typing the command **C:** and pressing the Enter (⏎ or Return) key. (If the hard disk that contains Quattro Pro for Windows is not C, substitute the appropriate letter in the command.)

2. Type CD\WINDOWS and press Enter to switch to the Windows directory.

3. At the C:\WINDOWS> prompt, type WIN and press Enter. Depending upon what programs are already installed in Windows, your screen will resemble Figure 1.4. As you can see,

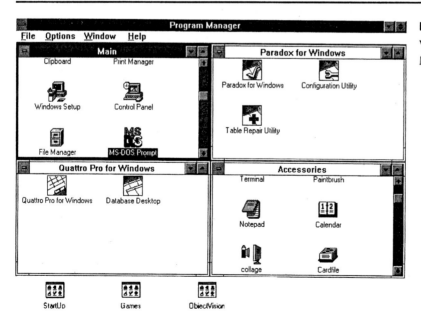

FIGURE 1.4:

Windows Program Manager screen

one of the windows contains the Quattro Pro for Windows icon and title. Double-click the left mouse button on this icon.

THE README FILE

Last-minute changes and corrections to the program and manuals are stored on the Quattro Pro for Windows System Disk, which comes with your software package. The very first time you start using Quattro Pro for Windows, a dialog box appears asking you if you want to read the README file. Click on OK and the text appears.

While the README file is displayed, you can click on the scroll box on the right side of the document window to scroll through the document. To leave the README file and return to the Program Manager, click on the Minimize document button, or open the Control menu box and click on Close.

The Quattro Pro for Windows Screen

The various parts of Quattro Pro for Windows' opening screen are named in Figure 1.5. The following sections describe the purpose of each part.

All of the windows in the example figures have been *maximized* unless otherwise noted. To maximize the application window, click on the Control menu box and then click on Maximize. Next, maximize the document window by clicking on the up arrow in the upper right corner of the document spreadsheet window.

Across the very top of the screen is the Title Bar, which includes the name of the program, Quattro Pro for Windows, and the name of a notebook file if one is loaded. When you begin working in Quattro Pro, the default or automatic file name is NOTEBK1.WB1. At the far left of the Title Bar is the Application Control menu box; at the far right are the Application Minimize and Maximize buttons.

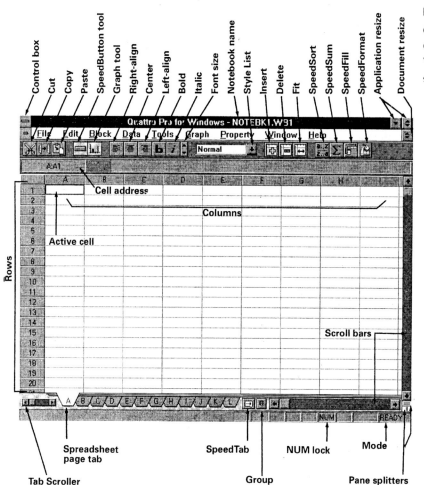

THE MENU BAR

The second line down from the top of the screen is a series of words beginning with *File* and ending with *Help*. These are the *menu* names; the menus themselves are "pulled down" over the Quattro Pro screen when activated. Each of them has a letter that is underlined. For example, in the menu called File, the letter *F* is underlined. The letter *F* is the access letter for the File menu, the letter *E* for the Edit menu, and so forth. At the far right is the Restore button, which resizes document windows.

THE SPEEDBAR

The SpeedBar contains icons for the most frequently used spreadsheet commands. For example, the scissors icon on the far left of the SpeedBar stands for the Cut command. Each of the SpeedBar icons is described below.

The Cut Button

The scissors button at the far left is the Cut button. After selecting a block, click on this button to remove the contents of the selected cells and place them on the Clipboard. Next you can move the mouse pointer to a different position on the spreadsheet page, or to a different page, and *paste* the cell contents (see below). You can even copy a single cell to multiple cells.

The Copy Button

The Copy button is to the right of the Cut button. After selecting a block, click on the Copy button to copy the selected cell contents to the Clipboard. Then you can move the mouse pointer to a different position on the spreadsheet, or to a different page, and paste the contents to other cells.

The Paste Button

The next button to the right is the Paste button. When you click on it, a copy of the contents of the Clipboard is inserted at the position of the mouse pointer. You can make multiple copies of the same information by clicking on the Paste button at different cell locations.

The SpeedButton

The SpeedButton tool is used to create macro buttons. A macro button, when clicked, executes the attached macro that you have created.

The Graph Tool

Next to the right of the SpeedButton is the Graph Tool. There are two types of graphs on Quattro Pro: regular graphs that take up an entire screen, and floating graphs that can be placed anywhere on a spreadsheet page. The Graph Tool creates floating graphs. After selecting a block of cells, click on the Graph Tool to create a bar graph of those cell values. The mouse pointer changes to a small bar graph. You can scroll the spreadsheet page to locate an open space on the spreadsheet, or place the graph directly on top of occupied cells. You can do this because the graph "floats" above the spreadsheet page and is not attached to it, although it remains with the page.

The Alignment Buttons

The next three buttons are used to align information in cells. The default alignment for information is left for labels, right for numbers. You can left-align, center, or right-align the contents of cells, by selecting the block and then clicking on the appropriate button. The block remains selected until you click on a different area of the spreadsheet, so you can click on another alignment button if you are unhappy with the results.

The Bold Button

The large lower-case "b" button is for bolding cell contents. After selecting a block, click on this button to make the contents display (and print) in bold format. This button is a toggle: click on it again to un-bold the cell contents.

The Italics Button

The italic "i" button is for italicizing cell contents. After selecting a block, click on this button to make the contents display (and print) in italics. This applies to all types of cell entries—labels, numbers, or dates. This button is a toggle: click on it again to remove the italics from the cell contents.

The Enlarge and Reduce Buttons

The Enlarge and Reduce buttons are the up- and down-pointing arrows next to the Italics button. Select a block and click on the up arrow to enlarge the contents of the block, or on the down arrow to reduce them. The height of the block is also adjusted according to the size of the contents.

The Style List

The Style List, when selected, reveals a list of block formats for display purposes. For example, the cell contents can be formatted to include Commas, as Currency, Date, Fixed, as a Heading, as a Percentage, or as a Total. The Total format inserts a double line at the top of the selected block.

When you move the cell selector to a specific cell, the Style List window displays the type of format used in that cell.

The Insert Button

When you build a spreadsheet, you frequently need to insert extra rows or columns. Quattro Pro makes it very easy to insert rows, columns, or even spreadsheet pages as needed, with a click of a button. The Insert button has a plus sign (+) on it.

The Delete Button

You may also need to delete rows, columns, or spreadsheet pages. The Delete button, marked with a minus sign (–), is very similar to the Insert button. As with inserting, you can delete rows, columns, or entire spreadsheet pages.

The Fit Button

The default length of a cell in Quattro Pro is 9 spaces. When you enter labels longer than 9 spaces, Quattro Pro allows the label to overflow into the cells to the right, provided those cells are empty. If they are not empty, the label is cut off at 9 characters. With numbers longer than 9 spaces, Quattro Pro truncates the number using scientific notation. If a date is longer than 9 spaces, a series of asterisks (*******) appears in the cell.

When you click on the Fit button, Quattro Pro automatically adjusts the width of the column to accommodate the widest entry in the column. See Lesson 3 for an exercise using this technique.

The SpeedSort Button

The SpeedSort button is actually two buttons. The top half of the button has the letters a..z and the bottom half z..a on it. The a..z button sorts the entries in a selected block alphabetically or sequentially; the z..a button sorts in reverse order.

The SpeedSum Button

The next button to the right, marked with the Greek letter Sigma (Σ), is the SpeedSum button. This is a specialized macro button for inserting a summing formula at the bottom of a column or to the right of a row of numbers.

The SpeedFill Button

The SpeedFill button, to the right of the SpeedSum button, is used to insert a series of numbers, dates, or labels into a selected block of cells.

The SpeedFormat Button

To the right of the SpeedFill button is the SpeedFormat button. This button is used to apply preset formats to selected blocks of cells.

The specific use of each SpeedBar button is introduced as needed to build a spreadsheet. All of the SpeedBar commands can also be accessed through the menu system. The SpeedBar simply accelerates the process of using the commands.

THE HORIZONTAL BORDER

Across the top of the spreadsheet is the *horizontal border*, which initially contains the letters A through I. These letters are the names of the *columns* in the spreadsheet. Although you cannot see the additional columns now, they are lettered A to Z, then AA to AZ, BA to BZ, and so forth up to column IV, for a total of 256 columns.

THE VERTICAL BORDER

The *vertical border* on the left side of the screen contains *row* numbers. Now you can only see rows 1 through 20, but there are many more of them—8192 to be exact.

THE CELLS

At the intersection of each row and column lies an individual spreadsheet *cell*, whose function is to store data and formulas. Every cell is identified by an address, which is simply its column and row position. For example, the cell in the upper-left corner (column A, row 1) is named

A:A1. The first letter A indicates that the cell selector is in spreadsheet A, and in cell address A1. The cell to the right of A:A1 is A:B1, directly beneath cell A:B1 is A:B2, and so on to the bottom-most right corner, cell A:IV8192.

THE CELL SELECTOR

The *cell selector,* positioned on cell A:A1 in Figure 1.5, highlights the current cell on the spreadsheet. Any information you typed now would be placed in this cell. Later in the chapter you'll see how to move the selector to other cells on the spreadsheet.

THE INPUT LINE

The *input line* is directly underneath the menu bar and above the horizontal border. It's where the data first appear as you type them in. The input line displays the address and contents of the selected cell.

At the far left is the cell address box. The first letter always indicates which spreadsheet in the notebook you are in. The letter and number combination that follows indicates the current cell address of the cell selector.

THE SPREADSHEET PAGE TAB

At the bottom of the spreadsheet page is the Spreadsheet Page Tab. There are 256 tabs, one for each spreadsheet in the notebook, labeled with letters.

To move to spreadsheet page B in the notebook, move the mouse pointer to the tab labeled B and click on it. In the cell address box, the indicator reads B:A1, as you are now working in spreadsheet B. Click on the tab labeled A to return to the A spreadsheet.

THE TAB SCROLLER

There are two methods to accelerate moving from one spreadsheet page to another. First, the Tab Scroller is located in the bottom left corner of the notebook window and operates in the same way as the spreadsheet scroll bars, described later in this chapter. Second, the SpeedTab button is located in the bottom middle of the notebook window and has an arrow pointing to the right when you open the notebook file.

Click on the SpeedTab button, and the spreadsheet page is replaced by the Graphs page, as indicated on the Tab. At this point, you have not created any graphs and therefore no graph icons appear on the page. The arrow in the SpeedTab button is now pointing to the left. Click on the SpeedTab button again. The A spreadsheet page appears. The SpeedTab button jumps you from the current spreadsheet page to the Graphs page and then back again.

THE GROUP BUTTON

To the right of the SpeedTab button is the Group button. This is used for advanced formatting.

THE PANE SPLITTER BUTTONS

Below the vertical scroll bar lie the two Pane Splitter buttons. These are used for breaking a notebook window into two panes and viewing a different part of the notebook in each.

THE STATUS LINE

At the very bottom of the screen is the *status line*. The left side displays a brief explanation of any highlighted menu command, and the right side the spreadsheet mode, such as **READY** or **EDIT.** When the spreadsheet is in Edit mode, the contents of the current cell are displayed on the left side of this line. If the Caps Lock or Num Lock key is activated, **CAP** or **NUM** also appears.

DIALOG BOX ERROR MESSAGES

When you make a mistake, an error message will appear in a dialog box on the center of the screen. The message will try to convey to you the type of error you made. (Further information about error messages is available through the Help system, described later in this chapter.) Don't be too concerned about making mistakes. Quattro Pro will just beep and display the error message in response. When this occurs, you can simply click on the OK button and try again.

THE ARROW KEYS

Although this book describes cell selector movement predominantly with the mouse pointer, you can also move the cell selector to any cell on the spreadsheet by using the ↑, ↓, →, and ← keys on your keyboard. Hitting an arrow key moves the cell selector one cell in the appropriate direction; holding it down advances it continuously. On some keyboards, these are combined respectively with the numbers 8, 2, 6, and 4 on the numeric keypad; on other keyboards, there is a separate set of arrow keys.

Note that if your keyboard has the arrow keys on the numeric keypad, they will not work when Num Lock is on. As the name suggests, Num Lock locks the numeric keypad in the numbers mode. You can always tell it is on when you see **NUM** on the status line. So to use the arrow keys, make sure Num Lock is off.

THE ENTER KEY

The Enter key sends whatever you type from the input line to the current cell. You will use this key quite regularly in your work with Quattro Pro for Windows (and computers in general), so be sure to become familiar with its location now, if you have not done so already. Note that on some keyboards only the ↵ symbol appears on the Enter key. On other keyboards, the Enter key may be labeled Return.

THE ESCAPE KEY

When first learning Quattro Pro for Windows, you will occasionally make a mistake or feel a bit lost. When you find yourself in unfamiliar territory, you can usually press the Escape key (labeled Esc, Escape, or Cancel) to move backwards through the series of steps you've just taken. In a dialog box, you can click on the Cancel button instead.

THE NUM LOCK KEY

As mentioned just a moment ago, the Num Lock key controls the numeric keypad on your keyboard. When Num Lock is off, the arrow, Home, End, PgUp, and PgDn functions are in effect, instead of the numbers, and **NUM** does not appear on the screen. (You can use the row of numbers above the letters Q through P, rather than those on the keypad, regardless of the Num Lock setting.)

THE BACKSPACE KEY

The Backspace key is used in the same manner as on a typewriter. When you hit it, the cursor moves back one space—on the input line, in this case. Note that the Backspace key erases as it moves backward, and that Backspace and ← are *not* the same keys.

Getting Help from Quattro Pro for Windows

While using Quattro Pro, you can get help at any time. If a Dialog box is open, click on the Help button; otherwise click on the Help menu. You can also press F1 to get help. Because the Help feature is *context sensitive*, the screen that appears will usually relate to whatever task you are working on at the moment.

For instance, select Help ➤ Contents while the opening screen is displayed. Your screen will then display a broad overview of all of Quattro Pro for Windows' Help Contents in a second window on the right of the screen, as shown in Figure 1.6.

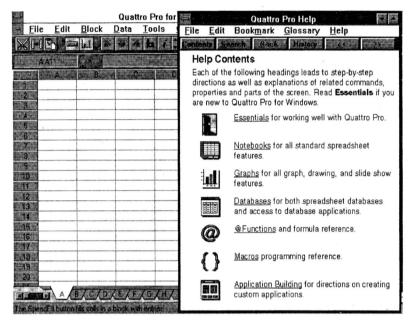

FIGURE 1.6:

The Quattro Pro for Windows Help Contents screen

You now have various options from which to choose. The various help topics are listed with a short explanation of what is contained in that section.

For example, suppose you wish to get help on the Essentials for working well with Quattro Pro for Windows. Move the mouse pointer to that topic. When you do, the arrow changes to a hand with the index finger extended. Click the left mouse button. The Help Contents window is replaced by a new window (as shown in Figure 1.7) that lists key concepts and gives a brief explanation of each. To see the previous help screen, click on the Back button at the top of the screen.

You can continue to make selections from the Help Topics screen and see what information is provided. To return to the spreadsheet, click on the Minimize button at the upper-right corner of the document window. The Help screen will disappear and return you to the spreadsheet.

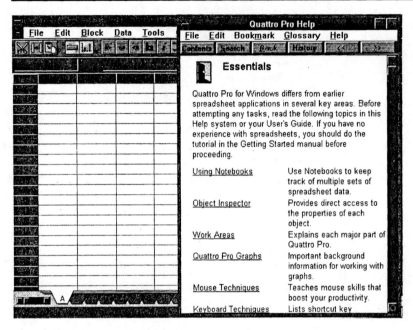

FIGURE 1.7:

The Help screen for the menu commands

While exploring the various Help screens, you'll notice that each one leads to another. The next screen will provide either more in-depth information about the topic or other information related to the option you selected at the opening menu. Remember, clicking on the Minimize button of the document window will always return you to the spreadsheet when you are finished.

As you perform the exercises in this book, use the Help screens whenever you want to review information pertaining to the topic at hand. If you need to, you can use the Maximize button to enlarge the Help window so that it fills the entire window.

The Notebook Concept

Quattro Pro for Windows introduces a totally new concept for spreadsheets: notebooks. This concept is very similar to paper and pencil ledger sheets. For example, a company may have several divisions, all of which contribute to the profit and loss statement. The top page of the ledger might be a consolidation of all the divisions' financial data. By turning the pages in the ledger book, you could examine the individual data of each division. Similarly, Quattro Pro for Windows allows you to use the top spreadsheet, labeled A on the tab at the bottom, as the spreadsheet in which you can consolidate data from the other 255 spreadsheets in the notebook. This does not mean you must use the A spreadsheet for consolidations, but you have that option. The reason we're touching upon this now has to do with cell addresses. Each page of the notebook is a separate spreadsheet, so there are 256 spreadsheet pages to each notebook. In order for you and Quattro Pro to find specific cells, the cell address begins with the spreadsheet page. If the cell is in spreadsheet A, and the active cell is in column B row 3, the complete cell address is A:B3. Likewise, if the cell is in spreadsheet page T, and the active cell address is column H row 18, the complete address is T:H18.

Navigating a Spreadsheet

Now that you've had an overview of the mouse, the screen, and the Help system, it's time to start interacting directly with the Quattro Pro spreadsheet. In this section, we discuss techniques that allow you to position the cell selector on any cell in the spreadsheet, and therefore, any cell in the notebook.

MOVING THE CELL SELECTOR

Let's try some simple exercises. Assuming that the cell selector is currently in cell A:A1 (spreadsheet A, cell A1), move the mouse pointer arrow down to cell A3 and click on it. The cell selector will move down two rows to cell A3, making A3 the "active cell." Next, move the mouse pointer arrow across to cell B3 and click on it. The cell selector will move one column to the right to cell B3, which becomes the "active cell." Take a look at the input line in the upper-left corner of the screen. It now indicates that the cell selector is indeed on cell A:B3, making it the active cell.

The Scroll Bars

Experiment with the mouse pointer for a while and watch the cell selector move from cell to cell. To move quickly across the spreadsheet, use the scroll bars. These are located at the right side and bottom right of the document window. For example, to scroll the spreadsheet to the right, click on the small right-pointing arrow inside the scroll bar. The spreadsheet moves one column to the right. Notice that the small box inside the scroll bar moves too. This is the scroll box. You can also click and drag the scroll box inside the scroll bar and move the spreadsheet with it. Or click inside the scroll bar next to the arrow pointing in the direction you wish to go.

The scroll bar on the bottom left scrolls the tabs at the bottom of the spreadsheets. Although the tabs are scrolled, the spreadsheets do not scroll. When you click on the desired tab letter, the spreadsheet appears. When you have finished experimenting, press the Home key to move the cell selector quickly back to cell A1.

MOVING TO A SPECIFIC CELL

The Go To command lets you move the cell selector quickly to a specific cell on the spreadsheet. Either select Edit ➤Goto, or press F5, which is named Go To on the Quattro Pro for Windows template that came with your software package. The Go To dialog box appears. Because the cell selector is currently in cell A:A1, that cell's address appears in the dialog box.

To move to a different cell, type in the cell's address, then click on OK. For example, if you type in **B6** and click on OK (or press Enter), the cell selector will jump to cell B6. Also, you can include the spreadsheet tab letter and the cell address in the Go To dialog box. For example, if you wanted to move to spreadsheet B and cell D6, you could type B:D6 and then click on OK.

MOVING THE SPREADSHEET WINDOW

When you first look at the Quattro Pro spreadsheet, you see only a small portion of the worksheet. As mentioned earlier, each spreadsheet actually contains 256 columns and 8192 rows—a total of 2,097,152 cells!

Because it can't fit all the cells on your screen at once, Quattro Pro for Windows displays only a portion of the larger worksheet. Figure 1.8 shows how you can envision the screen as a fragment of the whole, a window into the huge electronic spreadsheet.

Let's move this window around to view the other parts of the spreadsheet, using keystroke combinations.

1. Press the Home key to move the cell selector back to the upper-left corner of the spreadsheet—cell A:A1.

2. To jump to the extreme upper-right corner of the spreadsheet, press the End key, followed by the → key. The cell selector

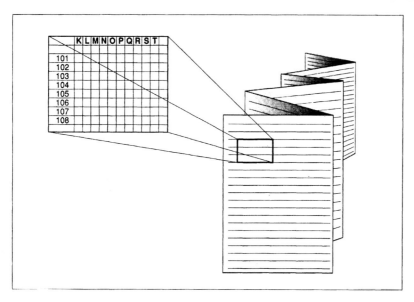

FIGURE 1.8:

The screen as a window into the larger spreadsheet

will move onto cell IV1 (column IV, row 1). Notice that the entire window has moved to the right as well, showing columns IN to IV.

3. To move to another corner of the spreadsheet, press the End key and the ↓ key. This time the cell selector moves to the extreme bottom-right corner of the spreadsheet, to cell IV8192. Now the bottom-most rows, numbered 8170 to 8192, are visible.

4. Pressing the End and ← keys will now move the cell selector to the extreme lower-left corner of the spreadsheet. Try this. The window now shows columns A through H and rows 8170 to 8192.

5. To return to cell A1, hit the Home key.

At this point, we've made a trip around the four extreme corners of the spreadsheet, as Figure 1.9 illustrates.

THE NOTEBOOK PARADIGM

Just as the foregoing figures illustrated the concept of the spreadsheet being larger than the computer screen, Figure 1.10 shows the layered aspect of notebook spreadsheets. The bottom or last spreadsheet contains the graph icons. Each icon stands for graphs you have created in any of the individual spreadsheets.

Summary of Quattro Pro for Windows Special Keys

Although this book emphasizes the mouse, at times you may prefer to use the keyboard to move the cell selector around on the spreadsheet. Table 1.1 lists all the special keys you can use for this. In this table, a hyphen between two key names means that you should hold down the first key while pressing the second. For example, Ctrl→ means hold

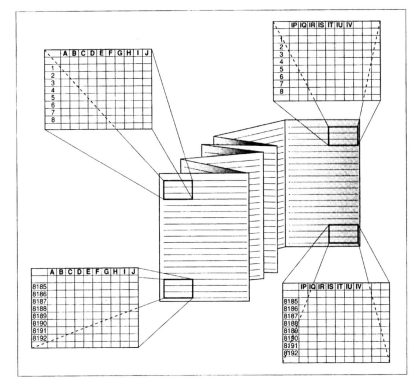

FIGURE 1.9:

The window moved to four corners of the spreadsheet

down the Ctrl (Control) key while tapping the→ key. Similarly, Shift–Tab means to hold down the Shift key while hitting the Tab key.

You may want to practice using the keys listed in Table 1.1 for a while. When you have finished, press Home to move the cell selector back to cell A1.

Leaving Quattro Pro for Windows

To exit Quattro Pro for Windows, click on the File menu. Click on the Exit command. Quattro Pro for Windows closes and the Program Manager reappears. There are two other ways to execute the Exit command after opening the File menu. One is to type the letter X, as it is

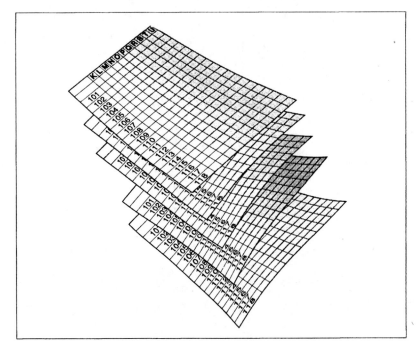

FIGURE 1.10:

The notebook of spreadsheets

the access letter for the Exit command. Another is to use the ↓ key to move the highlight to the word Exit and then press Enter.

If at any time in your work you have entered or changed information on a spreadsheet and then selected Exit from the File menu without having previously saved your work, the screen will display the message

Save changes in C:\QPW\ (file name)
Yes No Cancel

If you select Cancel, you will stay in Quattro Pro for Windows. If you select No, you'll be sent to the Program Manager, from which you first started Quattro Pro for Windows. Now you can exit Windows and turn off the computer, or run another program. If you select Yes, Quattro Pro for Windows will open the Save File dialog box and ask you to name the notebook file if it has not already been named. After you name it,

KEY	ACTION
→	Moves cell selector one cell to the right
←	Moves cell selector one cell to the left
↑	Moves cell selector up one cell
↓	Moves cell selector down one cell
Home	Moves cell selector "home" to cell A1
PgUp	Moves window up one screen
PgDn	Moves window down one screen
Tab	Moves cell selector one screen to the right
Ctrl-→	Same as Tab
Shift-Tab	Moves cell selector one screen to the left
Ctrl-←	Same as Shift-Tab
End, Arrow keys	Moves cell selector to the beginning or end of a block in the arrow's direction, or else to the far end of the spreadsheet
F5	Moves cell selector to any cell you specify

TABLE 1.1:

Keys for moving the cell selector

the computer will save the file and send you to the Program Manager.

For now, you have not done any work worth saving, so if the above dialog box appears in the middle of your screen, type the letter **N**, or move the highlight to the word No and press Enter. You'll be returned to the Program Manager shortly.

In the next chapter, you'll learn valuable techniques for actually putting the spreadsheet to work, using the menus, and saving your work for future use.

2 CHAPTER

Building a Spreadsheet

FEATURING

Entering
Information

Erasing mistakes

Building
formulas

Saving your
work

In this chapter, we discuss the basic techniques for building your own spreadsheets. These include entering data, creating formulas to calculate results, and saving your work. We start with a fairly simple example—a family budget. But as you will see later in the book, you can use these same techniques to build business spreadsheets of any size and sophistication.

Types of Cell Entries

There are several types of information that you can enter into any cell on the spreadsheet:

- Labels (words, sentences, and any other nonnumeric data)

- Numbers (real numbers on which you perform calculations)

- Dates

- Times

- Formulas (entries that perform calculations)

- Functions (built-in, complex formulas that come with the software)

- Macros (shortcuts for oft-repeated keystrokes)

- Graphs (pictures placed inside blocks of cells)

The sample spreadsheet we develop will include each of these *data types*.

If you exited Quattro Pro for Windows at the end of the last chapter, you need to start it again. Refer to the beginning of Chapter 1 if you need a refresher on this.

Entering Your Text in a Cell

To enter a label into a cell, simply move the cell selector to where you want the label to appear, type the label, and click on the check mark next to the input line. Suppose, for example, that you want to title your first sample spreadsheet, "Monthly Budget for the Dorf Family." Here are the steps to do just this:

1. Move the cell selector to cell A1 by pressing the Home key.

2. Type **Monthly Budget for the Dorf Family**. You'll notice that as you type, the letters appear on the input line.

3. If you make a mistake, you can erase it with the Backspace key (but not the ← key).

4. When you have finished typing, click the left mouse button, or click on the check mark next to the input line, or press Enter.

The label appears in cell A1 (though it overflows onto other cells), as shown in Figure 2.1.

That was easy, wasn't it? Notice that the label appears on the input line, just above the horizontal border. As you can see in the input line, Quattro Pro for Windows automatically added an apostrophe (') to the beginning of the label. That's a *label prefix*, which we'll discuss later.

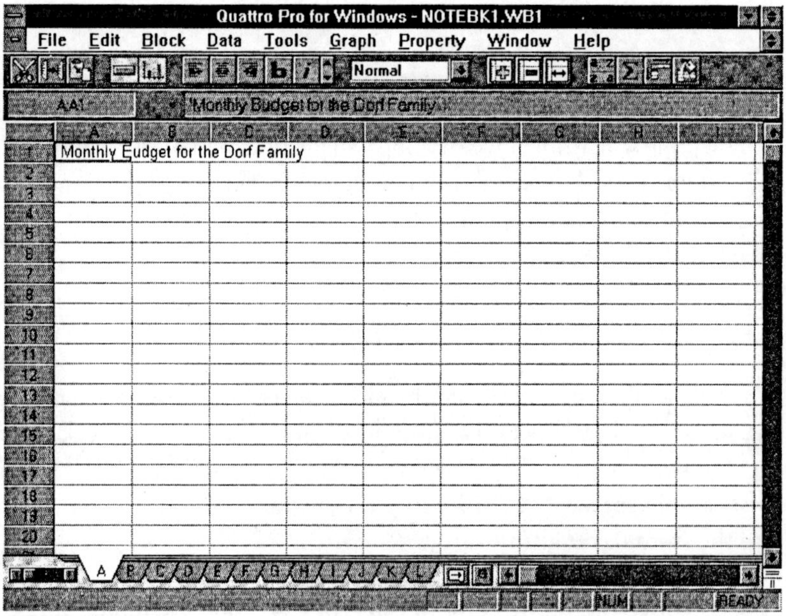

FIGURE 2.1:

A label entered into cell A1

Now that you have a title for your spreadsheet, let's add some other labels. Point the arrow at cell A6 and click. Check the cell address box to the left of the input line to make sure that the cell selector is in the correct cell.

SIMPLIFYING DATA-ENTRY WITH THE ARROW KEYS

Your next task is to enter labels that identify the numbers you will begin entering in the cells. In a family budget, there is a source of income—normally from jobs—and several expenditures. In this example, we'll assume that both the husband and wife work. In cell A6 type **Income**. Then press the ↓ key.

As you can see on your screen, the label Income is now in cell A6, and the cell selector has moved down to cell A7 to await another entry. Are you wondering why we told you to press ↓ rather than clicking on the check mark, as you have done so far? It's because clicking on the check mark would have left the cell selector at position A6. Making many sequential entries this way—a row of column headings or a list of data—would involve many wasted keystrokes: click, arrow, click, arrow, etc. Better, then, to use just an arrow key, if you know in advance the direction you want the cell selector to move in. (You can simply click on the next cell you want to use, without clicking on the check mark; but it is generally easier and more precise to use the arrow keys.)

For a little more practice, press ↓ to move the cell selector to cell A8, and type the label, **Ralph, job**. Press ↓ again to move the cell selector to cell A9, and enter **Alice, job**.

Move the cell selector to cell A11, type the label **Total Income**, and press ↓. At this point, your screen should resemble Figure 2.2.

Then enter the labels shown in Figure 2.3 onto your spreadsheet. When you get to row 20, click on the vertical scroll bar until rows 21

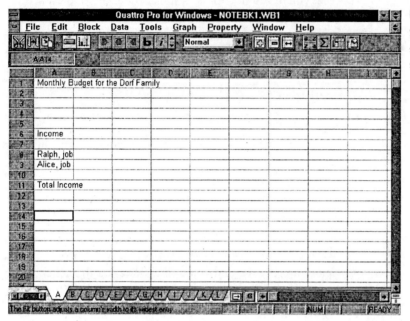

to 24 appear. If you make any errors along the way, try to correct them using some of the techniques listed above. (Note that the label JUNE is in cell C6, JULY in cell D6, and AUGUST in cell E6.)

Underlining Text

The hyphen (–), which you might want to use to draw underlines in a spreadsheet, has a special meaning in Quattro Pro for Windows—it is used to subtract numbers or identify negative numbers. Therefore, you çannot enter an underline into a cell simply by typing-------. Try it and you'll get the Error message: **Syntax Error**. (To cancel, click on OK in the Error message box and then on the X button in the input line, or hit the Escape (Esc) key three times.)

You can, however, enter lines by using the repeat-character label *prefix*, which is a backslash (\). Follow the backslash with the character

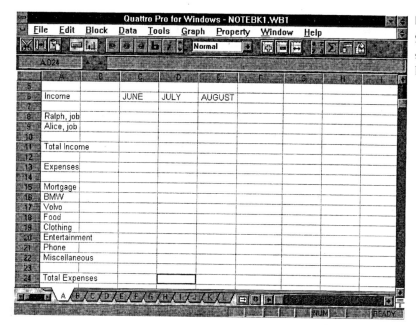

FIGURE 2.3:

Sample spread-
sheet with many
labels

you wish to repeat. For example, to place a line in cell C10, follow these steps:

1. Move the cell selector to cell C10.

2. Type \ –.

3. Click on the check mark or press Enter.

Cell C10 will fill with hyphens:--------. Now move the cell selector to C23 and enter \ – once again to put in another line. (Remember to click on the check mark, press Enter, or press an arrow key after typing \ –.)

Correcting Mistakes

Unless you are a superb typist, you will probably make mistakes quite regularly while entering information into a spreadsheet. You can correct these mistakes in several ways:

1. If you *have not* yet clicked the left mouse button, clicked on the check mark, pressed Enter, or pressed an arrow key after your typo, you can press the Backspace key to erase what you've just typed. To erase all the characters at once, hold down the Ctrl key and press Backspace, or just press Escape. You can also click the X button next to the check mark.

2. If you *have* already entered the mistake into the cell, simply place the cell selector back on that cell and reenter the information. The new entry will replace the old completely.

3. If you wish to erase the contents of a cell, move the cell selector to that cell and select Edit ➤ Clear. (You can also press the Delete (Del) key.)

There are some other ways to correct errors and make changes, which we'll discuss later.

Entering Numbers

Entering numbers into cells is no different from entering labels. Be aware, though, that for the computer to recognize an entry as a number (and not a word), it must begin with either a digit (0–9), a minus sign (−) for negative numbers, or a decimal point. You cannot put commas in numbers. For example, you can type 20000, but not 20,000. (Later, you'll see how to display numbers with the commas inserted.)

Let's put some numbers now into the sample spreadsheet for practice. Suppose Ralph earns $2000 per month, which you wish to show in cell C8. Use the mouse to move the cell selector to cell C8 and type 2000. Then press the ↓ key. Ralph's salary will appear in cell C8.

Furthermore, suppose that Alice earns $4000 per month, which you wish to put in cell C9. Since you entered the previous salary with the ↓ key, the cell selector should already be on cell C9, so just type **4000** and press Enter. Your screen should look like Figure 2.4.

Now you can enter some expenses into column C. Remember, you can use the techniques discussed earlier to correct any mistakes. Enter the following values into the cells below:

Enter **1550** into cell C15

Enter **330** into cell C16

Enter **275** into cell C17

Enter **400** into cell C18

Enter **200** into cell C19

Enter **75** into cell C20

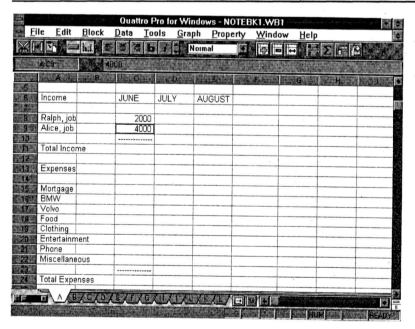

FIGURE 2.4:

Salaries entered in the sample spreadsheet

Enter **50** into cell C21

Enter **300** into cell C22

Figure 2.5 shows how the sample spreadsheet should look. Now, you don't have to add up these numbers on a calculator and enter the sum in cell C4; we will later use a formula to find the total expenses instead.

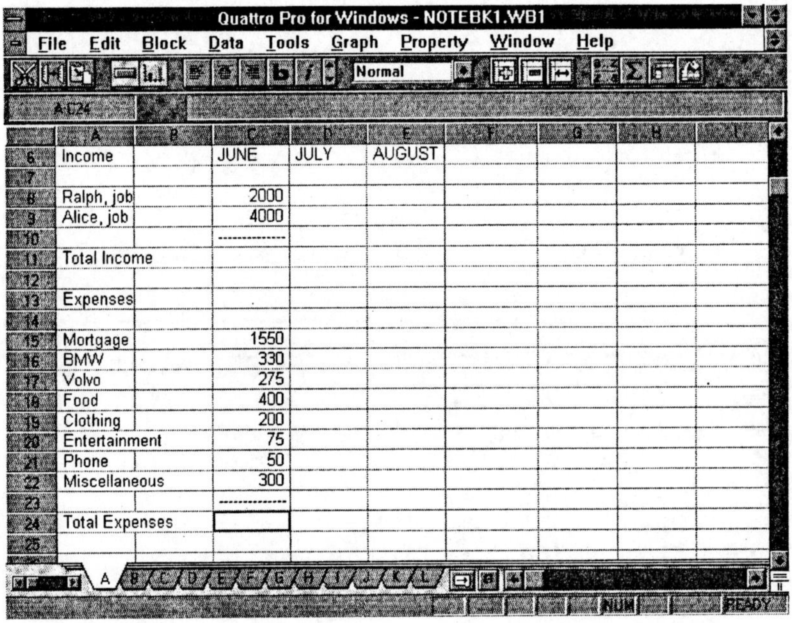

FIGURE 2.5:

Income and expenses in the sample spreadsheet

Entering Dates

There are several methods for entering dates into spreadsheet cells, but only a few techniques will allow you to perform *date arithmetic*, which means treating dates as numbers so you can use them in formulas. The best (and easiest) way is to use the command Ctrl-Shift-D and type the date in a *day-month-year* format.

Suppose, for example, you wish to put the current date near the upper-right corner of the sample spreadsheet in cell F1:

1. Move the cell selector to cell F1 using the mouse pointer or arrow keys.

2. Hold down the Ctrl key and the Shift key and type the letter **D**. (Note that **DATE** replaces **READY** at the right end of the status line.)

3. Enter today's date in *dd-mmm-yy* format (01-Dec-93 for December 1, 1993, for example).

4. Press Enter. The cell fills with a series of asterisks. Quattro Pro is indicating that the entry in the cell is too long to fit the cell. This happens because numeric or date entries are not allowed to spill over like label entries.

5. Click on the Fit button, which is third to the left of the Style List in the SpeedBar. Quattro Pro automatically sizes the column to properly display the date.

See the date appear in cell F1. But on the input line (while the cell selector is still at cell F1), there's a five-digit number, 34304. This is a *serial date* that Quattro Pro uses for date arithmetic.

SERIAL DATES

Serial dates are calculated based on the number of days elapsed since December 31, 1899, which is assigned the number 1. Thus the serial date 2 is January 1, 1900 and the serial date 34154 is July 4, 1993. The farthest date in the future that Quattro Pro accepts is 12/31/2099 (serial date 73050). To enter dates past 12/31/1999, enter the year in full, as in 7/4/2036. (Doing so, though, will fill the cell with asterisks, indicating that the column is too narrow to accomodate all the numbers. Chapter 3 will show you how to change a column's width, so you can display such an entry properly.)

You can also enter dates from the last century, if you want. These have negative serial dates, since they came before December 31, 1899. Thus the serial date 0 is 12/30/1899 and −24756 is 3/20/1832. The earliest date that Quattro Pro for Windows accepts is 3/1/1800 (serial date −36463).

Serial dates are very handy. Here are just a few of the tasks you can perform with them:

- Calculate how many days there are between two dates by subtracting one from the other.

- Fill a row of cells with dates that are all one week (or 5 days or 63 days) apart.

- Find a date 90 days in the future (or past) by taking today's date and adding (or subtracting) 90.

Using Simple Formulas

Formulas are cell entries that perform calculations on other cells. The operators you use in formulas are similar to the operators you use in everyday math. These are the most common ones:

+   Adds

−   Subtracts

*   Multiplies

/   Divides

To help Quattro Pro for Windows distinguish formulas from labels, numbers, and dates, most spreadsheet users begin a formula with a plus sign (+). Other characters are allowed, but for now just try to begin all formulas with a plus sign.

Now let's look at a simple formula to add Ralph and Alice's incomes and display the result next to the **Total Income** label on the spreadsheet.

When creating formulas, it is better to have them refer to the addresses of cells that contain numbers, rather than the numbers themselves. That way, if you change one of the numbers in a cell, the formula will automatically recalculate the answer. More on this a bit later.

To display the sum of Ralph and Alice's income in cell C11, follow these steps:

1. Move the cell selector to cell C11.

2. Type the formula *exactly* as shown below:

+C8+C9

3. Press Enter.

You should see that cell C11 now displays **6000**—the sum of Ralph and Alice's income. If you look at the input line near the top of the screen (as in Figure 2.6), you'll see that the cell actually contains the formula +C8+C9.

The formula +C8+C9 says to Quattro Pro, "In this cell, display the sum of the contents of cells C8 and C9." Note that if you had omitted the leading plus sign and entered the formula as C8+C9, Quattro Pro would have interpreted the entry as a label (because it began with a letter), not as a formula.

RECALCULATING A FORMULA WITH DIFFERENT DATA

Suppose Ralph suddenly gets a raise and is now earning $3000 per month. Do you need to enter a new formula? Absolutely not, because the formula +C8+C9 says, "Add whatever is in cell C8 to whatever is in cell C9 and display the total in cell C11." Hence, when you move the cell selector to cell C8, type **3000**, and hit Enter, the total income will immediately be recalculated, and cell C11 will display the correct result: **7000**. (See Figure 2.7.)

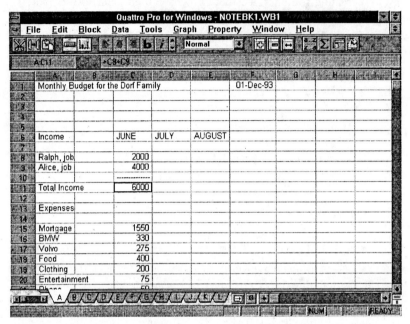

FIGURE 2.6:

Total income
calculated with
a formula

For the time being, however, let's assume that Ralph did not get a raise. Move the cell selector back to cell C8, type **2000**, and press Enter. The total income immediately returns to **6000**.

Functions vs. Formulas

The formula you just created added the total value of two income cells. Looking at the Expenses section of the Dorfs' budget, you can see that there are many cells that need to be totaled in order to determine the couple's expenses. You could take the time to enter the address of every cell (+C15+C16+C17... and so on), but that would be laborious and prone to error. It is simpler to total the cells as a group, or *block*. Before you can sum a large group of numbers, however, you need to know how to define a block of data.

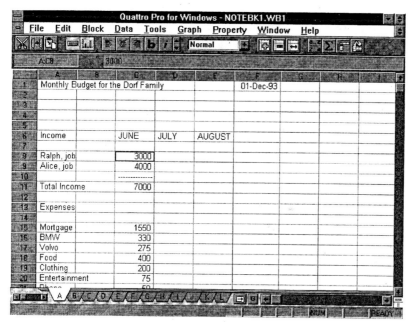

FIGURE 2.7:

Total income automatically recalculated

WHAT IS A BLOCK?

A block is any rectangular group of cells on a spreadsheet page. It is designated by the cell addresses of its upper-left and lower-right corners, with two periods in between. For example, the block A1..B3 consists of the row of cells A1 through A3 and the row of cells B1 through B3. The smallest possible block is a single cell, such as A1..A1. The largest block is the entire spreadsheet, A1..IV8192. Figure 2.8 shows examples of several blocks on a spreadsheet.

Note that all the sample blocks have an even, rectangular shape. You *cannot* define blocks that have any other shape, such as an L, U, T, triangle or pear. This is important to remember when you are deciding how to enter and list your data.

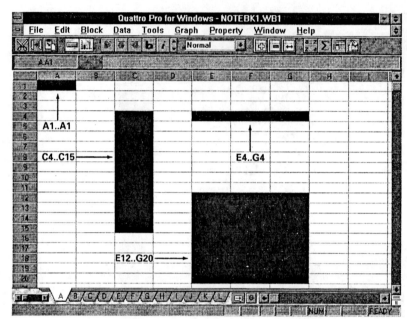

FIGURE 2.8:

Examples of blocks on a spreadsheet

USING A FUNCTION TO SUM A BLOCK OF NUMBERS

Rather than write your own formulas, you may be able to use one of Quattro Pro's preprogrammed functions, which are far too numerous to discuss right now. (We will discuss them in Chapter 15.) You only need the @SUM function to accomplish your present goal.

Notice that the function name begins with the @ (at) sign. All Quattro Pro functions begin with an @ sign, followed by a word and a pair of parentheses that enclose the *argument* of that function. Arguments are the data that the function uses in its calculation. (*Argument* may sound strange, but it is a term that mathematicians use regularly.) After the function finishes its calculation, it *returns* a result.

The @SUM function uses the general syntax @SUM(*block(s)*), where *block(s)* is the block (or blocks) of numbers to be summed. For example, @SUM(C15..C22) says, "Sum all the numbers in the block of cells from C15 to C22." Let's go ahead and use @SUM to total the Dorfs' expenses. You'll want to display the sum in cell C24, so follow these steps:

1. Move the cell selector to cell C24.

2. Type in the function exactly as shown below:

@SUM(C15..C22)

3. As usual, click the left mouse button, click on the check mark, or press Enter when you're through.

You should see the answer, 3180, in cell C24, and the actual function on the input line, as shown in Figure 2.9. Of course, if you were to change any of the expenses in block C15..C22, @SUM would calculate

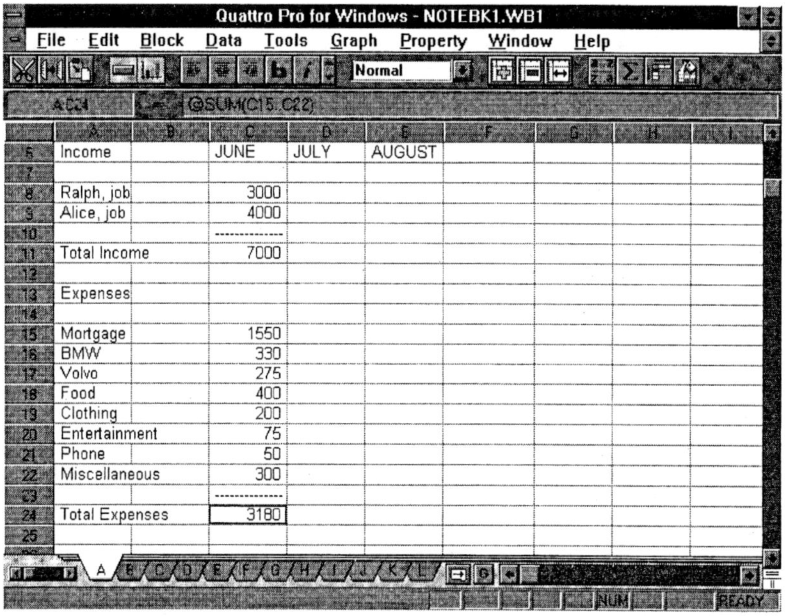

FIGURE 2.9:

Cell C24 showing the sum of the expenses

the new results immediately. You'll get much more experience with formulas and Quattro Pro for Windows functions in future chapters.

USING THE SPEEDBAR TO ENTER A SUMMING FORMULA

The SpeedSum button (marked Σ) is used to enter the @SUM function and a formula to total a block of cells. To use the SpeedSum button, follow these steps:

1. Move the cell selector to cell C24 (if it is not already there).

2. Click on the Cut button, select Edit ➤ Clear, or press Delete, to erase the current cell entry.

3. Click on the SpeedSum button.

Quattro Pro automatically enters the @SUM function, the parentheses, and the cell block C15..C23 (as opposed to the block C15..C22 from the previous example). Although it makes no difference in this particular example (because cell C23 does not contain a numerical value), be aware that this may affect your results in other circumstances. Whenever you click on the SUM button, Quattro Pro tries to create a formula using the SUM function and all of the contiguous cells in either the column or row, depending on where the cell selector is when you click the button. If the cell selector is at the end of a row of numbers, Quattro Pro tries to total all the numbers in the row either right or left. The cell selector must be in a blank cell for the button to work.

Do you want to take a break? Before you walk away from the computer, save your work so that you can use this sample notebook in later chapters.

Saving Your Work

All the work you have done so far on your notebook is stored in the computer's main memory (also called *random access memory*, or RAM). Unless you take specific steps to save a copy of this notebook on the computer's disk as a file, it will be erased completely when you exit from Quattro Pro for Windows or turn off the computer. To save your work, you need to set some options (or commands) from the Quattro Pro menu system.

To access the File menu, point to and click on the File menu name. At the end of Chapter 1, you opened the File menu and used the Exit command to leave Quattro Pro for Windows. Remember, to select an option on any menu, you can move the mouse pointer and click, use ↑ or ↓ to move the highlight to the option you want and press Enter, or type the option's highlighted access letter.

To save the notebook with this spreadsheet as a file on your disk, you need to select the Save option. So either click on the Save option or type **S**. Quattro Pro for Windows includes another command on the File menu, Save All. It is discussed in Chapter 8.

NAMING YOUR SPREADSHEET

After you've selected File and Save from the menus, Quattro Pro will display the Save File dialog box, as seen in Figure 2.10. The format for file names is as follows:

drive:\directory**.WB1**

The exact description of the *drive:\directory* portion depends on where you installed Quattro Pro for Windows. If it is installed on the C drive in the QPW subdirectory, the screen will read as in Figure 2.10.

The name you enter for the notebook can be no more than eight characters long, must not contain any blank spaces, and should not contain any punctuation marks other than the underline character (_). To make the name of the file easy to remember in this example, simply type **DORF** and press Enter.

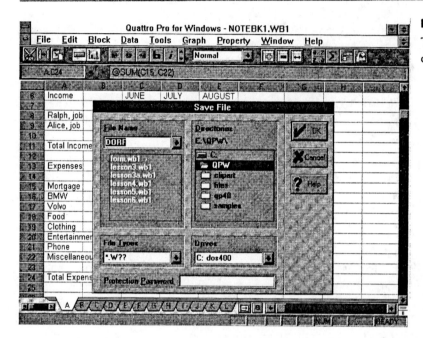

FIGURE 2.10:

The Save File
dialog box

You may notice that a disk-drive light comes on as Quattro Pro saves the file. After you've completed the steps for saving your work, a copy of the spreadsheet will remain on the screen.

Congratulations! You have successfully built a Quattro Pro spreadsheet that includes several types of entries: labels, numbers, a date, and formulas. Before moving on to more advanced techniques, you'd be wise to become familiar with the different data types. Take some time to read the rest of this chapter, and by all means feel free to experiment on a new blank spreadsheet page if you like.

One important point to note here is that you should save files regularly during the course of your work. If the power goes out, the work you've sweated over could be gone in an instant. Exiting from Quattro Pro without saving your work will also wipe out a notebook.

At this point, with the notebook safely stored on disk, you can exit Quattro Pro for Windows if you like. Click on the File menu and select Exit.

Aligning Labels

As we mentioned earlier, Quattro Pro automatically places the apostrophe label prefix in front of any label you enter. This prefix tells Quattro Pro to left-justify the label within the cell. Label prefixes and their effects are listed below:

' (apostrophe)	Left-justifies label
^ (caret)	Centers label
" (quotation mark)	Right-justifies label
\ (backslash)	Repeats label

To use a label prefix, simply type it in before you type the first letter of the label. For example, to center the letters *ABC* within a cell, position the cell selector to the appropriate cell and type **^ABC**. Then press Enter.

Figure 2.11 shows examples of labels entered with various prefixes. Note that any label long enough to spill over into adjoining cells will always be left-justified within its cell, regardless of the label prefix you assign. Also note that long labels will spill over only into empty cells. For example, in Figure 2.11, cell A10 contains the label **This is a long label.** But because cell B10 contains the number **999,** the fragment *long label* spilling out of A10 is cut short at the beginning of cell B10.

Cell A6 contains the label \=. Because the backslash label prefix fills the cell with whatever character(s) follows it, cell A6 is filled with equal signs.

Cell A12 contains a long label that appears to be centered within row 12. It isn't, though. Instead, there are simply blank spaces between the label prefix and the label itself. The cell actually contains the phrase, *This is a long label with leading spaces,* with some blank spaces in front of it. To enter such a label, simply position the cell selector, press the space bar a few times to insert blank spaces, type in the label, and hit Enter.

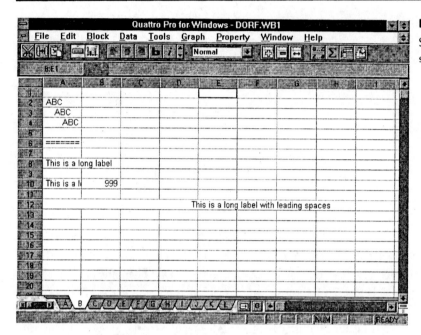

ALIGNING LABELS WITH THE SPEEDBAR

You can use the SpeedBar to set label alignment for a cell or cell block.

1. Move the cell selector to the first cell you want to modify.

2. Click and drag the cells that you want to realign. The cells are then highlighted (except for the active cell).

3. Click on the appropriate alignment button in the SpeedBar. The cells stay highlighted. If the alignment is not what you want, click on a different alignment button.

Entering Labels That Start with a Number

In some cases, you'll want to enter labels that do not begin with a letter—for example, an address such as 123 Oak Tree Lane. If you simply enter this text, Quattro Pro will display the error message

Invalid cell or block address

because it does not know whether the entry is a number (123) or a label (Oak Tree Lane). (Click on OK to clear the message.) Labels that begin with a number *must* be entered with a label prefix. So you should enter the street address as '123 **Oak Tree Lane** (or ^123 **Oak Tree Lane** or "123 **Oak Tree Lane**).

Rectify the problem now by moving the mouse to the beginning of the label and clicking, typing an apostrophe (or ^ or "), and pressing Enter. This puts the prefix where it belongs and stores the corrected label in the cell.

Rules for Entering Numbers

Here are some rules to keep in mind when entering numbers into a spreadsheet:

- A number can contain only digits (0–9), a leading plus (+) or minus (−) sign, and a decimal point (.). A trailing percent (%) sign is also acceptable. Commas, blank spaces, dollar signs, and other nonnumeric characters are not allowed.

- A number can contain only one decimal point.

- If you have a habit of using the letter *l* for the number *1* and the letter O for the number 0 on a standard typewriter, you'll need to break that habit now. Quattro Pro distinguishes between letters and numbers and will not accept one for the other. Use the number keys on the top of the keyboard or on the numeric keypad to enter all numbers.

- The number you enter into a cell can be extremely large or small, as long as it does not exceed 254 digits. If you enter a number that is too wide for a cell, the number will not spill over into an adjacent cell. Instead, the cell will display the number in scientific notation. You can use the Fit button to widen the cell so that a lengthy number can fit. Unlike labels, numbers are automatically right-justified.

- You can include a % sign at the end of a number to indicate percentage values. Quattro Pro will convert the number to a decimal value. For example, if you type **9.375%** into a cell, Quattro Pro will display it as 0.09375 (unless you change the display, discussed in Chapter 5).

EXAMPLES OF VALID AND INVALID NUMBERS

If all those rules for entering numbers are confusing you, take a look at examples of valid and invalid numbers in Table 2.1. It will help summarize the rules for you.

NUMBER	VALID OR INVALID?
1	Valid—nothing unusual about this number
123.45	Valid—nothing unusual about this number
+123.45	Valid—same as 123.45
−123.45	Valid—a negative number
22%	Valid—displayed as 0.22
12 ¾	Invalid—contains a space (12 + ¾ is okay, though)
12,345	Invalid—contains a comma
$123.45	Valid, though Quattro Pro will ignore the dollar sign
640K	Invalid—contains a letter
6.3E+9	Valid—the letter E (or e) can be used to express scientific notation, which is 6.3×10^9 in this example

TABLE 2.1:

Examples of valid and invalid number entries

In the next chapter, you'll learn some more advanced techniques for using the Quattro Pro for Windows menus and simplifying the development of larger spreadsheets.

3 C H A P T E R

FEATURING

Retrieving a spreadsheet

Editing cell entries

Inserting and deleting rows and columns

Enabling Undo

Erasing blocks of data

Learning Basic Editing Techniques

f you exited from Quattro Pro for Windows in Chapter 2, be sure to get it up and running on your computer again. If you did not exit but did save the DORF notebook, click on the File menu and select New. Quattro Pro opens a new notebook in which to work.

Retrieving Your Spreadsheet

Recall from the last chapter that you used the Save command from the File menu to save a notebook as a file named DORF. Quattro Pro for Windows always adds the *extension* .WB1 to any notebook file name you provide, so your notebook is actually stored under the file name DORF.WB1 in the QPW directory on your computer's hard disk.

Go ahead and retrieve DORF now:

1. Click on the File menu and then on Open. Quattro Pro will display the Open File dialog box with a list of the saved files, as shown in Figure 3.1.

■ Remember that the application window and the document window have been maximized in the example figures.

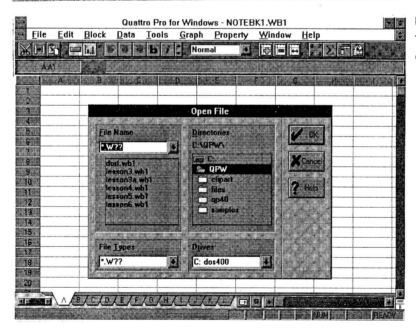

FIGURE 3.1:

The Open File dialog box

- Quattro Pro lists the previously saved notebooks in the File Name part of the dialog box. The asterisk and question mark are DOS *wild-card* specifications, ∗ standing for any number of characters and ? standing for any single character. Thus ∗.W?? represents all files in the QPW directory whose extension begins with *W*.
- In the right portion of the Open File dialog box, Quattro Pro displays the current directory and drive letter.

2. To select the file you want to retrieve, either type its name (DORF in this example) or click on the name of the file, then click on OK. You can also double-click on the name instead of clicking on OK.

If DORF is already open, Quattro Pro gives you an error message: **Notebook is already open.**

You'll see the spreadsheet reappear on the screen as shown in Figure 3.2. (Depending on where you positioned the cell selector when you last saved the notebook, you may see a different range of rows than that shown.)

Retrieving vs. Opening

Retrieve and Open are not the same command. Notice that when you highlight Retrieve in the File menu, the status line reads, **Load a notebook into the active window.** This means that whatever is in the current window will be erased to make room for the newly loaded notebook. This wasn't a problem just a moment ago when you retrieved DORF, because you were just loading it into an empty workspace. If you had been in danger of losing your current screen, Quattro Pro for Windows would have prompted you, **Lose changes in C:\QPW\DORF.WB1**, to which you could have answered Yes or No.

By contrast, selecting Open lets you **Load and display an existing notebook,** as per the status line. In this case, your newly loaded

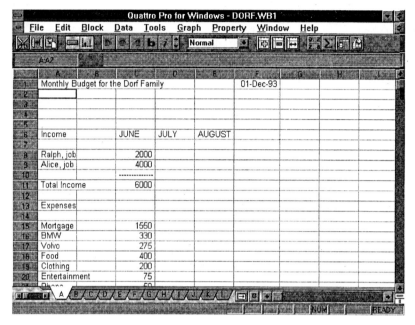

FIGURE 3.2:

The DORF file retrieved from disk

notebook will fill a new window that overlies the current window. You can open quite a number of different notebooks in this way—in fact, as many as 50.

Setting up a particular group of notebooks and spreadsheets in a certain manner is called *configuring the workspace*. Once you establish a configuration of windows that suits your work best, you can save your workspace for later use. For now, you'll be working with just one notebook.

Editing a Cell Entry

In Chapter 2 we discussed some simple ways to correct cell entries. In this section, you'll learn how to edit without having to retype or delete an entry—except for dates (but more on that later).

EXPLORING THE EDIT MODE

To change the contents of any cell, simply click on the cell containing the data you want to change. The contents of the cell will appear on the input line. Click on the input line to place an insertion point in the entry. The word EDIT will appear at the far right of the status line. (You can also press the Edit key (F2) after selecting the cell. Pressing F2 puts then insertion point at the end of the entry on the input line.)

Let's get some hands-on practice with the Edit mode right now. Start with the label in cell A1 and change *Dorf* to *Smith*:

1. Move the cell selector to cell A1 by using the mouse or pressing Home.

2. Click on the end of the input line or press F2. The input line will then read:

'Monthly Budget for the Dorf Family_

where _ denotes the insertion point's position.

3. Click on the space in front of the *D* in Dorf, to move the insertion point like so:

'Monthly Budget for the _Dorf Family

4. Hit Insert to switch from Insert to Overwrite mode. The Overwrite indicator (**OVR**) will appear on the status line, meaning that whatever you type now will replace the characters ahead of the insertion point.

5. Type **Smit** and you will notice that the *S, m, i,* and *t* replace the *D, o, r,* and *f*:

'Monthly Budget for the Smit_Family

6. If you insert the *h* in *Smith* now, you'll overwrite the blank space and end up with **SmithFamily**. To avoid this run-on, first return to the Insert mode by pressing Insert again. The Overwrite indicator will disappear.

7. Now type **h**. Note that the blank space and the word *Family* shift to the right, making room for the new letter:

'Monthly Budget for the Smith_Family

8. Click on the check mark to finish the edit.

After you click on the check mark, the modified label will return to cell A1.

Now let's practice deleting some text from a cell entry. With the cell selector still on cell A1, follow these steps:

1. Start editing by clicking on the input line or by pressing F2.

2. Click on the space in front of the *S* in *Smith:*

'Monthly Budget for the _Smith Family

3. Hold down the mouse button and drag so that the name *Smith* is selected.

4. Release the mouse button.

5. Select Edit ➤ Clear.

'Monthly Budget for the   _Family

6. Make sure that you are in the Insert mode.

7. Type **Dorf** so the label reads:

'Monthly Budget for the Dorf_Family

8. Click on the check mark, or press Enter. The original label is now back in cell A1.

Of course, you're not limited to editing labels; you can edit any kind of entry you like.

EDITING DATES: A SPECIAL CASE

Cells that contain dates entered with the Ctrl-Shift-D key combination require a slightly different technique for editing. For example, in the previous chapter you entered a date into cell F1. Move the cell selector to cell F1 and click on the input line so that the serial date appears on the input line. Unless you happen to know the serial number for the new date you wish to place in the cell, this method won't do you much good. Click on the X button or press Escape to cancel the edit.

To enter a new date, it is easier to follow the same procedure you used to enter the date in the first place. Move the cell selector to the cell containing the date, press Ctrl-Shift-D, and enter the new date in *DD-MMM-YY* format. Then click on the check mark, press Enter or press an arrow key.

THE AUTOMATIC EDIT MODE

Whenever you enter an incorrectly syntaxed number, formula, function, etc., into a cell, Quattro Pro will display an error message. After you click on OK or hit Escape, it will automatically put you in the Edit mode.

You saw an example of this when you attempted to enter the label *123 Oak Tree Lane* in Chapter 2. Quattro Pro rejected the entry because you put letters in a number—and so it thought you were entering an invalid cell or block address. (You weren't, but it thought you were.) You corrected the entry by moving the cursor to the beginning of the label, typing an apostrophe to identify the entry as a label, and then clicking on the check mark.

Changing a Column Width

By default, Quattro Pro for Windows sets the width of all columns in the spreadsheet to nine spaces. But you can easily change that width. As you saw in Chapter 2, if you enter a number that is too long to fit into a cell, Quattro Pro will display it in scientific notation, such as **1.23E+08** for 123,000,000. Widening the column will allow the software to display the number in the more familiar format.

In Chapter 2 you used the Fit button to change a column width. Here is another method.

To widen or narrow a single column, first move the cell selector to the column you wish to change. Then click the right mouse button to open the Active Block dialog box. In the following steps, we'll change the width of column D to demonstrate how this works:

1. Move the cell selector to cell D5.

2. Click the right mouse button. The Active Block dialog box shown in Figure 3.3 appears.

3. Click on Column Width in the column headed Numeric Format. The contents of the Active Block dialog box change to resemble Figure 3.4.

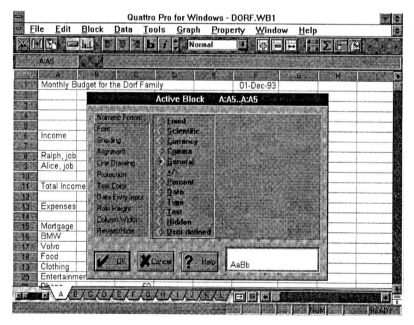

FIGURE 3.3:

The Active Block dialog box

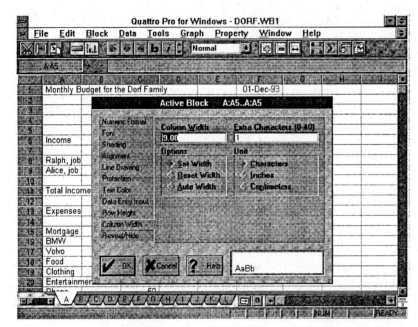

4. Make sure Characters is selected in the Unit column. If not, click on the diamond beside Characters to select it, then click in the Column Width box.

5. Type 4 in the Column Width box to replace the default value of 9.00.

6. Click on OK.

As you can see in Figure 3.5, column D is now just wide enough to accommodate the July heading.

A third way to change column width is to move the mouse pointer to the horizontal border and drag the relevant line. When the mouse pointer changes to a two-headed arrow, click and drag the line left or right to the width you want. (Similarly, you can change row height by dragging the lines in the vertical border.)

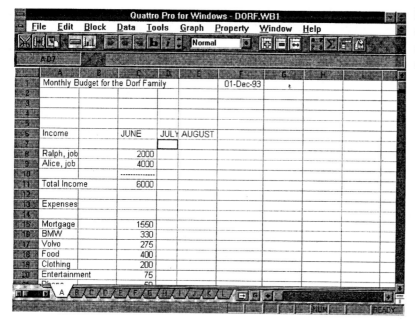

FIGURE 3.5:

Column D narrowed to four spaces

REINSTATING A COLUMN WIDTH

If you change your mind about a column width and wish to revert to the default width of nine spaces, move the cell selector to the appropriate column and click the right mouse button. In the Active Block dialog box click on Column Width, Reset Width, OK. Try this to reset column D to a width of nine spaces.

CHANGING ALL COLUMN WIDTHS

If you prefer to adjust the widths of all columns in the current spreadsheet simultaneously, click on the Active Page command on the Property menu. For example, to set all the columns in your spreadsheet to a width of 15 spaces, follow these steps:

1. Click on the Property menu.

2. Click on Active Page. The Active Page dialog box appears as in Figure 3.6.

3. Click on Default Width.

4. Type **15** to replace the default setting of 9.00 spaces.

5. Click on OK, or press Enter.

To reset the columns to their width of nine spaces, select Property ➤Active Page. In the Active Page dialog box, click on Default Width. Type **9** to replace the 15.00, then click on OK.

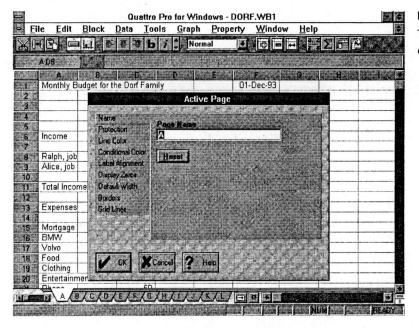

FIGURE 3.6:

The Active Page dialog box

Inserting a Row

Suppose you wish to add some new categories to the Expenses portion of the spreadsheet. To do so, first you need to add some blank rows to the spreadsheet to accommodate the new information. The SpeedInsert button will allow you to do this. Let's try this by inserting a few rows beneath the row labeled *Phone* (row 21) in the current spreadsheet:

1. Move the cell selector to the row above which you wish to place a new row. In this case, move it to cell A22.

2. Click and drag the mouse pointer so that cells A22 to A24 are highlighted.

3. Click on the Insert button in the SpeedBar, the button marked with a plus sign (+). The Insert dialog box appears as in Figure 3.7.

4. At the top of the dialog box Quattro Pro displays the location of the cell selector and the block of cells that is highlighted,

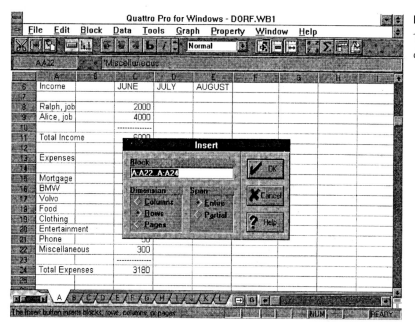

FIGURE 3.7:

The Insert dialog box

A:A22..A24. Notice the dot by the word Rows in the column headed Dimension, indicating that Rows is selected.

5. Click on OK.

Three new rows will appear beneath row 21, as shown in Figure 3.8. (You may have to scroll down a few rows to see them.) These new rows run across the entire length of the spreadsheet page. Because you highlighted a total of three rows, three rows are inserted. The rows are inserted beginning with the active cell.

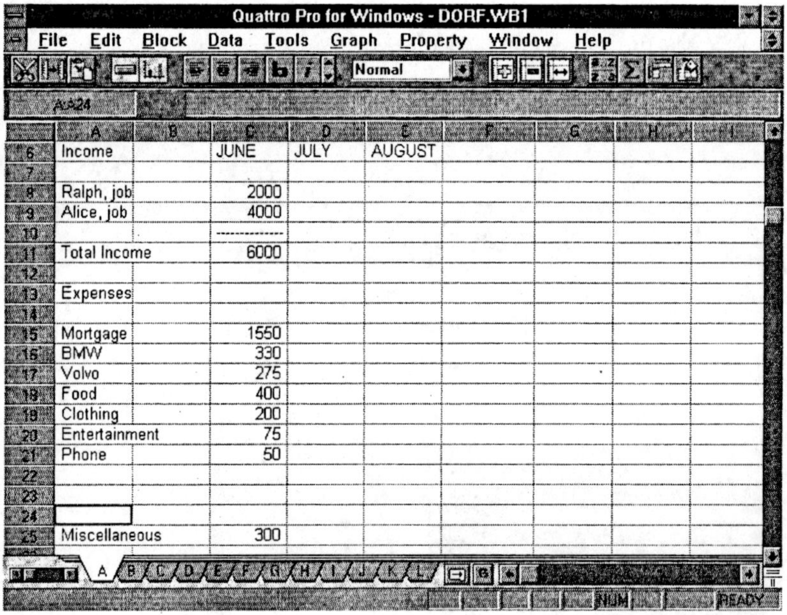

FIGURE 3.8:

Three new rows entered in DORF

Inserting a Row Block

The previous section showed you how to insert an entire row or rows across a spreadsheet. Suppose, however, that you want to insert a row space in only a single column. To execute this task, called inserting a row block, follow the steps below.

1. Move the cell selector to cell A20.

2. Click on the Insert button.

3. Click at the end of the cell address in the box under the Block heading.

4. Erase the A20 at the end of the field entry and replace it with A18, so that the block entry reads A:A20.. A:A18.

5. Under the Span heading, click on Partial. A dot now precedes the word.

6. Click on OK.

As you can see, column A now has three row spaces between **Volvo** and **Food**. The numbers entered in column B did not separate, however; the space insertion affected only column A.

Inserting a Column

The technique for inserting new columns is identical to that for inserting new rows, except that you select Columns rather than Rows in the Insert dialog box. To demonstrate, we'll insert a new column between **JUNE** and **JULY** in the current spreadsheet:

1. Move the cell selector to column D. (In this example, click on cell D6, so you will be able to see the results better.)

2. Click on the Insert button.

3. Under the Dimension heading, click on the word Columns. A dot now precedes the word.

4. In the previous example, we changed the Span from Entire to Partial. Now switch it back by clicking on Entire.

5. Click on OK.

The new column is inserted to the left of the previously highlighted column as shown in Figure 3.9. If you wanted to insert more than one column, you would indicate the number of columns by entering a block address, such as **D6..F6**, in the Insert dialog box. Quattro Pro would then insert three columns.

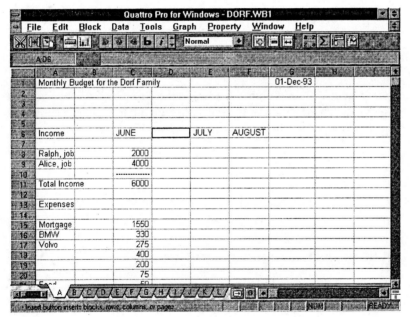

FIGURE 3.9:

Column inserted between JUNE and JULY

Inserting a Column Block

The previous section showed you how to insert an entire column or columns into the spreadsheet. Suppose, however, you want to insert space between two columns, without inserting an entire column.

We'll use our DORF budget as an example. Let's assume that the Dorfs have just moved to a new state and have not yet started working. They already have expenses, however. With the Insert button, we can insert a block of space that will move the income numbers under the July label but leave the expense numbers in their original location.

1. Move the cell selector to cell C8.

2. Click and drag the mouse pointer so that cells C8..D11 are highlighted.

3. Click on the Insert button in the SpeedBar. The Insert dialog box will appear.

4. In the Insert dialog box, click on Columns under Dimension and on Partial under Span. Quattro Pro has inserted the block address A:C8..D11 for you.

5. Click on OK.

Notice that space has been inserted in only the selected column block. The income data is now in column E under **JULY**. The block remains highlighted until you click on a different cell.

Deleting a Row Block

You can easily delete the row block that you inserted earlier by using the Insert dialog box. Follow these steps:

1. Click on cell A20.

2. Click and drag the mouse pointer so that cells A20 to A18 are highlighted.

3. Click on the Delete button in the SpeedBar. It is to the right of the Insert button and is marked with a minus sign.

4. Click on Rows under the Dimension heading and on Partial under the Span heading.

5. Click on OK. Cells A18 to A20 are removed, and the cells below are moved up to replace them. The cells will remain highlighted until you click on a different cell.

Deleting a Row

Before you delete a row from a spreadsheet, remember that you will dump the *entire* row, from column A to column IV, unless you select Partial from the Delete dialog box. Afterwards, all the rows beneath will move up to replace the deleted one. (To erase only the *contents* of a row, or a portion thereof, you can use the Cut button or the Edit ➤ Clear option, which are discussed later in this chapter.)

To delete a row, then, position the cell selector on the row you wish to delete (or the topmost row if you wish to delete several) and click on the Delete button. To remove row 22:

1. Move the cell selector to any cell in row 22.

2. Click on the Delete button.

3. Click on Entire under Span, and make sure that Rows is selected under Dimension.

4. Click on OK.

■ To delete several rows, click and drag the block of cells before you click on the Delete button. Or if you have not highlighted the block before opening the Delete dialog box, type the cell address in the Block box. For example, to delete rows A22, A23, and A24, type A:A22..A24.

■ If you change your mind and do not wish to delete a row after all, and you have not yet clicked on OK, simply click on Cancel.

Deleting a Column

When you erase a column from a spreadsheet, beware that you will trash the *entire* column, from row 1 to row 8192. Afterwards, all columns to the right will shift left to replace the deleted one. (To erase only the *contents* of a column, or a portion thereof, use the Cut button or the Edit ➤ Clear option, which are discussed next.)

Go ahead and delete the new column D that you just inserted:

1. Move the cell selector to any cell in column D (though preferably to cell D6 in this example, so that you can best see the results).

2. Click on the Delete button.

3. Under Dimension click on Columns, and under Span click on Entire.

4. Click on OK.

To delete several columns, click and drag the columns before accessing the Delete dialog box, then click on OK. Or type the addresses of the block of columns you want to delete in the Block box in the Delete dialog box, then click on OK or press Enter. For example, to delete several columns type **D6..F6**.

Deleting a Column Block

The column block you inserted earlier with the Insert dialog box can be deleted easily. Because you have already deleted a single column, the cells that you are going to delete are C8..C11. This moves the income numbers back to the June column.

1. Click on cell C8.

2. Click and drag the mouse pointer until the cells C8..C11 are highlighted.

3. Click on the Delete button in the SpeedBar.

4. Click on Columns under Dimension and on Partial under Span.

5. Click on OK.

Erasing a Block of Data

As we mentioned above, deleting an entire row or column affects a very large portion of the spreadsheet—well beyond what you see on the screen. To limit the erasure to a particular block of cells, use the Cut button or the Edit ➤ Clear option.

Erasing portions of a spreadsheet used to be hazardous work—you could accidentally erase the wrong block and get stuck. Fortunately, Quattro Pro for Windows has a built-in safeguard against just that problem, a feature called Undo. When you take any action that changes the spreadsheet, and find that the result is not as you intended, you can select Edit ➤ Undo to undo the previous action. It's like pretending the error never happened. In the following example, you will erase a block and then use Undo to return the spreadsheet to its prior state.

ENABLING UNDO

Before erasing anything, make sure that the Undo option is enabled— i.e., set to work.

1. Click on Property to pull down the Property menu.

2. Click on Application. The Application dialog box appears, as shown in Figure 3.10.

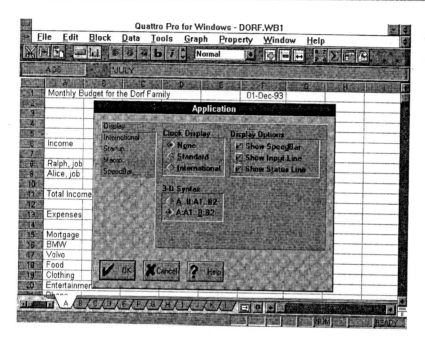

FIGURE 3.10:

The Application dialog box

3. Undo is considered a Startup setting in Quattro Pro for Windows, so click on the word Startup. The Startup options appear in the Application dialog box, as shown in Figure 3.11.

4. Undo is not enabled yet. Click on Undo enabled, so that a check mark precedes the words.

5. Click on OK.

ERASING THE BLOCK

Now you can use the Cut button or the Edit ➤ Clear feature with impunity. The first step is to move the cell selector to the upper-left corner of the block you want to erase. For this exercise, erase the labels and expenses from rows 15 through 21.

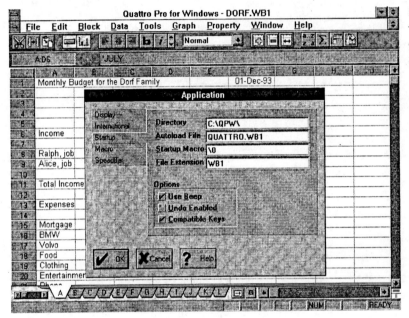

FIGURE 3.11:

The Application Startup options in the dialog box

1. Click on cell A15.

2. Click and drag the mouse pointer until the cells in the block A15..C21 are highlighted, as in Figure 3.12.

3. Click on the Cut button or select Edit ➤ Clear.

As soon as you click on the Cut button (or on Clear), the area that was highlighted will be completely erased, as shown in Figure 3.13.

RECOVERING FROM DISASTER WITH UNDO

But wait a minute. Suppose you change your mind and realize that you didn't want to cut this large block of cells after all. No need to worry Quattro Pro for Windows knows what you did, and can reverse the action with Undo.

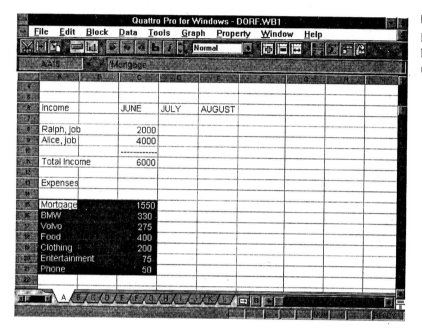

FIGURE 3.12:

Block of
highlighted cells
to be erased

Click on the Edit menu, then click on Undo Cut. Immediately, all of the cells are restored as before.

Undo is a wonderful tool for recovering from a mistake—whether it is a deletion or an addition. You can even undo something you have already undone! Just select Edit ➤ Redo. But you must either enable Undo when you start a session with Quattro Pro for Windows or change the default Application setting so that it is always enabled.

There are two things to note here. First, Undo and Redo work only on your most recently issued command. So if you erase a block of cells and then delete a row, selecting Edit ➤ Undo will return only the deleted row. When you make a mistake, undo it *immediately!*

Second, the Undo and Redo commands change to include your last operation. In this case Undo appears as Undo Cut, and Redo as Redo Cut. You will also see Undo Block Delete, Undo Property Set, and so on.

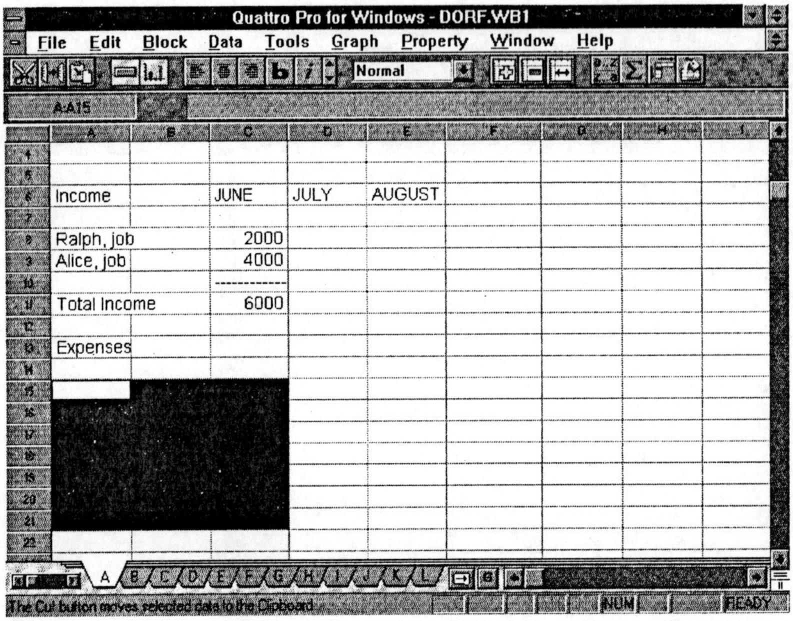

FIGURE 3.13:

The highlighted block erased

Erasing the Entire Spreadsheet

If at any time you want to erase the spreadsheet screen completely and start with a clean slate, click on the Select All button at the intersection of the row letters and column numbers, in the upper left corner of the spreadsheet border. When you click on it, the entire spreadsheet is highlighted as a single block of cells. Click on the Cut button, select Edit ➤ Clear Contents or press Delete. The entire spreadsheet is erased. Remember to enable Undo before you take such drastic actions.

As with Block Delete and all Quattro Pro operations, this deletion affects only the copy of the spreadsheet that is currently in memory. It has no effect on the most recently saved disk copy. Therefore, if you've recently saved your notebook and then accidentally erased the entire thing, you can still retrieve your work by opening another copy of the file. If Undo is enabled, you can also reverse the accidental erasure by selecting Edit ➤ Undo, provided that you have not done anything else in the meantime.

The Importance of Saving Your Work

In this chapter you've seen some general techniques for changing, adding to, and deleting segments of your spreadsheet. You've also learned that enabling the Undo option is crucial if you wish to restore accidental erasures.

Undo is helpful, but even it cannot save your work during the past hour (or more) if there is a sudden power failure—in such a case you will certainly lose all of your work since the last time you saved the notebook. To avoid such a catastrophe, save your work often. This ensures that you won't lose more than 15–20 minutes' worth of your work, or whatever time interval you choose.

Before leaving this chapter, be sure to save the notebook. Select File ➤ Save, as before. Note that if you use File ➤Save As instead, and type in the name of a file that already exists, Quattro Pro will display the Save File dialog box with these words:

File already exists:
Replace   Backup   Cancel   Help

What are these options about?

- **Replace** saves your notebook as DORF and, in so doing, throws away the old version.

- **Backup** saves your notebook as DORF, but it also keeps the old version. It manages this by changing the extension of the old file from .WB1 to .BAK. Now you'll have two files on disk, DORF.WB1, the most recent version of the Dorfs' family budget, and DORF.BAK, the version of the notebook that existed before you made the changes that are now in DORF.WB1.

- **Cancel** closes the dialog box and sends you back to the notebook, as though you had never asked to save anything.

- **Help** gives you information on saving your files.

Making backups of your notebooks is always a good idea. It ensures you don't lose vital information that perhaps you once thought was not important. However, you have not really created any vitally important documents now, so just choose Replace to save your modified DORF notebook.

In the next chapter, you'll learn some more advanced techniques for copying and moving blocks of data on the spreadsheet, and get a little more practice with formulas as well.

4 C H A P T E R

FEATURING

The click and drag method

Copying information

Moving information

Relative and absolute cell references

▼

Copying and Moving Blocks of Data

In this chapter, you will learn some more advanced techniques for copying and moving blocks of data on the spreadsheet. You'll also build formulas and copy them, and learn how to make them absolute or relative.

Simplifying Your Work with the Pointing Method

As you learned in Chapter 2, you can place cell addresses and block references (such as A1..C5) in functions. Pointing, clicking and then dragging allows you to do that by highlighting a cell or block, rather than by typing the address. You used the click and drag technique in Chapter 3 to highlight a group of cells for erasing.

You can use this same point, click, and drag technique to create functions and copy and move information easily. Because it is so visually oriented, you don't have to waste time looking up the address of a cell or block and then keying it in—and then erasing typos. With pointing, clicking and dragging, you enter the address as you look it up.

Creating a Function with the Pointing Method

Recall that in Chapter 2 you entered the function @SUM(C15..C22) to sum the expenses on the spreadsheet. You entered this function simply by typing it in. If you were lucky, you didn't have to retype it. Now let's look at the other way you can create this function.

Move the cell selector to C26, where the function is located, and erase it. The cell should be empty now. To reenter the function:

1. Click on cell C26.

2. Type the beginning of the function:

@SUM(

Capital letters are not important, so **@sum(** will work just as well. (Quattro Pro just converts the letters to uppercase later on anyway.) It is far more important to include the opening parenthesis.

3. Begin the click and drag operation by pressing the left mouse button. Notice that the function on the input line reads **@SUM(C26** and the mode indicator in the lower-right corner reads **POINT**.

You are in Point mode, and now you'll see how to stretch the cell selector over the cells you wish to include in the function.

4. Move the cell selector to cell C15 with the mouse pointer.

5. Now you want to anchor the cell selector to this cell before stretching it over the numbers you want to sum. To do this, click the left mouse button. The function on the input line now reads **@SUM(C15**.

6. To stretch the cell selector, click and drag the mouse pointer until all the numbers in cells C15 through C24 are highlighted, as shown in Figure 4.1.

7. Complete the function by typing the closing parenthesis. The function on the input line now reads **@SUM(C15..C24)**. Notice that the cell selector jumps back to its original location, cell C26.

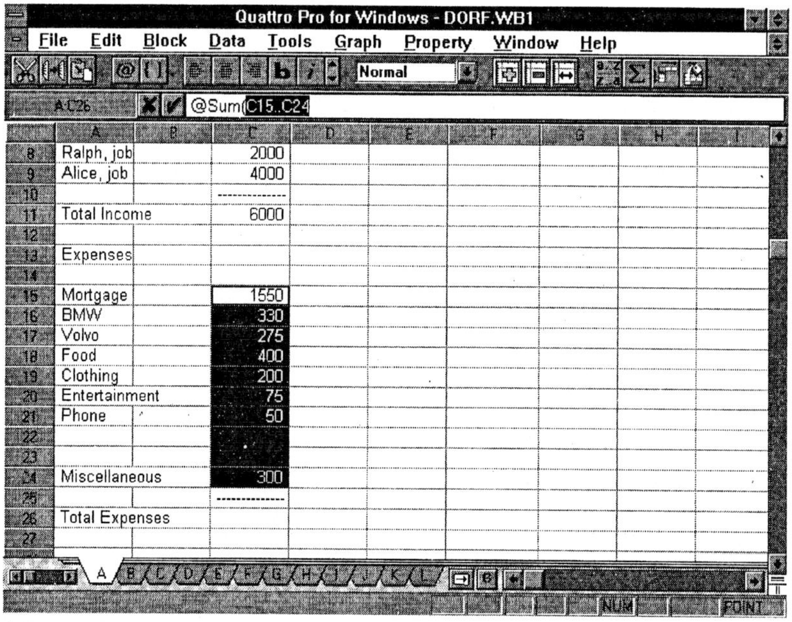

FIGURE 4.1:

The cell selector highlighting the numbers being summed

8. Click on the check mark to complete the function.

The sum of the expenses, 3180, now appears in cell C26. You can see the actual function, @SUM(C15..C24), on the input line, as shown in Figure 4.2.

After learning a few rules about pointing and clicking, you can employ some fancy tricks. Both are discussed in the rest of the chapter.

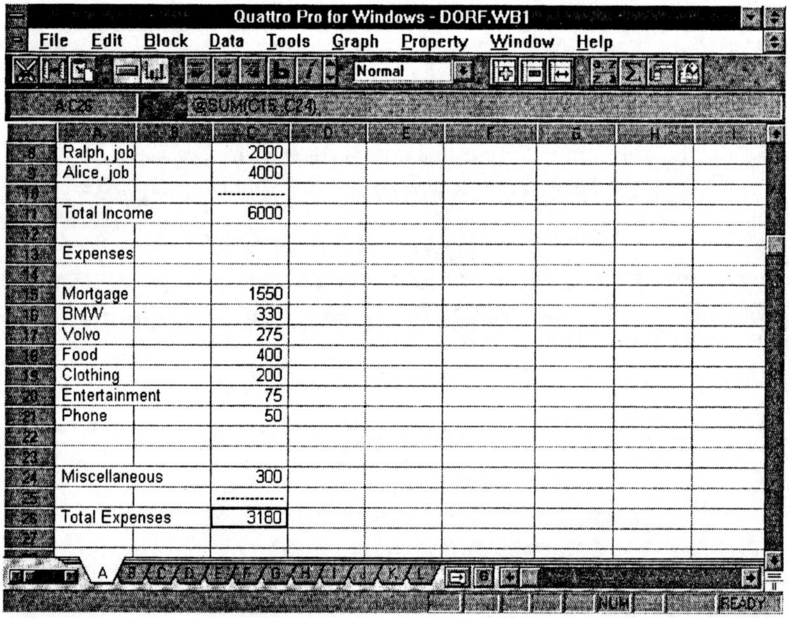

FIGURE 4.2:

An @SUM function in cell C26

Copying Information from One Cell to Several

Up to this point, the spreadsheet has contained information just for the month of June. Now it needs data for July and August as well. To speed things along, we'll show you how to copy entries rather than having to type them in again.

Copying data, such as numbers, labels, and dates, is a relatively straightforward operation. Position the cell selector on the cell you wish to copy, or on one corner of the block of cells you're copying. Click the left mouse button and hold it while you drag so that the highlight covers all of the cells that you want to copy.

Suppose you want to copy Ralph's income from cell C8 to D8 and E8:

1. Move the cell selector to cell C8. The number 2000 will be highlighted.

2. Click on the Copy button, the second button from the left in the SpeedBar. The contents of cell C8 are copied onto the Clipboard.

3. Select the cells you want to copy to. Click and drag cells D8 and E8.

4. Click on the Paste button, the next button to the right of the Copy button.

Immediately, the contents of the source block (cell C8) are copied to the cells in the destination block (D8..E8), as shown in Figure 4.3.

You can also copy by selecting a source block, then selecting Block ➤ Copy. The Block Copy dialog box appears. You then enter the cell address of the destination block into the To section, and click on the check mark. We'll try this next.

Copying Blocks of Information

In the last example, you copied a single cell's contents to two other cells. You can also copy the contents of several cells at once. For this you could use the Copy button again, but this time we'll use the Block ➤ Copy command.

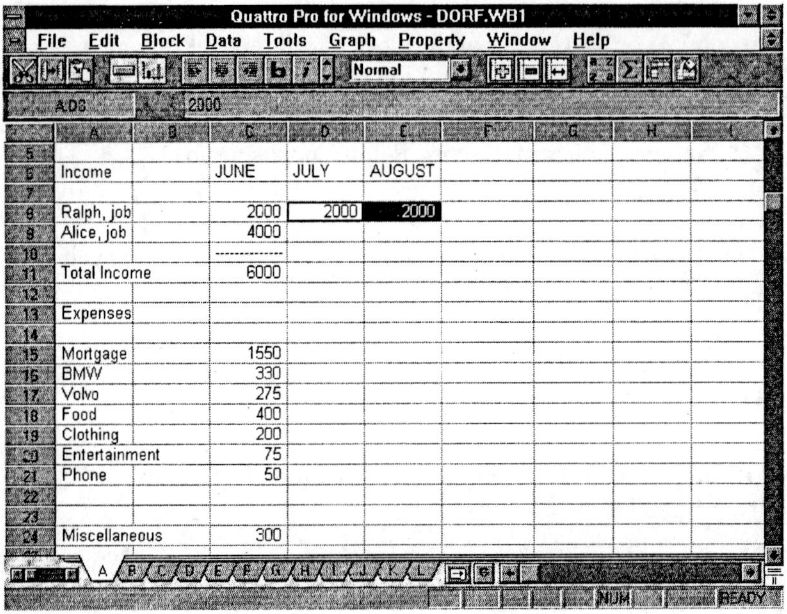

FIGURE 4.3:

Cell C8 copied to cells D8 and E8

Suppose that the monthly expenses in cells C15 through C26 are fairly constant, so you just want to copy June's expenses to the July and August columns:

1. Move the cell selector to cell C15.

2. Click and drag the mouse pointer so that the cells in block C15 to C26 are highlighted.

3. Click on the Block menu and then click on Copy. The Block Copy dialog box appears (as in Figure 4.4) with the From box displaying the cell address A:C15..C26. The To box displays the same block address.

4. Double-click on the To box. The dialog box is moved up to cover part of the SpeedBar and is reduced in size, leaving only

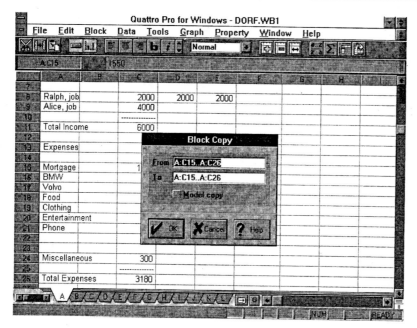

FIGURE 4.4:

The Block Copy
dialog box

FIGURE 4.4:

The Block Copy
dialog box

the top border visible, as shown in Figure 4.5. The input line
now displays the current cell block address, A:C15..C26.

5. Click and drag cells D15..E15. These are the cells to which
we want to copy the information from cells C15..C26.

6. Click on the up arrow in the Block Copy dialog box border.
The full dialog box reappears, with the To box displaying the
cell address D15..E15. (See Figure 4.6)

7. Click on OK.

Your screen should now match Figure 4.7.

Notice that Quattro Pro for Windows was rather clever about copying
the expenses. Even though you did not specify the entire destination block
D15..E26, Quattro Pro performed the copy flawlessly. Quattro Pro always
copies the entire source block, even if the destination block you specify

The Block Copy
dialog box
reduced and the
block of cells
C15..C26
highlighted

contains fewer cells than the source block. For example, if you high-lighted a large block as the source, but highlighted only a *single* cell as the destination, Quattro Pro for Windows would still copy the entire source block. (The single cell at the destination would just become the upper-left corner of the copied block.)

At first this may sound a bit confusing, but you'll find that with practice the procedure will become intuitive. Let's move on to some more topics concerning copying.

A Slight Diversion

Alice's income is expected to increase by 10 percent in August, so you can't just copy her income from column C. Instead, you can calculate her August income with a formula.

To begin with, move the cell selector to cell D9 and enter July's income—4000. (We could have copied 4000 from cell C9, but in this example

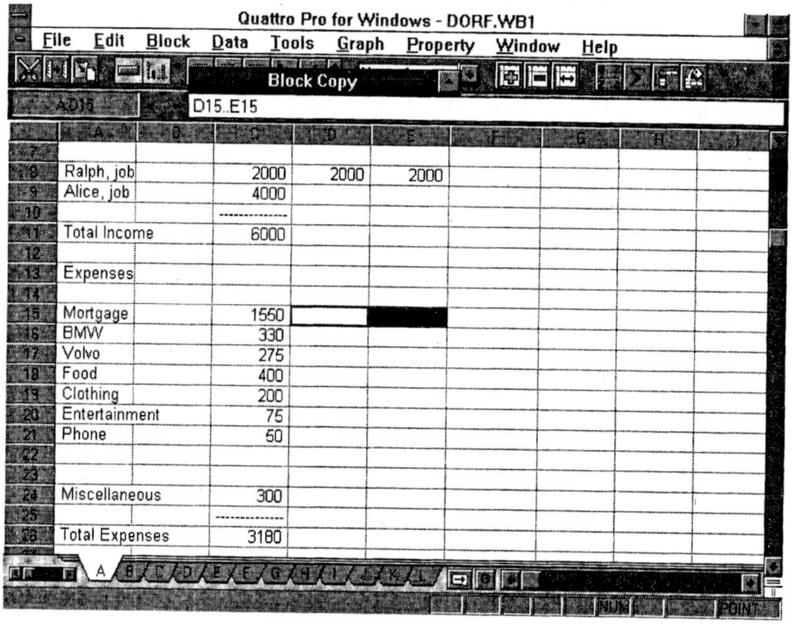

FIGURE 4.6:

The block D15..E15 highlighted

it is probably easier to type **4000**.) Now to calculate August's income, you need to increase July's income by 10 percent.

To increase a value by a percent, multiply the value by one plus the percentage. So Alice's new income will equal 1.10 times her July income. Let's enter the appropriate formula:

1. Move the cell selector to cell E9.

2. Type the formula **+D9*1.10**.

3. Click on the check mark to complete the formula.

The result, 4400, appears in cell E9.

It is simple to calculate the 10 percent increase without using the spreadsheet; however, this example serves to illustrate the use of a formula that refers to another cell. Don't forget to copy the dotted line

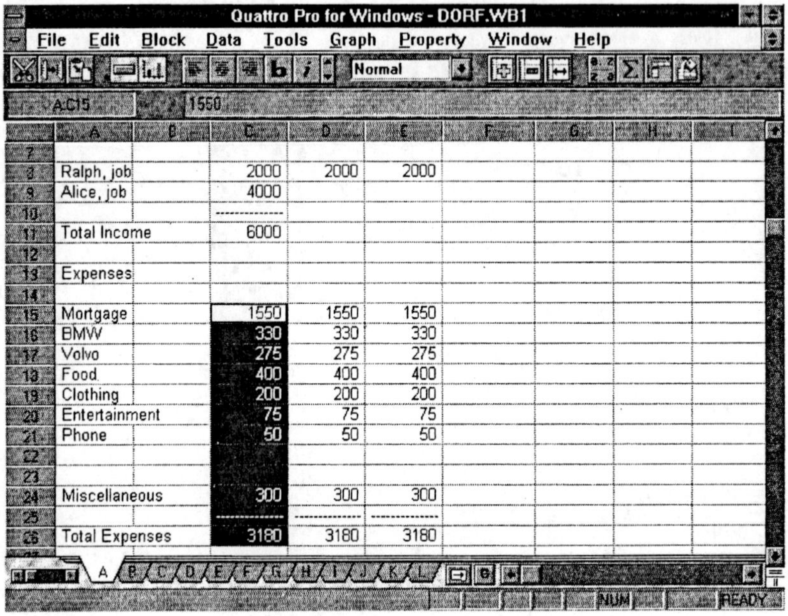

FIGURE 4.7:

The Expenses
section copied to
July and August

from C10 to cells D10 and E10.

Now, let's get back to the main topic of this chapter— copying.

Copying a Formula

The menu selections and the steps for copying formulas are the same as those for copying data. Quattro Pro for Windows treats formulas a little differently, however, in that it attempts to retain their meaning as it copies them. (You got a hint of this in the previous example, but let's deal with this topic independently here.)

Suppose you want to copy the summing formula in cell C11 to cells D11 and E11. Here are the steps to do so:

1. Move the cell selector to cell C11.

2. Click on the Copy button.

3. Click on cell D11 and drag to E11.

4. Click on the Paste button.

Observe that 6000 appears in cell D11, but 6400 appears in E11. You may have thought that Quattro Pro would simply copy the formula +C8+C9 to each of these cells. But this is not exactly the case. If you move the cell selector to E11, you will see on the input line that it actually contains the formula +E8+E9! So the copied formula was adjusted to apply to column E, which contains Ralph's income and Alice's recently increased income. If you move the cell selector to cell D11, you'll see that cell D11 has also been adjusted. It contains the formula +D8+D9. Figure 4.8 shows the "logic" that Quattro Pro used to copy the formulas.

In other words, Quattro Pro for Windows did not copy the formulas *exactly*. Instead, it made sure that the copied formulas would retain their original meaning in a different context, which in this example was to display the sum of the numbers in the two rows above. This copying feature is handy because a spreadsheet often contains several copies of a given formula.

The formula you just copied was a simple one, and the cells it worked on easy to find, but this feature of retaining a formula's "meaning" applies even to complex formulas nested in a complex spreadsheet.

Understanding Relative and Absolute Cell References

In the previous example, you saw how Quattro Pro adjusted the cell addresses inside a formula as it copied the formula to two cells. In some cases, however, you will not want Quattro Pro to adjust such *cell references*. For example, if cell B2 contained a 15 percent discount rate, any formulas that included that discount would have to refer always to cell B2, no matter where they were situated in the spreadsheet.

To prevent Quattro Pro from adjusting such a reference while it is copying a formula, you must change it from a *relative* to an *absolute* reference. You've seen what a relative reference is: it refers not to one specific

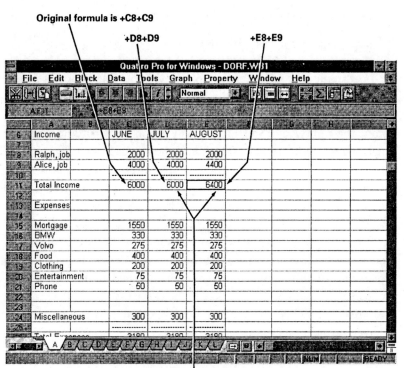

FIGURE 4.8:

Quattro Pro for Windows' adjustment of the formulas as it copied them

Original formula is +C8+C9

+D8+D9

+E8+E9

Both formulas adjusted to retain the "meaning" of the original formula

cell's address, but to a cell that is located *relative* to the formula's position. In the previous section's example, the formula you copied summed the two numbers above—i.e., 2000+4000 in July's column and 2000+4400 in August's column.

However, an absolute reference—indicated by a dollar sign ($) in front—always refers to a *specific* cell's address, no matter where the formula is located.

Imagine you have the formula +B2*C3 in cell C2. As written, it multiplies two numbers together—the number in the cell to the left of the formula by the number in the cell underneath. That is what the formula really means. But these references are relative, so if you relocate the formula to cell K25, Quattro Pro for Windows will have to rewrite it as +J25*K26 to keep its original "meaning" intact.

Now, if you make the references absolute—so the formula reads +$B$2*$C$3—the formula will take on a different, more specific meaning altogether: multiply the number in cell B2 by the number in C3. No matter where this formula is actually situated, it will always generate the same answer (unless, of course, you change the numbers in cells B2 or C3).

Creating Absolute References

There are two ways to put a dollar sign in a cell reference to make it absolute. One is simply to type it as you enter the formula. The second is to press the Absolute (Abs) key (F4) to change the reference from relative to absolute automatically. This latter method is preferable when you are creating a formula with the pointing method.

Each time you press the Abs key, Quattro Pro will adjust the cell reference. For example, if you begin a formula with a reference such as +C9 on the input line and then press F4, the reference will change to +$A:$C$9. The second time you press F4, the reference will turn to +$A:C$9, in which case column C is relative but row 9 is absolute. Pressing F4 a third time will change the reference to +$A:$C9, in which case the column is absolute and the row is relative. The fourth time you press F4, the reference appears as +$A:C9—spreadsheet A is still absolute, but the cell reference is relative. Pressing F4 a fifth, sixth and seventh time gives you the first three options again, but this time with no spreadsheet reference: +$C$9, +C$9, and +$C9 respectively. Pressing F4 one last time will bring the formula back to the fully relative +C9.

In the example above, the Abs key produced two *mixed references* in its cycle: +$A:C$9 and +$A:$C9. (For the moment we won't worry about the relative and absolute spreadsheet values. Chapter 8 examines this topic in greater detail.) In mixed references, one part of the reference is relative and the other is absolute. Hence, if you were to copy the

formula +$A:C$9 to a new cell in a different column, the column reference would adjust itself to the new cell's column but the row would still
refer to row 9. Alternatively, copying the formula +$A:$C9 to a new cell
in a different row would adjust the row but leave the column referring
to column C.

Let's test the F4 key. Suppose the Dorf family has an outstanding,
interest-free loan of $1000 from their friends. They want to see how
paying off 25 percent of this loan each month will affect their finances.

First, set up two columns in which to store the loan information:

1. Move the cell selector to cell A22 and enter the label **Loan %**.

2. Move to cell B22 and enter the label **Loan $**.

3. Move to cell A23 and enter the percentage that the Dorfs will
   pay off each month—**25%**. (It will appear as **0.25** in the cell.)

4. With the cell selector in cell B23, enter the loan amount—
   1000.

Now you can begin entering the formulas to see what happens if
the Dorfs pay off 25 percent of their loan each month:

1. Move the cell selector to cell C23.

2. Type + to start entering a formula.

3. Move the cell selector to cell A23. The formula on the input
   line now reads **+A23**.

4. To make this cell reference absolute for copying, press the
   Abs key (F4). The formula now reads **+$A:$A$23**.

5. Type * (for multiplication) to continue entering the formula.
   The formula now reads **+$A:$A$23*** and the cell selector
   jumps back to cell C23.

6. Click on cell B23. The formula now reads **+$A:$A$23*B23**.

7. Press F4 to make *that* reference absolute as well. The formula now reads **+$A:$A$23∗$A:$B$23.**

8. Click the left mouse button, or click on the check mark.

Cell C23 now contains the formula **+$A:$A$23∗$A:$B$23**, and the cell displays **250** (because 25 percent of 1000 is 250).

Now copy this formula into the columns for July and August:

1. With the cell selector still on cell C23, click on the Copy button.

2. Click on cell D23 and drag to E23.

3. Click on the Paste button.

At this point, your spreadsheet should look like Figure 4.9.

Nothing is ever immutable in a spreadsheet. Suppose the Dorfs decide to pay off only 10 percent of the loan each month. To see what effect this has on their monthly expenses, simply move the cell selector to cell A23. Type in the new percentage figure, **10%**, and click on the check mark. (The 10 percent appears as **0.1** in the cell.)

Quattro Pro immediately recalculates the monthly payments on the loan so that each month displays 100, rather than 250. Figure 4.10 shows this.

Copying Only the Cell Contents

When you copy a cell or block of cells, Quattro Pro for Windows assumes that you want to copy the contents of the cell and cell formulas together. However, there may be times when you want to copy just the cell contents and not the underlying formulas. To do so, highlight the cells you want to copy and select Block ➤ Values. In the Block Values dialog box, double-click on the To box and then select the cells you want to copy the values to. Click on the Maximize button on the Block Values title bar, then click on OK. Only the contents of the cells are copied, not the formulas that generated the values.

Original formula
is+$A:$A$23∗$A:$B$23

Both copied formulas are also
+$A:$A$23∗$A:$B$23
(absolute cell references
were not adjusted)

Changing Existing References

As mentioned in Chapter 3, you can click on the input line or use the Edit key (F2) to change any existing cell entry, including formulas. You can even modify a formula by converting one of its references to a relative, absolute, or mixed reference. This saves you from having to retype the formula.

For example, suppose you want to change the existing absolute reference in the formula in cell C23 to either a mixed or relative reference. You need to get rid of some of the dollar signs in +$A:$A$23*$A:$B$23.

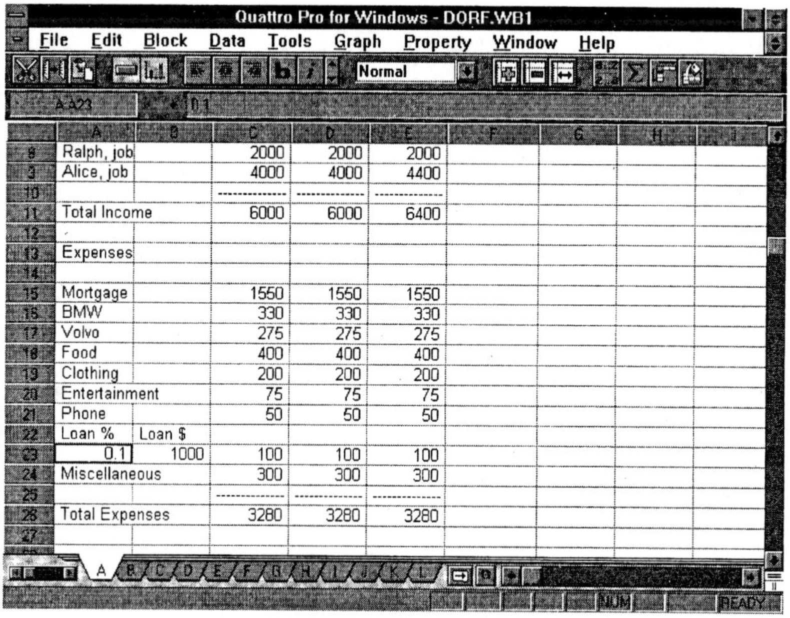

	A	B	C	D	E
8	Ralph, job		2000	2000	2000
9	Alice, job		4000	4000	4400
10			------------	------------	------------
11	Total Income		6000	6000	6400
12					
13	Expenses				
14					
15	Mortgage		1550	1550	1550
16	BMW		330	330	330
17	Volvo		275	275	275
18	Food		400	400	400
19	Clothing		200	200	200
20	Entertainment		75	75	75
21	Phone		50	50	50
22	Loan %	Loan $			
23	0.1	1000	100	100	100
24	Miscellaneous		300	300	300
25			------------	------------	------------
26	Total Expenses		3280	3280	3280
27					

FIGURE 4.10: Loan payments reduced to 10 percent in cell A23

Click on cell C23, then click on the input line or press the Edit key (F2). The formula appears on the input line:

+$A:$A$23*$A:$B$23

The position of the insertion point on the input line will depend on where you click. Next, to change the way that $A:$A$23 is referenced, move the insertion point with the mouse pointer anywhere in that reference (i.e., in front of the first $, the second A, the second $, the 2, or the 3). Then press F4.

Notice how that part of the formula becomes a mixed reference: $A:A$23. Hit F4 again and it will change to $A:$A23. Hit F4 again and you'll see $A:A23, a fully relative reference. Hit F4 once more and the reference will revert back to $A$23, but without the spreadsheet reference. Press F4 four more times to restore the full reference.

Move the cursor to the second half of the formula, $B$23, and hit F4 a few times. The same changes will occur, in a cycle, from absolute (both dollar signs) to mixed (one dollar sign) to relative (no dollar signs). Be sure that the formula returns to the state that you found it in (i.e., with six dollar signs in it) before reading on, by pressing Escape twice.

Moving Data

Moving information around a spreadsheet is much like copying, except that you use the mouse Move option, rather than the Copy option. Let's give it a whirl.

First press Home to move the cell selector up to cell A1. You'll notice that there are several blank rows near the top of the spreadsheet, as shown in Figure 4.11.

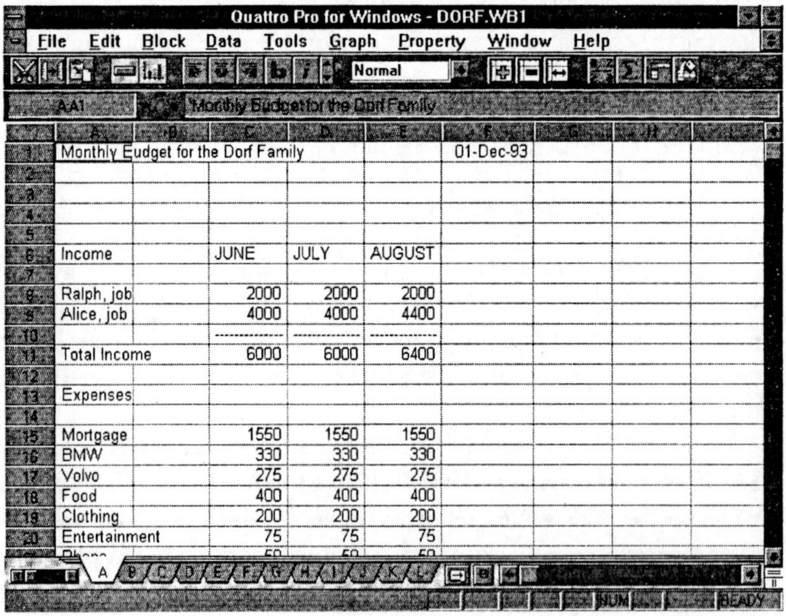

FIGURE 4.11:

The spreadsheet with a few blank rows

To move the data beneath the blank rows upwards, you could either delete rows 3, 4, and 5 (using the Delete button described in Chapter 3) or else move all the information below row 6 up a few rows. Let's try the latter method:

1. Position the cell selector in the upper-left corner of the block being moved (cell A6 in this example).

2. Click and drag cells A6..E26.

3. Release the mouse button.

4. Move the mouse pointer to the middle of the block of cells.

5. Press and hold the left mouse button. The mouse pointer arrow shape is transformed into a right hand shape.

6. Still holding the mouse button, move the hand upwards towards the top of the spreadsheet, until the top of the outline appears between rows 2 and 3.

7. Release the mouse button. The block moves to the new position, and remains highlighted. To remove the highlighting, click on a cell that is not in the block.

You've just moved a significant block of cells! If you ever have the sudden realization that you moved a block to a wrong part of the spreadsheet, do not panic. As with all commands, this one can be undone with Edit ➤ Undo. Try it with the block you've just moved. Provided that the Undo option was already set to Enable, and you didn't do anything else since the move, you'll see the block jump back to its original position. Be sure to put the block back in its new location (starting at row 3) before reading on. Use Edit ➤ Redo if you like.

As Figure 4.12 shows, the entire highlighted block moved up and closed the gap beneath the spreadsheet title in cell A1. If you scroll around the spreadsheet and look at the calculations, you'll see that all

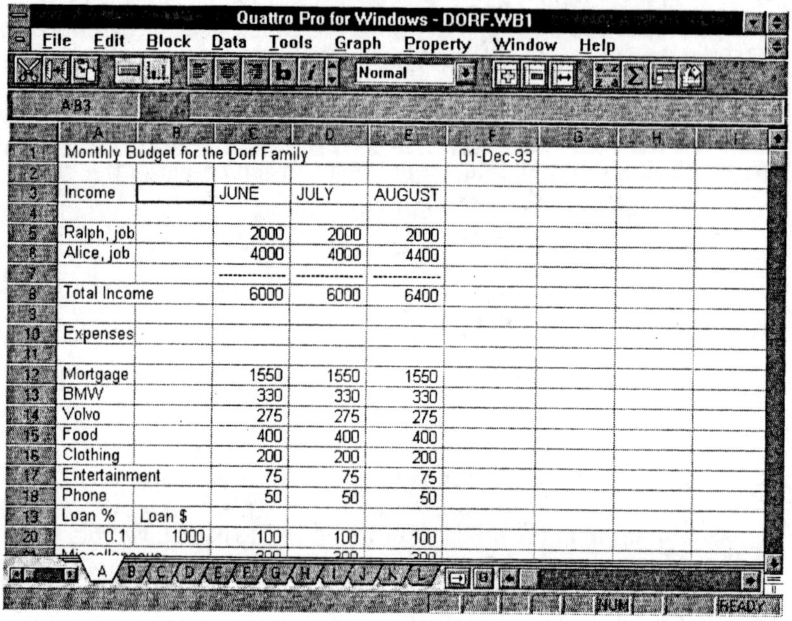

FIGURE 4.12:

Data moved up on the spreadsheet

the formulas still display correct results. That is because the Move command always adjusts formulas, even those with absolute references, to their new location. With Move, you can rely on Quattro Pro for Windows to adjust all formulas within the moved block automatically.

Some Finishing Touches

On a budget spreadsheet, you'll probably want to know how much cash remains after all expenses have been paid. You can easily add the appropriate formulas to DORF.WB1 using techniques we have already discussed. The first steps required to do this are as follows:

1. Move the cell selector to cell A25, and enter the label **Remainder**.

2. Click on cell C24, and enter \= to fill the cell with double lines (=========).

3. In cell C25 enter the formula to subtract the total income from the total expenses: +**C8**–**C23**. Click on the check mark, and the cell should show the result: **2720**.

To extend the lines and copy the formula to the July and August columns, follow these steps:

1. Click on cell C24.

2. Click and drag cells C24 and C25.

3. Click on the Copy button.

4. Click and drag cells D24..E25.

5. Click on the Paste button.

Now the total remaining cash is displayed at the bottom of each column, as shown in Figure 4.13.

Saving the Modified Notebook

Since you've made quite a few changes to DORF.WB1 so far, save this new version of the notebook for future use. As at the end of Chapter 3, you can use the usual Save command to do so. Click on the File menu and then click on Save.

Now that you have saved the file safely, feel free to experiment with the numbers in the spreadsheet—the income and expenditure values, the loan-repayment percentage in cell A20, and the loan amount in cell B20—to try out various fanciful what-if scenarios: e.g., what if Ralph or Alice earned more or less money, what if they traded in their BMW for a VW, etc. Don't type values directly into the cells in rows 8

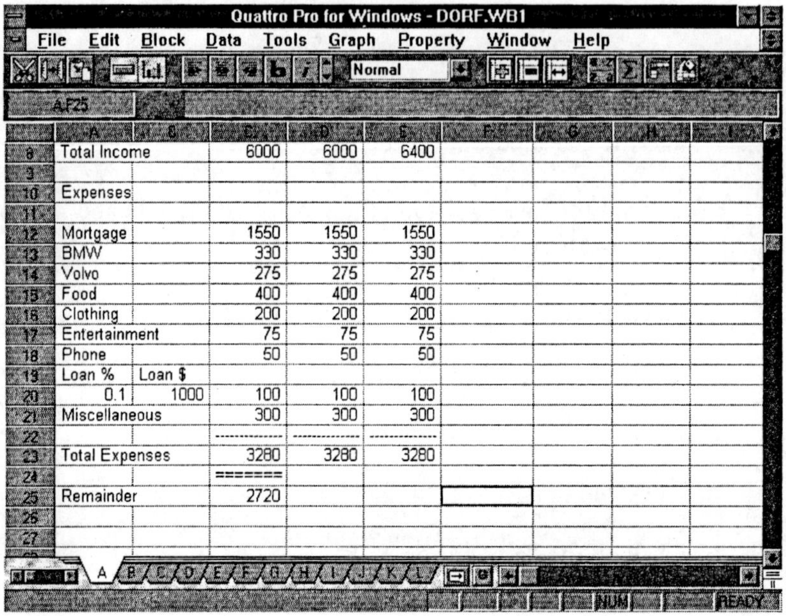

FIGURE 4.13:

Remaining cash calculated in row 25

Quattro Pro for Windows - DORF.WB1

File   Edit   Block   Data   Tools   Graph   Property   Window   Help

Normal

A:F25

	A	B	C	D	E
8	Total Income		6000	6000	6400
9					
10	Expenses				
11					
12	Mortgage		1550	1550	1550
13	BMW		330	330	330
14	Volvo		275	275	275
15	Food		400	400	400
16	Clothing		200	200	200
17	Entertainment		75	75	75
18	Phone		50	50	50
19	Loan %	Loan $			
20	0.1	1000	100	100	100
21	Miscellaneous		300	300	300
22			-------------	-------------	-------------
23	Total Expenses		3280	3280	3280
24			=======		
25	Remainder		2720		
26					
27					

A / B / C / D / E / F / G / H / I / J / K /

NUM   READY

or 23, however, as these contain formulas. (You'll learn about a way to protect such cells from accidental changes in Chapter 7.) When you're through playing around, be sure that you do *not* save the notebook as DORF.WB1. Choose a name of your own.

So far, you've learned a great deal about building spreadsheets— not only how to enter data and formulas, but also advanced techniques for changing spreadsheets, copying information, and using the pointing method. For more advanced techniques for creating formulas, and an overview of the complete range of functions (such as @SUM) that Quattro Pro for Windows has to offer, see Chapter 15. In the next chapter, we'll examine ways of enhancing your spreadsheet's appearance.

5 CHAPTER

Enhancing Your Spreadsheet's Appearance

When you enter numbers, dates, times, and labels in a cell, they don't just appear; they are displayed in a default format of some sort. This chapter shows you how to change the way that data are displayed in your spreadsheet, without having to change the data.

Before continuing, open an empty spreadsheet page so that you can experiment with some of the formatting styles that will be discussed in this chapter. To open a blank spreadsheet page, click on the B tab at the bottom of the notebook window.

Formatting Numbers

By default, numbers (including the results of numeric calculations) are automatically displayed to as many decimal and integer places as fit into a cell. To change the format of a number (or block of numbers), follow these steps:

1. Position the cell selector on the cell or in the upper-left corner of the group of cells you wish to format.

2. Click and drag the cells you wish to format.

3. Click on the Style List button in the SpeedBar.

4. Choose the style you want from the options displayed (see Table 5.1).

We'll provide some exercises for you at the end of this chapter. For now, just take a moment to review the various format options for numbers, as listed in Table 5.1. (Note that you can modify currency settings and numeric punctuation for foreign countries with the international settings discussed in Chapter 13.)

Formatting Dates and Times

As you've seen, when you enter a date by pressing Ctrl-Shift-D, Quattro Pro for Windows automatically formats the cell to display the date in *dd/mmm/yy* format. When you enter dates or times with the functions @DATE, @DATEVALUE, @NOW, @TIME, @TIMEVALUE, or

FORMAT	DESCRIPTION	EXAMPLES
Comma	Shows commas in thousands places, and displays negative numbers in parentheses	(123.00) 12,345,678.90
Currency	Displays leading currency sign, commas in thousands places, and negative numbers in parentheses	($123.00) $123.46 $12,345,678.90
Date	Displays numbers as per specified date format	see Table 5.2
Fixed	Displays numbers to a fixed number of decimal places (0–15), rounded as appropriate	~123.00 ~123.46 ~12345678.90
Heading 1	Changes the selected block contents to 18-point Helvetica type	**Heading 1**
Heading 2	Changes the selected block contents to 12-point Helvetica type	Heading 2
Normal	Displays numbers as entered or calculated and rounds to nearest decimal value as space permits in cell	−123 123.987654 31264598.9
Percent	Displays numbers as percentages	12.75% 9.38% 12.00%
Total	Inserts a double line at the top of the cell (or block of cells)	$11,001.00

TABLE 5.1:

Format Options for Displaying Numbers

@TODAY (see Chapter 15 for an examination of these functions), Quattro Pro displays only their serial numbers. For example, if you type **@DATE(93,12,31)** into a cell, Quattro Pro returns the serial date **34334** rather than **12/31/93.** If you enter **@TIME(12,30,0),** it returns **0.520833** rather than **12:30 PM.**

To display *dd/mm/yy* dates or serial dates and times in different formats, follow these steps:

1. Move the cell selector to the cell or to the upper-left corner of the block containing the date(s) or time(s) you want to format.

2. Click and drag the cells containing the values you want to format.

3. Select Property ➤ Current Object (or press F12, or click the right mouse button) to open the Active Block dialog box, as shown in Figure 5.1.

4. Click on either the date or the time to find the format you want (see Table 5.2). Click on OK.

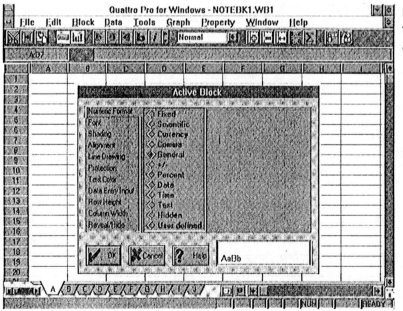

FIGURE 5.1:

The Active Block dialog box

FORMAT	DESCRIPTION	EXAMPLES
Date 1	*dd-mmm-yy* format	23-Dec-92
		01-Jan-00
		27-Jul-20
Date 2	*dd-mmm* format	23-Dec
		01-Jan
		27-Jul
Date 3	*mmm-yy* format	Dec-92
		Jan-00
		Jul-20
Date 4	Long International format	12/23/92
		92-12-23
		12.23.92
Date 5	Short International format	12/23
		12-23
		12.23
Time 1	*hh:mm:ss* a.m./p.m. format	01:20:31 AM
		01:20:31 PM
		12:00:00 AM
Time 2	*hh:mm* a.m./p.m. format	01:20 AM
		01:20 PM
		12.00 AM
Time 3	Long International format	13:20:31
		13.20.31
		13,20,31
		13h20m31s

TABLE 5.2:

Date and time formats

FORMAT	DESCRIPTION	EXAMPLES
Time 4	Short International format	13:20
		13.20
		13,20

TABLE 5.2:

Date and time formats (continued)

Descriptions and examples of various date and time formats are listed in Table 5.2.

Formatting Labels

As you learned in Chapter 2, you can use label prefixes to left-justify, right-justify, or center a label within a cell. Using the Alignment option, you can change the label alignment in an entire group of cells. The steps for formatting labels are as follows:

1. Move the cell selector to the cell or to the upper-left corner of the block containing the label(s) you want to format.

2. Click and drag the cells you want to format.

3. Click on the appropriate alignment button in the SpeedBar. For example, click on the left-justify button to left-justify the labels.

4. The highlighting remains on so that if you decide that the choice you made is incorrect, you can click on a different SpeedBar alignment button.

5. When you are satisfied with the appearance of the data, click on any cell outside the highlighted block.

Note that any label that is too wide for its cell will be left-justified automatically.

Reformatting Entries on a Sample Spreadsheet

In the previous chapters, we created and saved the DORF notebook file. Open the DORF notebook using File ➤ Open. This spreadsheet, before formatting, is shown in Figure 5.2. Now we'll format the spreadsheet to give a much neater display.

FORMATTING THE INCOME NUMBERS

Suppose you wish to format the numbers in the income portion of the spreadsheet page as currency and the loan interest as percent values. Here are the steps to do so:

1. Click and drag cells C8..E8.

2. Click on the Style List button in the SpeedBar. The Style List is displayed, as in Figure 5.3.

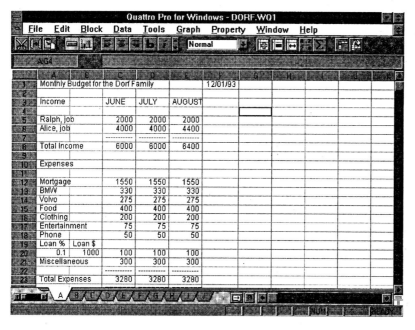

FIGURE 5.2:

The DORF spreadsheet before formatting

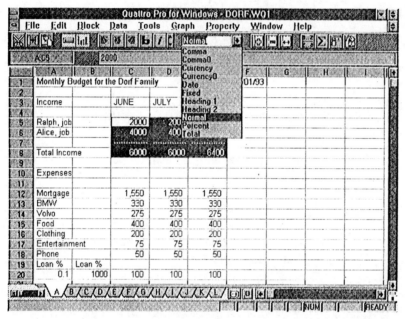

FIGURE 5.3:

The Style List

3. Click on Currency. The values are reformatted, but the cells are too narrow for the entry, and so display asterisks instead.

4. Click on the Fit button.

Now the values in cells C8..E8 are displayed with a leading $ sign with two decimal places, as opposed to Normal format.

To format the interest rate as a percent:

1. Move the cell selector to cell A20.

2. Click on the Style List button.

3. Click on the Percent item.

Now the percentage is displayed as **10.00** rather than **0.1**.

Formatting Multiple Blocks

The \- entry to separate the values and indicate totals in cells C7..E7 and C24..E24 can be eliminated because Quattro Pro for Windows includes a Total format on the Style List.

1. Click and drag cells C7..E7, then click on the Cut button.

2. Click and drag cells C24..E24, and click on the Cut button.

3. Click and drag cells C9..E9.

4. Press and hold the Control key.

5. Click and drag cells C26..E26. Both blocks are now selected and ready for formatting. Release the Control key.

6. Click on the Style List button.

7. Click on Totals. Both blocks are formatted with the Total format, a double-underline. Whenever you want to format multiple blocks, on the same page or on different pages, you can use the Control key and the mouse to select the blocks and perform the format.

Let's change the values in cells C12 to I21 to Comma with no decimal places.

1. Click and drag cells C12 to I21.

2. Click the right mouse button to open the Active Block dialog box.

3. Click on Comma. Enter 0 as the number of decimal places.

4. Click on OK.

Changing the Title Headings

In the DORF spreadsheet we have a main heading and two subheadings. Quattro Pro for Windows includes a Heading 1 and Heading 2 format that we can use to distinguish the headings.

1. Click on cell A1.

2. Click on the Style List button.

3. Click on Heading 1.

Finish the formatting by selecting the Income and Expenses labels and using Heading 2 as the format. The reformatted DORF spreadsheet appears in Figure 5.4.

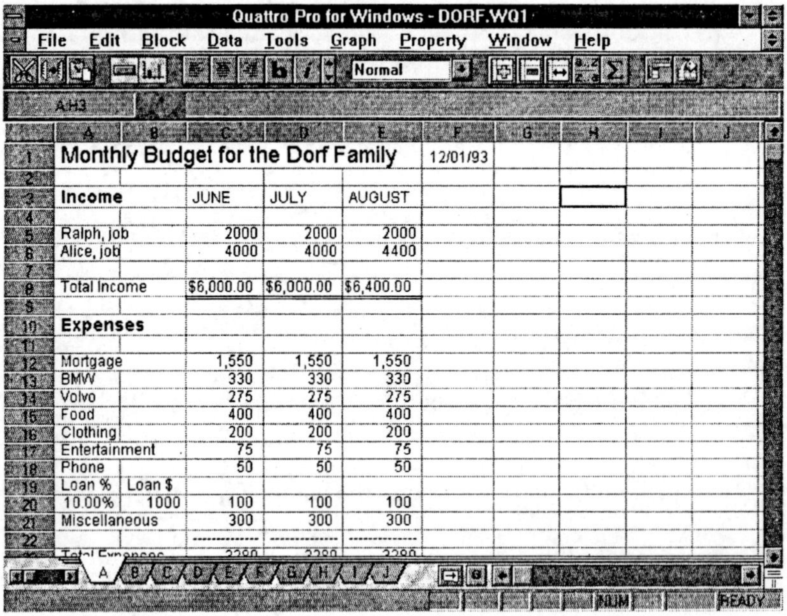

FIGURE 5.4:

The reformatted DORF spreadsheet

Changing the Row Height

When you reformatted the label using Heading 1, Quattro Pro automatically adjusted the size of the type and the height of the row. There may be occasions when you want to increase or decrease the row height a specific amount for display purposes. You can do this with the Active Block dialog box.

1. Move the cell selector to the row that you want to modify.

2. Click the right mouse button. The Active Block dialog box appears.

3. In the Active Block dialog box, click on Row Height. The Active Block: Row Height options appear, as shown in Figure 5.5. The current row height is displayed, along with the options to reset the row height to the default, and to change

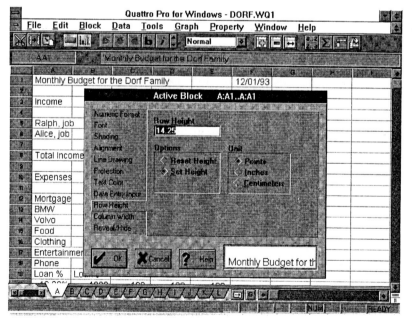

FIGURE 5.5:

The Active Block: Row Height options

the units used as a measurement from the default of points to inches or centimeters. If you select a different unit, Quattro Pro calculates the current row height in the new unit value and displays the corrected number.

4. Make the entries you want and click on OK to make the change.

Changing the Style List Defaults

The default formats on the Style List can be modified to your liking. For example, when you select Percentage as the style, you might want the decimals to be displayed to three places instead of two. Or you might want Heading 1 to be displayed in a different typeface that you have added to Windows.

1. Select Edit ➤ Define Style. The Define/Modify Style dialog box appears, as in Figure 5.6.

2. Click on the Define Style For button. The Style List is displayed.

3. Click on the style format that you want to modify. Quattro Pro for Windows shows you which properties can be changed for that particular style by inserting a check mark in front of the properties.

4. Click on the appropriate property. Another dialog box appears with the property settings. For example, if you want to change Heading 1, the Font dialog box appears. Select a new font. You can also select a different point size and other options such as bold or italics as the new default.

5. Click on OK in both dialog boxes to make the change.

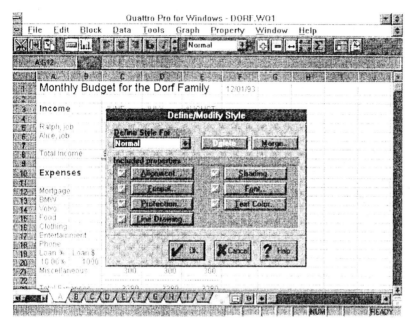

FIGURE 5.6:

The Define/
Modify Style
dialog box

6 CHAPTER

FEATURING

Filling blocks with data

Giving blocks names

Moving named blocks

Managing Blocks Effectively

In Chapter 4 you learned the basics of copying and moving blocks of data. This chapter will show you some more techniques for handling blocks so that you can easily make them an integral part of your work.

Filling a Block

Block filling is a useful technique that can help speed spreadsheet development. The Block ➤ Fill option lets you fill blocks of cells with numbers or dates and also lets you increment (and decrement) values along the way. Furthermore, the SpeedFill button in the SpeedBar allows you to select an initial number and a block of cells and then fill the selected cells with a sequence based on the initial number. The basic technique for using the Fill option is as follows:

1. Position the cell selector at the upper-left corner of the block you wish to fill.

2. Click on the Block menu name, then choose the Fill option. The Block Fill dialog box appears.

3. Specify a block you want to fill, either by using the pointing method or by entering block coordinates.

4. Enter a *start value*, a *step value*, and a *stop value*.

5. Click on OK.

To try this out yourself, start with a blank spreadsheet page and follow the steps below. (If you have any other work on your screen, save it first by selecting File ➤ Save. Then select File ➤ New to open an empty, new notebook.) Suppose now that you wish to type in the years 1993 to 1996 across row 2 of the blank spreadsheet. Here are the steps:

1. Move the cell selector to cell B2.

2. Type 1993.

3. Click on the check mark or press Enter.

4. Click and drag cells B2..E2.

5. Click on the SpeedFill button, which is the second from the right in the SpeedBar.

You'll see the years appear across row 2. The values that have been entered are not serial (date) values. To use the SpeedFill button to enter serial values, the initial cell must contain a date value. Try this next example to see how.

1. Move the cell selector to cell B6.

2. Hold down Control and Shift while you press D. In the status line the word **DATE** appears, indicating that you can make a date entry.

3. Type 12-DEC-93.

4. Click on the check mark. Because the entry is too long for the cell, a series of asterisks appears.

5. Click on the Fit button (the button with the double-headed arrow in the SpeedBar) to widen the column. The date appears as you typed it, and the serial number appears in the input line.

6. Click and drag cells B6..E6.

7. Click on the SpeedFill button. Again, asterisks appear in cells C6..E6.

8. Click on the Fit button to widen the columns. The dates are now displayed incremented by one day.

Quattro Pro for Windows assumes that you always want to increment the values by a factor of one, depending on the initial value. Let's examine a different way to enter numbers, using the Block ➤ Fill option.

1. Move the cell selector to cell B10.

2. Click and drag cells B10..E10.

3. Select Block ➤ Fill. The Block Fill dialog box appears, as shown in Figure 6.1.

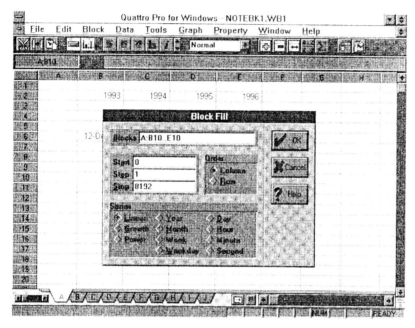

4. Click on the Start field and enter 1993.

5. Click on the Step field, or press Tab to move the cursor there. Then enter **5** as the step value.

6. Click on Year as the Series.

7. Click on OK.

Quattro Pro enters the dates as serial dates. Because 1993 represents the number of days that have elapsed since the turn of the century, the number displayed is 1905. Furthermore, you entered a Step value of 5, which means 5 years, so the remaining numbers are five-year increments from the beginning value.

Keep in mind, however, that the suggested Stop value of 8192 in the Block Fill dialog box will not be high enough for most date entries because it's the serial date for June 4, 1922. Since you're probably interested in dates that come much later in the century, you need to enter a much larger number instead.

When using Fill, keep a few simple points in mind. You can use any positive or negative number. For example, if you enter 100 as the start value, −25 as the step value, and 0 as the stop value, Fill will generate the numbers 100, 75, 50, 25, and 0 (provided the block contains at least five cells—i.e., enough room to accept the entire fill).

If you do not know the exact stop value for a fill operation, just enter any large number (or accept the suggested value of 8192—the maximum number of rows in the spreadsheet) and the operation will automatically stop when the specified block is filled or the ending number for the fill is reached. When decrementing past zero, enter a large negative number for the Stop value.

If you fill a block that consists of several rows and columns, the Fill option will automatically start at the top-left corner of the block, fill that column, and then proceed to the top cell of the next column, continuing until all the columns are filled. You can fill rows first by selecting Rows under Order in the Block Fill dialog box.

In Figure 6.2, the block D14..G19 was filled with the number 4500 as the Start value, −50 as the Step value, and 0 as the Stop value. (Here we chose a Stop value much smaller than 4500 because the Step value was a large negative number—i.e., decrementing quickly from 4500.) The Series setting was Linear.

Simplifying Your Work with Named Blocks

Although it is never actually *necessary* to name blocks in your work, giving blocks names makes it easier to build and use a single spreadsheet.

You can use block names (which can refer to a single cell as well) within functions and formulas (in place of cell references), in the Go To dialog box, and in other places. For example, suppose you assign the

First fill operation

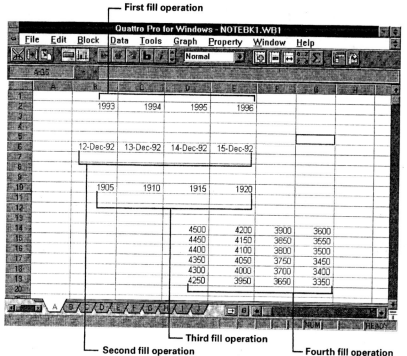

FIGURE 6.2:

Results of several
fill operations

Second fill operation

Third fill operation

Fourth fill operation

names *Principal, Interest,* and *Term* to cells containing the principal, interest, and term of a loan. You could then calculate the payment on the loan using the more readable function @PMT(*Principal, Interest, Term*) rather than one with cell references, such as @PMT(B1,B2,B3). (@PMT and other functions are covered in Chapter 15.) Furthermore, from anywhere in the notebook you could use Edit ➤ Goto (or press the F5 key) and enter the cell's name to move the cell selector quickly to that cell. This is a very handy technique if you want to manage a large notebook efficiently.

VALID BLOCK NAMES

There are a few simple rules to keep in mind when creating block names:

- A block name can have no more than 15 characters.

- A block name can contain only letters, numbers, and punctuation marks.

- Uppercase and lowercase letters are equivalent. For instance, *PRINCIPAL, Principal,* and *principal* are treated identically. (Actually, Quattro Pro automatically converts all block names to uppercase—that's why it doesn't matter how you enter them.)

You can invoke all the options for creating and managing block names from the Names submenu on the Block menu. The options under Names are:

- Create

- Delete

- Labels

- Reset

- Make Table

We'll discuss each of these options for creating and managing named blocks in the sections that follow.

Naming a Block

Naming a block is quite easy:

1. Move the cell selector to the upper-left corner of the block you want to name.

2. Click and drag the block.

3. Select Block ➤ Names ➤ Create. The Create Name dialog box appears, as shown in Figure 6.3.

4. Enter a name for the block in the Name field.

5. Click on OK.

To see the benefit of giving a block a name, select Edit ➤ Goto (or press F5) and enter the block name directly on the input line. The cell selector will jump to the first cell in that block from anywhere on the spreadsheet.

Click on the B tab near the bottom-left corner of the window to open a new spreadsheet page. We will enter some numbers in column B, then assign the name FIRSTYEAR to the data in column B.

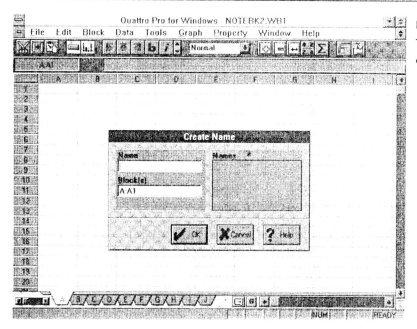

FIGURE 6.3:

The Create Name dialog box

1. In cell B2, enter the value 100.

2. Click and drag cells B2..B10.

3. Click on the SpeedFill button. A series from 100 to 108 is entered.

4. Select Block ➤ Names ➤ Create. The Create Name dialog box appears.

5. Enter **COLUMN** in the Name field.

6. Click on OK.

To experiment with the named block, first try entering a function that contains the block's name. For example, move the cell selector to cell B11 and enter the function **@SUM(COLUMN)**. You will then see the total, 936, appear in cell B11.

To move the cell selector to the upper-left corner of the block:

1. Select Edit ➤ Goto (or press F5). The Go To dialog box appears.

2. Click on COLUMN, then choose OK. The cell selector will move to the top of the named block.

We discuss the use of block names in functions and in conjunction with Go To in more detail below.

Cell Labels as Block Names

Rather than type in block names directly, you can use labels within the spreadsheet as block names. (These labels must conform to the rules for valid block names mentioned above.)

To demonstrate, Figure 6.4 shows a sample spreadsheet page with some data for a loan typed in. The number in cell B1 was formatted as currency by using the Style List button. The value in cell B2 (.10) was

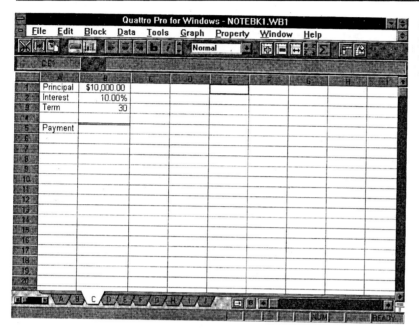

formatted as Percent by using the Style List. Cell B5 was formatted as Total using the Style List. Go ahead and create this spreadsheet now on a blank page of your notebook (we used page C). Remember to use the Fit button if necessary.

Now suppose you want to assign the labels in cells A1 through A3 to the corresponding cells B1 through B3:

1. Position the cell selector at the upper-left corner of the block of labels (cell A1 in this example), and drag cells A1..A3.

2. Select Block ➤ Names ➤ Labels. The Create Names From Labels dialog box appears, as shown in Figure 6.5. Quattro Pro needs to know where the yet-to-be-named cells are in relation to the labels. These cells can be located either one

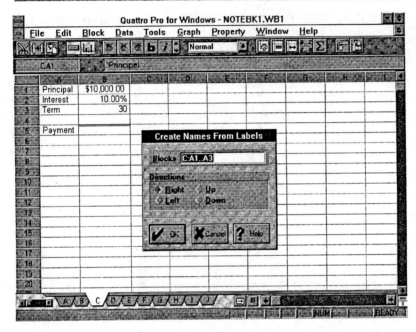

FIGURE 6.5:

The Create
Names From
Labels dialog box

column to the left or right of the labels, or one row above or below the labels. They cannot be farther away.

3. In this example, the cells to be named are to the right, so go ahead and click on Right. Then click on OK.

Though not much appears to have happened, you have assigned the name PRINCIPAL to cell B1, INTEREST to cell B2, and TERM to cell B3. You'll see how to use these new names next.

Placing Block Names in a Function

You saw in an example above how you could type a block name directly into the function @SUM(COLUMN). You can also use the Names key (F3) as a shortcut for entering block names. Let's experiment with the sample spreadsheet page you've been using so far. Suppose you wish to calculate the payment on the loan using the new block names. Here are the steps:

1. Move the cell selector to where you want the function to appear (cell B5 in this example).

2. Type **@pmt(** to begin the function.

3. Press the F3 key. You'll see a dialog box appear with the list of existing block names. (See Figure 6.6.)

4. Double-click on PRINCIPAL. The function now reads

   @pmt(PRINCIPAL

5. Type , (a comma) to continue the function, and press F3 again to call up the block names.

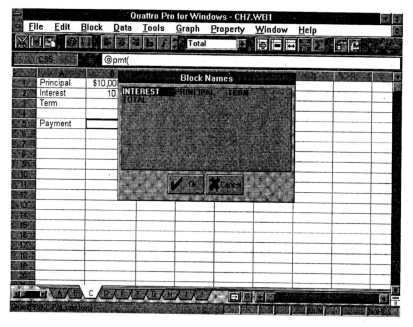

FIGURE 6.6:

The Block Names dialog box

6. Double-click on INTEREST.

7. Type /12 to divide the annual interest by 12. Then add a comma, so the function reads

   @pmt(PAYMENT,INTEREST/12,

8. Press F3 to bring back the menu of block names, then double-click on TERM. The function now reads

   @pmt(PRINCIPAL,INTEREST/12,TERM

9. Finish the function by typing *12) to multiply the term by 12 and complete the function. It now reads

   @pmt(PRINCIPAL,INTEREST/12,TERM*12)

10. Click the left mouse button, or press Enter.

The completed formula is placed in cell B5 and displays the calculated monthly payment. Now use the Style List button to format cell B5 as Currency, as shown in Figure 6.7.

This technique of selecting block names and using the Names key (F3) is not only fast, but also ensures that you will not misspell a block name or enter a nonexistent block name while creating a function or formula.

How to Go to a Named Block Quickly

As mentioned earlier, you can move the cell selector quickly to any named cell or to the upper-left corner of any named block using the Go To function. To try this out on the current spreadsheet, follow these steps:

1. Select Edit ➤ Goto or press F5. The Go To dialog box will present the prompt:

   Reference C:B5

The bottom of the dialog box displays a menu of block names.

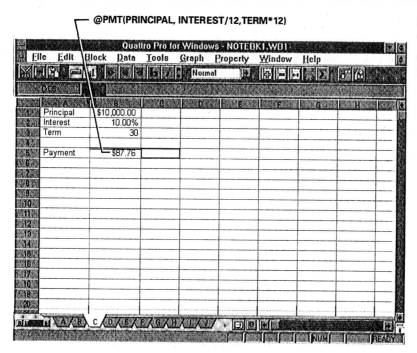

FIGURE 6.7:

The function calculating with block names

2. Double-click on the block name you want to go to. The cell selector will jump immediately to the named cell or block.

This simple technique is actually very handy when you're working on a large spreadsheet because it allows you to move quickly to a specific cell from anywhere in the notebook, with minimal typing and little room for error.

Save this notebook as CH6 now; you'll need it in the next chapter.

Giving Blocks Absolute and Relative Names

Named blocks can be treated as *absolute* or *relative* references when copying functions. For example, if you copy a function such as @PMT(PRIN-CIPAL,INTEREST/12,TERM*12) the copied function will attempt to adjust cell references for their meaning and may produce incorrect results. But if you copy or move @PMT($PRINCIPAL,$INTEREST/12,$TERM*12), the dollar signs will make the cell references absolute, so the function will not adjust to its new location.

When you attempt to edit a function that contains references to named cells or blocks, you'll notice that the input line displays the cell references—in this case, B1, B2/12, and B3*12—rather than their respective names. This makes it easy to convert the function's references from relative to absolute or mixed for moving or copying. As discussed in Chapter 4, you can simply position the cursor on the reference you wish to change and press the Absolute key (F4) until the appropriate dollar signs are inserted.

Moving a Named Block

Another advantage of named cells or blocks is that their names move with them. Therefore, any functions that refer to named blocks will still refer to them, and so retain their accuracy. For example, in the current spreadsheet, the function @PMT(PRINCIPAL,INTEREST/12,TERM*12) refers to the values in cells B1, B2, and B3. But moving any of these cells around the spreadsheet has no effect on it, so the function still calculates the proper payments.

To test this out for yourself, move the data in block A1..B3 to a new location. (Use the mouse hand or select Block ➤ Move.) You'll notice that the payment function in cell B5, @PMT(PRINCIPAL,INTEREST/12,TERM*12), still calculates the appropriate payment. In addition, if you press the F5 key and click on a block name to go to, you'll see the cell selector move to the *new* location of the named block.

BLOCK MOVES THAT OVERWRITE DATA

When you move data on a spreadsheet to an area that already contains data, they will completely overwrite (replace) that original data. If you inadvertently overwrite data in this way, they will be lost forever unless you use Edit ➤ Undo to undo your move. An even safer way to ensure that data are not lost is to save the notebook before you move anything.

EFFECTS OF BLOCK MOVES ON FORMULAS

Should you move data and/or formulas around on a spreadsheet, Quattro Pro for Windows will ensure that the formulas' meanings are retained. For example, if you move a formula such as +C1+C2 from one cell to another, its cell references will remain the same, regardless of whether they are relative or absolute. That is, moving the formula +C1+C2 from cell C4 to A4 leaves the formula as +C1+C2 in the new cell. But if you move the data to which the formula refers—or both the formula and the data—then the cell references will adjust accordingly, even if you move the formula to a different page of the notebook.

Look at Figure 6.8 to see how this makes sense. Cell C4 contains the formula +C1+C2. If you move only the formula in cell C4 to a new location (say, cell C18), it will still display the sum of cells C1 and C2—as it should. If, however, you move the the entire block of cells C1 through C4, so that both the data and formula are relocated, then the

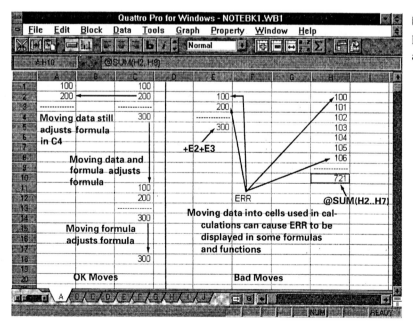

FIGURE 6.8:

Examples of OK and bad moves

formula in the new location will be adjusted to refer still to the two cells above it—+C11+C12 in this example. And if you move just the data—block C1..C2, in this case—to, say, A1..A2, then the formula in cell C4 will change from +C1+C2 to +A1+A2. In each case, Quattro Pro for Windows has the smarts to retain the original meaning of the formula.

AVOIDING BLOCK MOVES THAT CAUSE ERRORS

When you move data from somewhere on the spreadsheet to a new area that is already referenced by an existing formula, Quattro Pro may respond by changing the reference in the formula to ERR, which in turn makes the entire formula display **ERR** in its cell. This is a safety device that informs you when a data move may have caused a formula to calculate incorrect data.

For example, if cell E5 contains the formula +E2+E3 and a move of yours replaces the data in cell E2 with a new number, then the formula in cell E5 will become +ERR+E3 and the cell will display **ERR**. Quattro Pro is telling you that as a result of new data being moved into cell E2, the calculation performed by the formula in E5 may now yield an answer you're not expecting. If the move was intentional, you will need to edit or re-enter the formula in cell E5 so that it becomes +E2+E3 again.

If a function refers to an entire block, such as @SUM(H2..H7), then moving data into either of the *coordinate cells* H2 or H7 will change the function to @SUM(ERR). Note that this occurs *only* when you move data into one of the coordinate cells—those that define the upper-left and lower-right corners of a block. Moving data into any other cell within this block will not cause an error, but simply cause the function to recalculate and display the new value instead. Figure 6.8 shows examples of some bad moves that might cause a function or formula to display **ERR**.

Of course, all of this can seem quite confusing until you practice rearranging blocks on a spreadsheet some more. As discussed earlier, you can always use File ➤ Save to save the notebook before moving anything. You can also use Edit ➤ Undo to undo a move immediately after discovering you've made a mistake.

Reassigning a Block Name

When you name a block on a spreadsheet that already contains named blocks, Quattro Pro for Windows will display a dialog box list of existing block names and a prompt that awaits your entry. To change the location of an existing block name, click and drag the new block of cells. Then select Block ➤ Create. When the Create Name dialog box appears with the new block address in the Blocks field, click on the existing block name, then on OK. The new address replaces the old.

Deleting a Block Name

This procedure deletes only the block's *name*, not its data. To select this option, choose Block ➤ Names ➤ Delete. Then click on the name you wish to delete from the dialog box of block names that appears on the screen, and choose OK.

If you delete a block name that is used in a function, Quattro Pro will simply adjust the function to use the cell reference rather than the block name. For example, if you were to delete INTEREST from the sample spreadsheet in Figure 6.7, the payment function @PMT(PRINCIPAL,INTEREST/12,TERM*12) would automatically be rewritten as @PMT(PRINCIPAL,B2/12,TERM*12).

DELETING ALL BLOCK NAMES

To delete all the block names from a spreadsheet, select Block ➤ Names ➤ Reset. The screen will display the Reset Names dialog box with the prompt **Delete all names?** and provide you with the options Yes, No, and Help. To delete all block names, select Yes; to retain all block names, select No; or select Help for more information.

As with Delete, Reset only removes a block's *name*, not the data within it. The Reset option also replaces *all* references to named blocks within functions with regular cell references. So use this option with caution. After you have removed all the block names from a spreadsheet, the only way to replace them is to enter each one again. The Edit ➤ Undo command will also work, provided it has been previously enabled and that you invoke it immediately after the deletion. (Of course, if you saved the notebook before deleting the block names, you could always re-open the notebook from the disk.)

Listing Block Names

There are two ways to view a list of block names and the cells that they reference. The first is the same one you used when you created the @PMT function. After making an entry on the input line that includes a function or an operator, press F3. The list of named blocks will appear in the Block Names dialog box. Press + and the cell references for each named block will be displayed next to the names of the blocks. Pressing − returns the Block Names dialog box to its former width.

A second way of viewing block names and their coordinates is to make a table of block names directly on the spreadsheet. Quattro Pro for Windows can do this for you. Select Block ➤ Names ➤ Make Table. When prompted, move the cell selector to the upper-left corner of the area in which you want the table to appear (if you have not already done so). Click on OK, and the table will appear on the spreadsheet. Note, however, that this table will overwrite any data that were already in those cells, so be sure that you first move the cell selector to an area that has two columns of blank rows beneath it. Figure 6.9 shows both the Names menu and the table of block names created by Quattro Pro.

In this chapter, you've been introduced to some useful techniques for managing blocks of data on the spreadsheet. In the next chapter, you'll learn some advanced techniques for formatting the spreadsheet.

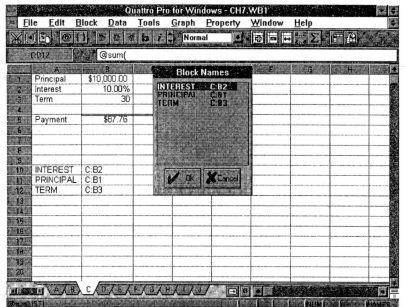

FIGURE 6.9:

Block names and coordinates displayed on the screen

7 CHAPTER

Making More Productive Use of Your Spreadsheet

FEATURING

Protecting your spreadsheet

Using Search and Replace

Viewing two spreadsheet areas simultaneously

Formatting cells for emphasis

Until now, you've learned many basic skills for creating spreadsheets and handling data in them. In this chapter, you'll learn some slightly advanced, though simple and ultimately essential, techniques for managing your spreadsheet more effectively.

Protecting a Spreadsheet

Suppose that your work requires you to build many notebooks and let other people use them to enter data and perform calculations. It's quite possible that less experienced people will make a mess of your work by accidentally replacing formulas with numbers or inadvertently erasing large blocks of text.

To guard against such catastrophes, you can protect spreadsheet pages while leaving specific cells open for later changes.

To set up a protection scheme for your notebook, first access the Protection option from the Active Page dialog box to specify which cells you want to unprotect. Then open the Property menu and the Active Page to turn on the global protection feature, which will allow you to modify only those cells that have been unprotected.

Consider the simple loan-payment spreadsheet you developed in the last chapter. Anybody using this spreadsheet to calculate loan payments only needs to change the loan parameters in cells B1, B2, and B3. For example, increase the principal to $50,000 so the spreadsheet resembles Figure 7.1. The labels in column A and the function to calculate the payment in cell B5 do not need to be changed. The following sections discuss how to protect cells.

UNPROTECTING DESIGNATED CELLS

The Active Block dialog box Protection option allows you to specify individual cells or a block of cells to protect or unprotect. In the following steps, we'll use this option to unprotect cells B1..B3:

1. Click and drag cells B1..B3.

2. Click the *right* mouse button to open the Active Block dialog box.

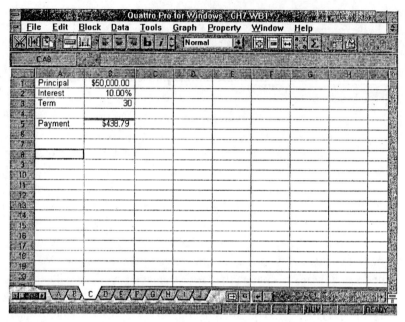

FIGURE 7.1:

A simple loan payment spreadsheet

3. Click on Protection. You'll see the Active
   Block: Protection dialog box, as shown in Figure 7.2.

4. Click on Unprotect.

5. Click on OK.

TURNING ON GLOBAL PROTECTION

At this point, you've unprotected cells B1 through B3, but you have not yet turned the page protection feature on, so it is still possible to change or delete the contents of any cell on the spreadsheet page. To turn on page protection:

1. Select Property ➤ Active Page or click the right mouse button on the page tab.

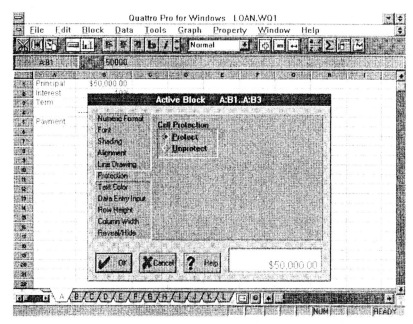

2. Click on Protection.

3. Click on Enable, then select OK.

To test the degree of protection, try changing any of the values in B1, B2, or B3. You'll see that Quattro Pro for Windows accepts the new data and recalculates the function accordingly. But try changing the contents of any other cell on the spreadsheet, and Quattro Pro will reject the action and display the alert message shown in Figure 7.3. Click on OK or press Escape to resume your work.

Note that after setting up a protection scheme, you should save the notebook so that the new protection scheme is saved as well.

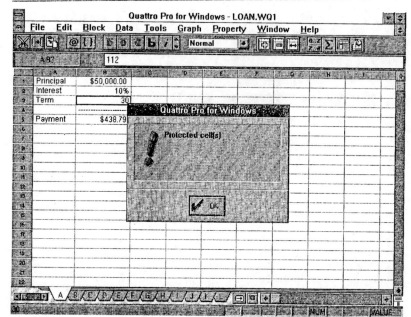

FIGURE 7.3:

The Alert message for protected cells

TURNING OFF GLOBAL PROTECTION

Of course, you may later decide to make changes to parts of the spreadsheet that are currently protected. To do so, select Property ➤ Active Page, then click on Protection, Disable, and OK. Once again, you'll be able to move the cell selector to any cell and add, change, or delete data, functions, or formulas.

REPROTECTING INDIVIDUAL CELLS

If you use the Active Block dialog box Protect option to unprotect a cell or group of cells, then later change your mind and decide to protect those cells, simply click and drag the cells and select the Protection option from the Active Block dialog box.

Remember to save the notebook with the spreadsheet's new protection scheme.

Reformatting Long Labels

Quattro Pro for Windows includes a text-formatting feature, similar to something you might find in a word-processing system, that changes the margin width of long text labels, and neatly adjusts the long label within the new margins. This is handy for entering memos or other long passages of text into a spreadsheet. In fact, you can enter a label with up to 1022 characters!

Figure 7.4 shows a sample spreadsheet with a long label typed into cell A1. The label actually spills over to column R, but you cannot see this on the screen.

Now suppose you wish to display the long label so that you can read it without having to scroll over to column R.

1. Move the cell selector to the beginning of the label (cell A1 in this example).

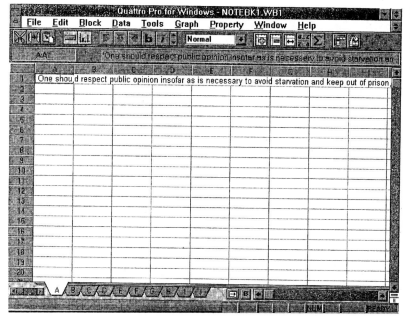

FIGURE 7.4:

A sample spreadsheet with a long label in cell A1

2. Select Block ➤ Reformat. The Block Reformat dialog box appears.

3. In the Block field, enter or select the block of columns you want the entry to span. For example, if you want to have the text read across three columns, you could enter A1..C1, either by typing the cell addresses, or by double-clicking on the Block field, and then clicking and dragging the columns.

4. Click on OK.

Figure 7.5 shows the same label after reformatting. Notice that the label is neatly *word-wrapped*—that is, lines are broken between words rather than within words.

If you reformat a label, any data and formulas beneath it in the same column will be pushed down to make room for the reformatted text. The

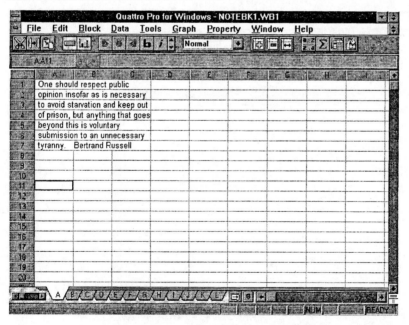

FIGURE 7.5:

The long label reformatted to fit within three columns

reformatted text occupies the cells specified, in this case A1..C1, physically—not just for display purposes.

However, data or labels in other columns will not be pushed down, and existing data to the right of the reformatted cell may block the display of the reformatted text. If this occurs, move the existing data and formulas to a new location on the spreadsheet using the mouse hand or Block ➤ Move. The reformatted labels will then appear on the screen after you complete the move operation.

Searching a Spreadsheet for a Specific Entry

Another handy technique that Quattro Pro for Windows offers for managing text is its global search-and-replace feature, which can be used to change all occurrences of text or numbers to some new value.

Figure 7.6 shows a sample spreadsheet with transactions for the month of December—that is, only the first 20 rows of the month's

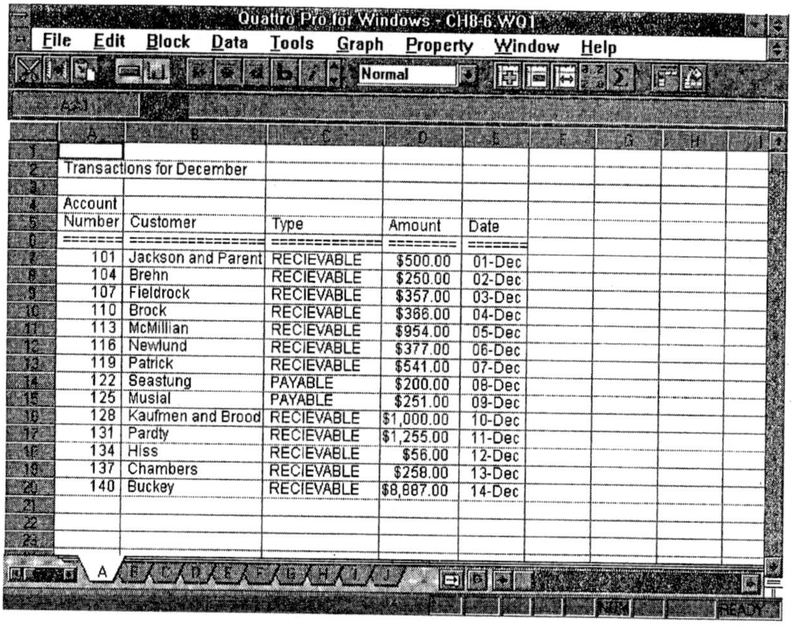

Transactions for December				
Account				
Number	Customer	Type	Amount	Date
======	==============	============	========	======
101	Jackson and Parent	RECIEVABLE	$500.00	01-Dec
104	Brehn	RECIEVABLE	$250.00	02-Dec
107	Fieldrock	RECIEVABLE	$357.00	03-Dec
110	Brock	RECIEVABLE	$366.00	04-Dec
113	McMillian	RECIEVABLE	$954.00	05-Dec
116	Newlund	RECIEVABLE	$377.00	06-Dec
119	Patrick	RECIEVABLE	$541.00	07-Dec
122	Seastung	PAYABLE	$200.00	08-Dec
125	Musial	PAYABLE	$251.00	09-Dec
128	Kaufmen and Brood	RECIEVABLE	$1,000.00	10-Dec
131	Pardty	RECIEVABLE	$1,255.00	11-Dec
134	Hiss	RECIEVABLE	$56.00	12-Dec
137	Chambers	RECIEVABLE	$258.00	13-Dec
140	Buckey	RECIEVABLE	$8,887.00	14-Dec

FIGURE 7.6:
A sample spreadsheet with misspellings

ledger. Note that within the Type column, the word *receivable* is consistently misspelled as *recievable*. The search-and-replace capability allows you to correct such misspellings.

To correct all the misspellings in the sample spreadsheet, follow these steps:

1. Move the cell selector to the top of the block with data to be changed (cell C7 in this example).

2. Click and drag cells C7..C20.

3. Select Edit ➤ Search and Replace. You will see the Search and Replace dialog box, as shown in Figure 7.7. The block containing the misspellings is already entered.

4. Click on the Find field, then enter the misspelled word: **RECIEVABLE**.

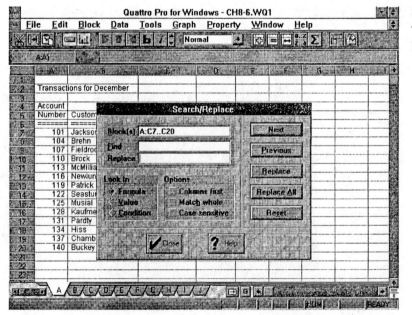

FIGURE 7.7:

The Search and Replace dialog box

5. Click on the Replace field, then enter the correct spelling: RECEIVABLE.

6. Select Replace All to replace all the occurrences of the word *recievable*.

Quattro Pro will instantly perform the entire search-and-replace operation. Figure 7.8 shows the sample spreadsheet after Quattro Pro has globally corrected all the occurrences of *recievable*.

Note that Quattro Pro pays attention to the case of search-and-replace characters. This means you can use Search and Replace to change case, as well as spelling. For example, you can search for "Loan" and replace it with "LOAN," simply by entering the replacing text in uppercase letters.

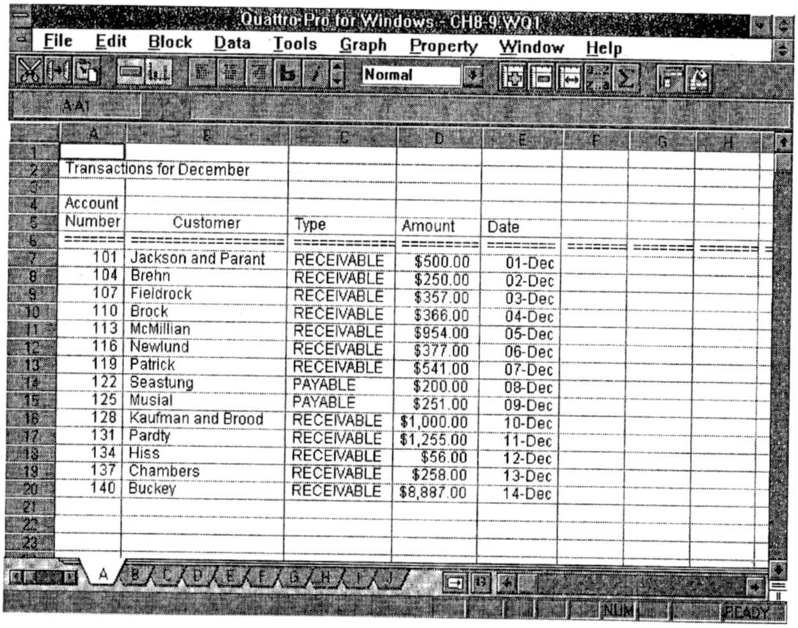

FIGURE 7.8:

The sample spreadsheet after globally replacing RECIEVABLE with RECEIVABLE

There are several other options presented in the Search and Replace dialog box:

COLUMN	OPTION	ACTION
Look In	Formula	Determines how a formula will be examined in the search process. The Formula choice searches for a formula only.
	Values	Searches only for the results generated by a formula.
	Condition	Allows you to include operators in your search. (For example, one conditional search might be ?>200, which instructs Quattro Pro to look for all values greater than 200.)
Options	Columns first	Searches the spreadsheet page by starting at the far left column and going down. The default is to search on a row-by-row basis.
	Match whole	If you select this option, Quattro Pro looks for all the letters entered into the Find field, as opposed to only a partial match. For example, if you enter "and" in the Find field, only the word "and" will be found. Otherwise, Quattro Pro finds words such as "land", "gland", and "sand."
	Case sensitive	Select this option to make Quattro Pro find entries with the specific case entered in the Find field.

The buttons activate the Search and Replace as follows:

BUTTON	ACTION
Next	Begins or resumes a forward search.
Previous	Begins or resumes a backward search.
Replace	Lets you decide on a case-by-case basis whether or not to replace a specific entry.
Replace All	Replaces every entry.
Reset	Erases the entries in the Block(s), Find, and Replace fields.

You can also use the Search and Replace option to change numbers in a spreadsheet. For example, suppose that the account number for Brock in the sample spreadsheet should be 103 rather than 110. You can then specify column A (i.e., block A7..A11) as the block to search and replace, 110 as the search string, and 103 as the replace string. Then select Next and proceed as discussed above.

Use this technique with caution. Suppose that you change a receivable amount from $500 to $550. Quattro Pro will blindly change *all* occurrences of $500, disregarding whose invoice they may actually be on. Keep this in mind when you use the Search and Replace command to make global changes to the price of an item or a similar value in a spreadsheet. Sometimes you *want* the computer to go about changing things indiscriminately, as when you corrected the spelling of *receivable;* often you don't.

Transposing Blocks

Typically, a spreadsheet consists of rows and columns of data, with headings in the top row and leftmost column. How you arrange the rows and columns is a matter of your own choosing. But just in case you change your mind about the way you've laid out the rows and columns in a spreadsheet, Quattro Pro for Windows offers a quick and easy method for changing the row headings into column headings, and vice versa.

Figure 7.9 lists probable voting turnouts by state in a hypothetical election. The columns are headed by state names, and the rows by politicians. Since there are only two candidates, but 50 states, this table would be easier to read if the states were listed by rows and the two contenders by columns. Typing the entries again would be pointless drudgery; *transposing* the columns and rows would be much faster.

To rearrange the spreadsheet, follow these steps:

1. Move the cell selector to the upper-left corner of the block you wish to transpose (cell A5 in this example).

2. Click and drag the block of cells containing the entries. In this example, the block is A5..G8.

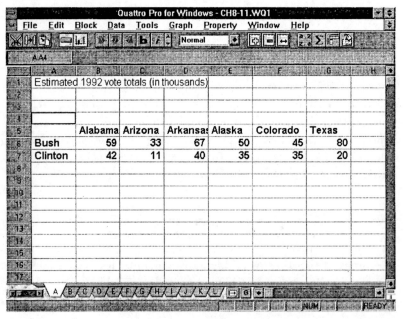

FIGURE 7.9:

Voting turnouts by state for Bush, and Clinton

3. Select Block ➤ Transpose. The Block Transpose dialog box appears. When you transpose the block, you must allow enough room for it. Quattro Pro is suggesting the same To block and From block.

4. Double-click on the To field to shrink the dialog box.

5. Click on cell A10.

6. Click on the up arrow in the Block Transpose dialog box title bar. The dialog box reappears with A10 in the To field.

7. Click on OK.

Figure 7.10 shows the transposed block, starting in cell A10.

You should be aware of two important points when using the Transpose option. First, chances are that formulas (both with absolute and relative references) will become inaccurate after a transposition

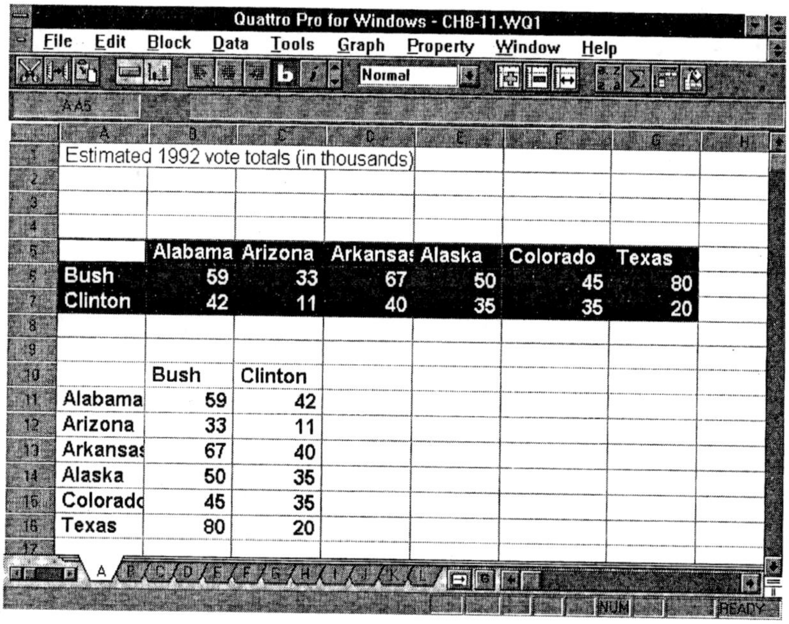

FIGURE 7.10:

The vote totals transposed

takes place, because Quattro Pro cannot alter a formula's variables to account for the change. That is, a formula that refers to, say, cell D4 in its calculation will continue to do so, even if a transposition has relocated the contents of cell D4 to cell A7. Note also that Transpose copies the data rather than moving it.

Second, if the block into which you transpose data already contains data, the transposed data will overwrite (replace) the data originally in the block. When that happens you can immediately use Edit ➤ Undo to reverse the command, unless you don't care about it.

To play it safe, then, save a spreadsheet *before* transposing data. If you find that the transposition creates problems, just select File ➤ Retrieve to bring up a copy of the original, unchanged spreadsheet.

Freezing Titles

With any spreadsheet that is too large to fit on a single screen, you need to scroll around to locate particular data. As you do so, column titles and other pertinent data may move off the screen, so that you see only rows and columns of numbers. To avoid sinking in this sea of digits, you can freeze column and/or row headings at the edges of the screen. In this way, you can scroll deep within the spreadsheet and still know what the rows and columns are called.

This Locked Titles option is found on the Windows menu. Before engaging this command, place the cell selector below the row of titles and/or to the right of the column of titles that you wish to freeze. Then select Window ➤ Locked Titles. The dialog box appears with the following options:

Clear
Horizontal
Vertical
Both

To freeze only those titles above the cell selector (i.e., only the column headings), select Horizontal. To freeze titles only to the left of the cell selector (i.e., only the row headings), select Vertical. To freeze both headings, select Both. (To unfreeze previously frozen titles, select Clear.) Then choose OK. When you return to the spreadsheet and scroll far to the right or downwards, the titles will remain on the screen.

Figure 7.11 shows a sample spreadsheet that displays a political campaign budget. Though not currently visible on the screen, the months extend to the right, out to December. There are also a few rows beneath row 21.

Figure 7.12 shows how the large spreadsheet looks if you scroll to the lower-right corner. Because all row and column titles have since scrolled off the screen, it is difficult to tell what the various numbers refer to. But you want to know what's what.

1. Move the cell selector to the cell where you want to freeze the titles. Here, click on B3, which is the first row beneath and the first column to the right of the titles that you want to freeze.

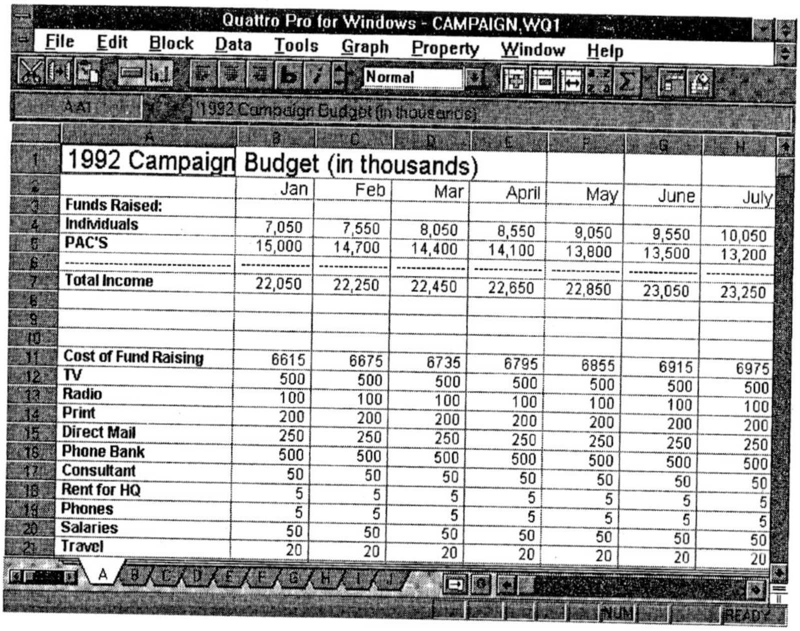

	A	B	C	D	E	F	G	H
1	1992 Campaign Budget (in thousands)							
2		Jan	Feb	Mar	April	May	June	July
3	Funds Raised:							
4	Individuals	7,050	7,550	8,050	8,550	9,050	9,550	10,050
5	PAC'S	15,000	14,700	14,400	14,100	13,800	13,500	13,200
6	----------	----------	----------	----------	----------	----------	----------	----------
7	Total Income	22,050	22,250	22,450	22,650	22,850	23,050	23,250
8								
9								
10								
11	Cost of Fund Raising	6615	6675	6735	6795	6855	6915	6975
12	TV	500	500	500	500	500	500	500
13	Radio	100	100	100	100	100	100	100
14	Print	200	200	200	200	200	200	200
15	Direct Mail	250	250	250	250	250	250	250
16	Phone Bank	500	500	500	500	500	500	500
17	Consultant	50	50	50	50	50	50	50
18	Rent for HQ	5	5	5	5	5	5	5
19	Phones	5	5	5	5	5	5	5
20	Salaries	50	50	50	50	50	50	50
21	Travel	20	20	20	20	20	20	20

FIGURE 7.11:
A sample campaign spreadsheet, top-left corner

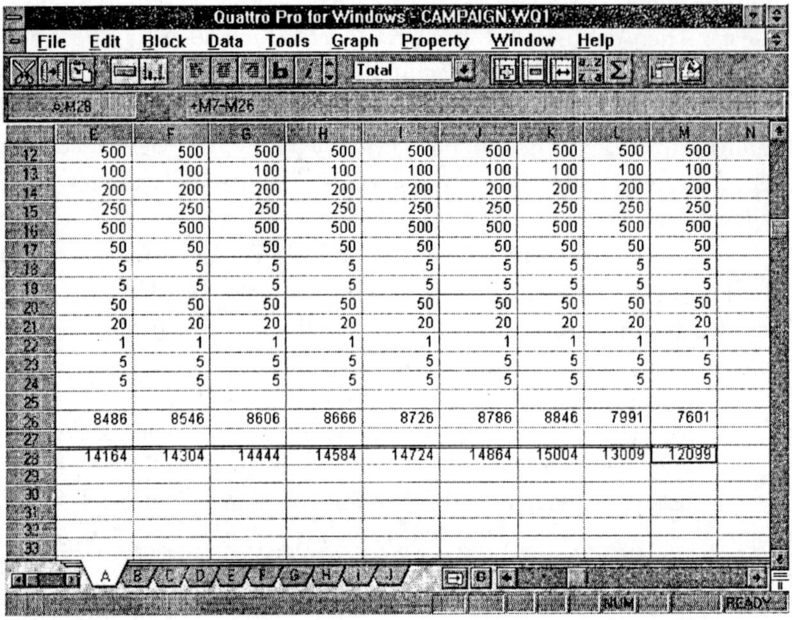

FIGURE 7.12:

The sample campaign spreadsheet when scrolled to the bottom-right corner

2. Select Windows ➤ Locked Titles. In the dialog box, click on Both.

Nothing appears to happen at first. But if you scroll down to the lower-right corner of a large spreadsheet, the column and row titles will remain on the screen, as shown in Figure 7.13.

There is one small disadvantage to freezing sections of the spreadsheet: after you freeze an area, you can no longer move the cell selector into that area to make changes. The arrow keys will not move the cell selector into the frozen area, and the mouse pointer changes to a circle with a diagonal line to indicate cells you cannot click on. If you need to make changes within the area, unfreeze the area by selecting Window ➤ Locked Titles, and then the Clear option. Then press the Home key to bring you to the part of the spreadsheet where the titles are.

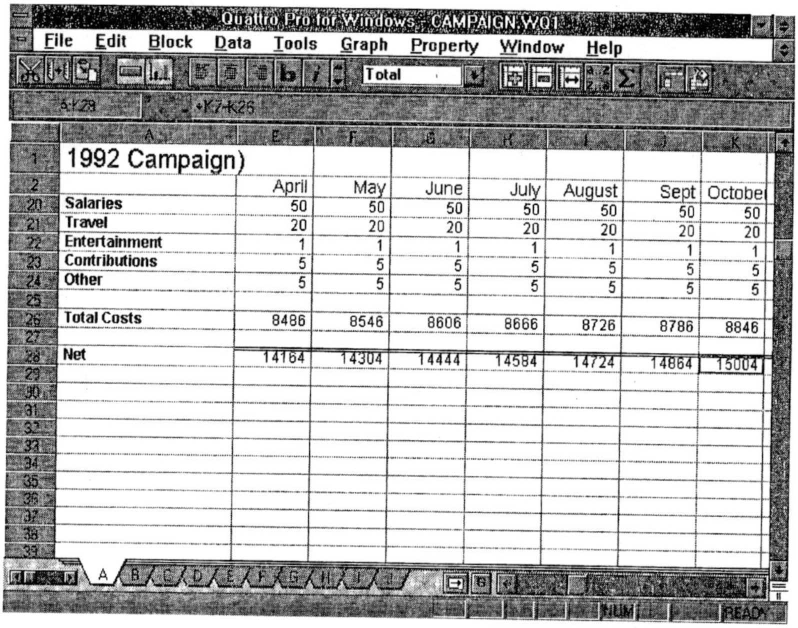

FIGURE 7.13:

The sample campaign spreadsheet scrolled with frozen titles

Viewing Two Areas of the Spreadsheet Simultaneously

Often you'll find yourself having to scroll back and forth between two areas of a large spreadsheet page. Rather than clicking on the scroll boxes, you can divide the screen in two, either horizontally or vertically, and scroll through the two separate sections independently.

Using the campaign budget spreadsheet shown earlier as an example, you would follow these steps to split the screen into two horizontal windowpanes.

1. If the titles are frozen, use Window ➤ Locked Titles and the Clear command to remove the lock. In the lower right corner of the spreadsheet page border are two equal signs, one horizontal and one vertical.

2. Move the mouse pointer onto the horizontal equal sign. When it is correctly positioned, the pointer changes to a two-headed arrow with a line across the center.

3. Click and drag the symbol. As you do, a dotted line appears horizontally across the screen indicating the position the split will assume if you release the mouse button.

4. Move the split symbol onto the border between rows 8 and 9 and release the mouse button.

At this point, the screen is split in half, and a new horizontal border appears between rows 8 and 9, as in Figure 7.14.

SWITCHING BETWEEN TWO PANES

The cell selector will operate in only one window at a time. To switch it from one pane to the other, click on the pane you want. If you move

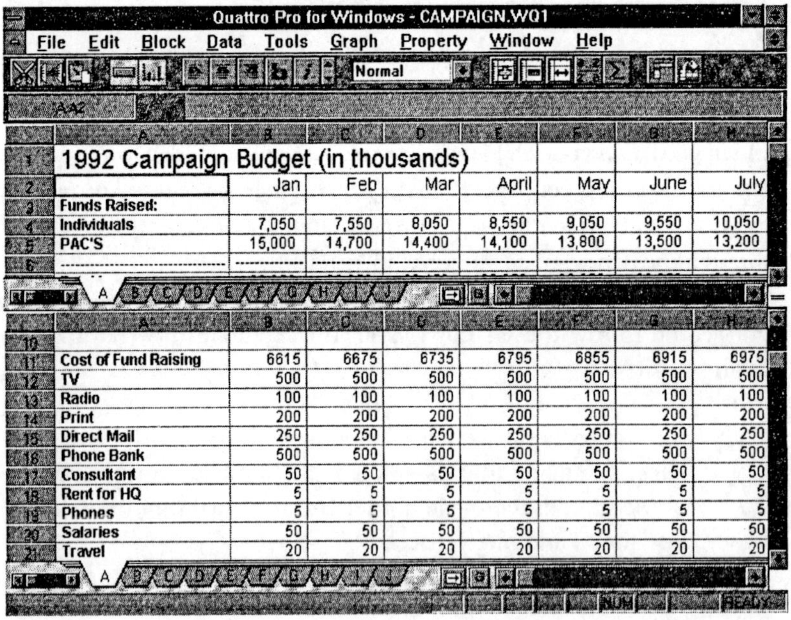

FIGURE 7.14:

The campaign spreadsheet divided into two windowpanes

the cell selector to the bottom window, you'll be able to scroll up and down through the expenses items without affecting the upper window.

SYNCHRONIZING THE SCROLLING OF TWO PANES

While a spreadsheet is split in two horizontally, take a moment to experiment with synchronized scrolling. If you click the horizontal scroll box, you'll notice that both windows scroll in synchronization, regardless of which window the cell selector is in. Note, though, that this joint scrolling holds for only one direction of motion: horizontal scrolling for a horizontally split screen and vertical scrolling for a vertically split screen (described below).

You can unsynchronize the windows if you want, by selecting Window ➤ Panes and clicking on the Synchronize option in the Panes dialog box. The default setting is Synchronize, so clicking on it once turns it off. Click on OK to close the dialog box. Notice that the windows no longer scroll together; instead, only the selected window scrolls. To return to synchronized scrolling, follow the same steps and click on Synchronize again.

You cannot split the screen both horizontally and vertically at the same time. Before switching from a horizontal split to a vertical split, then, you must first clear the existing window split.

CLEARING THE SECOND WINDOWPANE

To return the screen to a single windowpane, simply click on the split symbol at the far right of the split border and drag it to the top or bottom of the window.

CREATING A VERTICAL WINDOWPANE

The example above demonstrated a horizontal window break. To split the screen vertically instead, move the mouse pointer to the vertical equal sign and click and drag it to the position you want. Remember, synchronized scrolling will now work only vertically.

THE EFFECT AN OPEN PANE HAS ON SPREADSHEET CHANGES

While the spreadsheet page is split into two panes, any changes you make to numbers used in calculations will be reflected immediately in both windows. They are, after all, just two views of the same spreadsheet page.

Some cosmetic changes will not be automatically reflected in both panes, however. These include frozen titles and column widths. Think of the supplementary lower (or right) window as being superimposed on the upper (or left) one. Any cosmetic changes made to the second windowpane will disappear when you go back to the single-window mode; any made to the first will remain.

Emphasizing Special Cells

When you format cells for data entry, Quattro Pro for Windows automatically adds commas, currency symbols, or the appropriate number of decimals. To add even more emphasis to certain areas or cells of the spreadsheet (so that, say, negative numbers or unusual profits stand out), Quattro Pro offers several options in the Active Block dialog box.

You have the option of turning the grid lines that outline all of the cell borders off or on. The default setting is on. To turn the grid off, select Property ➤ Active Page. Click on Grid Lines in the Active Page dialog box, then click on both the Horizontal and Vertical options. Click on OK to close the dialog box with the changes.

One of the main attractions of Quattro Pro for Windows is that you can use the Active Block dialog box to add various types of emphasis to a cell block in a single step. Some of the ways to emphasize blocks are described in the following sections.

LINE DRAWING

The Line Drawing option in the Active Block dialog box allows you to insert lines on the outside, around, or on the inside of a block of cells.

Click and drag the cells you want to emphasize, then click the right mouse button to open the Active Block dialog box. Click on Line Drawing to open the dialog box shown in Figure 7.15. The three ways to add lines are All, which places lines all round the selected cells; Outline, which places the lines around the border of the selected cells; and Inside, which inserts the lines on the borders between the cells.

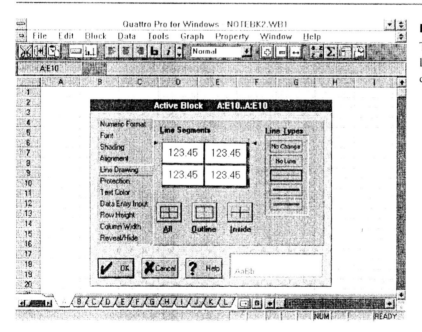

FIGURE 7.15:

The Active Block: Line Drawing dialog box

Choosing the Line Thickness

After selecting the line you want to add to the block of specified cells, select the type of line you want—No Line, single, thick, or double—and click on OK. Figure 7.16 shows all three types of lines drawn in several blocks.

Removing Lines

If you decide that the lines you have added to the spreadsheet are not appropriate, click the right mouse button. From the Active Block dialog box, select Line Drawing and, under Line Types, No Line. Click on OK. The lines will be removed from the block.

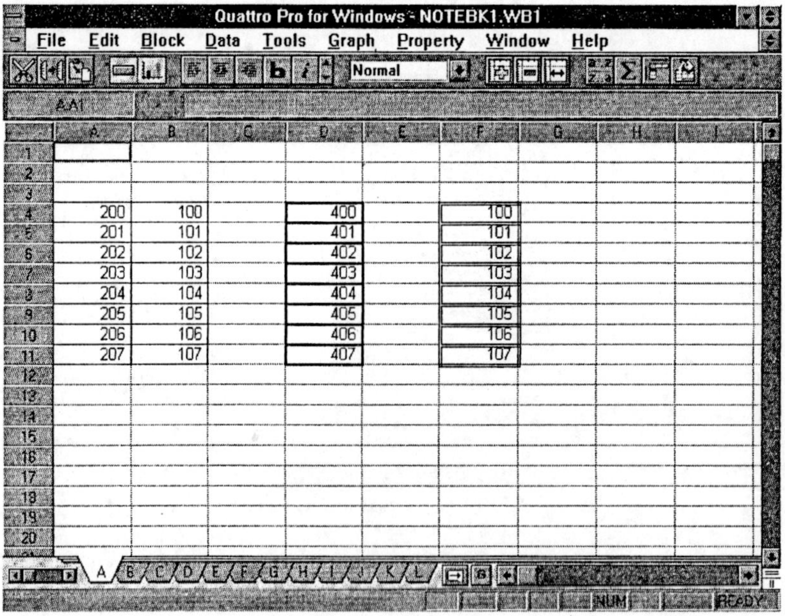

FIGURE 7.16:

Single, thick, and double lines drawn in blocks

SHADING A BLOCK OF CELLS

You can add blends of shading to a block of cells with the Active Block: Shading option. Click on one of the boxes under Blend. Quattro Pro then displays the manner of shading that you have selected in the lower right corner of the Active Block dialog box. You can also select colors to emphasize specific cells. You can use the colors in combination with a type of shading. Select a color from Color 1, a second from Color 2, and choose a suitable blend, then click on OK.

When you print the shaded cells on paper, they will appear in reverse, the cells darkened and the characters in white (unless you have a color printer).

Turning Shading On

1. Click and drag the block of cells you want to color or shade (or both).

2. Click the right mouse button to open the Active Block dialog box.

3. Click on Shading. The Active Block: Shading options appear, as shown in Figure 7.17.

4. Click on the color or shading (or both) to see the effect on the block.

5. Click on OK.

SELECTING FONTS

A *type font* determines the size of the printed character, the style, and the typeface. In addition, you can make cell entries bold, italic, underline or strikeout.

To specify a font for a block of cells:

1. Click and drag the block whose type font you want to change.

2. Click the right mouse button to open the Active Block dialog box.

3. Click on Font. The Active Block: Font dialog box appears, as shown in Figure 7.18. Note that this figure includes fonts that were installed using Adobe Type Manager.

4. Click on the scroll bar to find the typeface you want.

5. Click on the typeface. Look in the lower-right corner of the dialog box to see the effect of the typeface.

6. When you are satisfied with the typeface, click on Point Size to enlarge or reduce the type.

7. Click on OK.

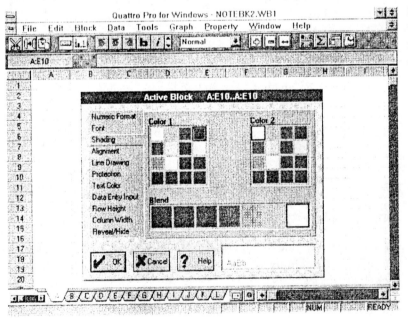

FIGURE 7.17:

The Active Block: Shading option dialog box.

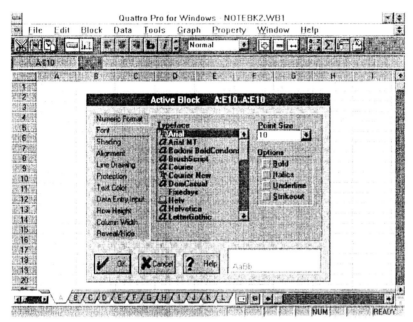

Figure 7.19 shows several types of cell emphasis.

This chapter examined ways to enhance your spreadsheet. The next chapter covers the use of multiple pages in a notebook and linking cells among spreadsheet pages.

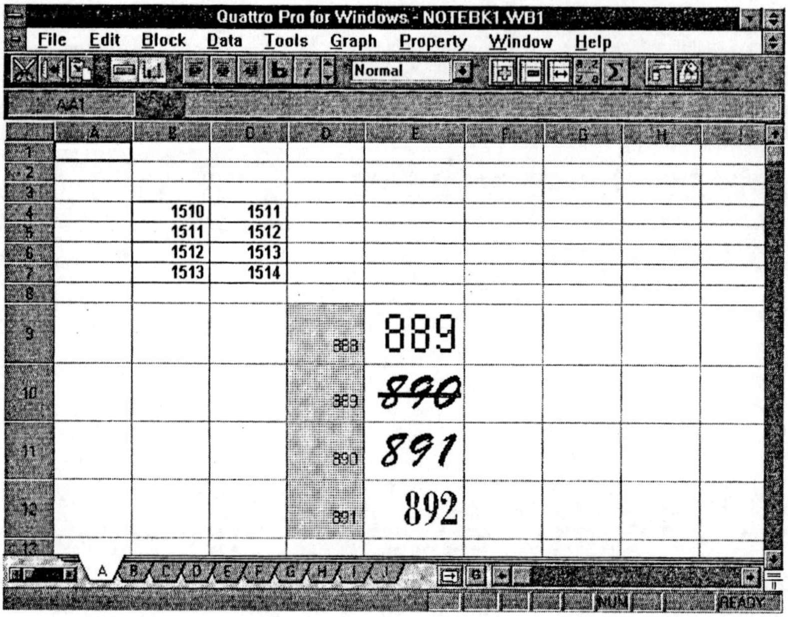

FIGURE 7.19:

Cells with emphasis

8 C H A P T E R

Working with Multiple Spreadsheet Pages

FEATURING

Linking multiple spreadsheet pages using Group mode

Arranging spreadsheet windows

Repositioning and resizing windows

n the last chapter, you learned how to view two different segments of a spreadsheet page simultaneously. This is helpful if you are working on a large spreadsheet and don't want to scroll back and forth constantly between the two areas. Quattro Pro for Windows allows you to call up a number of separate spreadsheet pages at the same time. In this chapter, we will work with multiple spreadsheet pages.

Opening a Second Spreadsheet Page

When you start Quattro Pro for Windows, the *default name* of the opened, blank notebook is NOTEBK1.WB1, opened to spreadsheet page A. After entering information, you will probably want to open another spreadsheet page while keeping the first one still on the screen, perhaps to add data. To do so:

1. Click on the Tab labeled B at the bottom of the window.

2. Click on the A tab to make that spreadsheet page active again.

Whenever you open a new spreadsheet page, Quattro Pro will place it directly over the previous spreadsheet page.

THE TAB SCROLLER

At the bottom left of the window is the Tab Scroller. Clicking on either arrow scrolls the spreadsheet page tabs one page at a time in the direction you have clicked. The scroll box can be clicked and dragged in the direction you want to open pages, too.

1. Click several times on the right arrow button in the Tab Scroller. As you can see, further spreadsheet page tabs are now visible.

2. Click on the left arrow button to return to the A spreadsheet page tab.

NAMING A SPREADSHEET PAGE

Let's suppose that you want to set up a notebook which records the sales and expenses for each day of a month for a business . Each week occupies an individual spreadsheet page. We will include a fifth page that totals the profit and loss for the entire month. First, let's name each of the pages.

1. Move the mouse pointer to the Tab for spreadsheet page A.

2. Click the right mouse button. The Active Page dialog box appears, as shown in Figure 8.1. The Name option is already selected.

3. Type 1stWeek as the page name. (Note that you cannot use spaces in a spreadsheet page name.)

4. Click on OK or press Enter. The spreadsheet page name appears on the spreadsheet page tab.

5. Click on the B spreadsheet page tab.

6. Click the right mouse button on the B spreadsheet page tab to bring up the Active Page dialog box.

7. Name this spreadsheet page 2ndWeek.

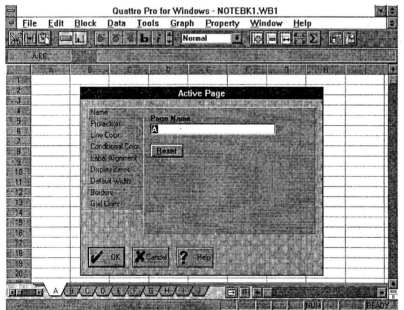

FIGURE 8.1:

The Active Page dialog box

8. Repeat the steps so that spreadsheet page C is named
3rdWeek, spreadsheet page D is named **4thWeek**, and
spreadsheet page E is named **WkTotals**. To move to spreadsheet page E, you may need to click on the right-pointing
arrow in the Tab Scroller.

Your notebook should resemble the one shown in Figure 8.2.

Return to spreadsheet page 1stWeek using the Tab Scroller. Let's
add the labels and titles that are common to each weekly spreadsheet
page. We can do this in one step using the Group mode of Quattro Pro
for Windows.

1. Click on the Tools menu name.

2. From the Tools menu, click on Define Group. The
Define/Modify Group dialog box appears, as shown in
Figure 8.3.

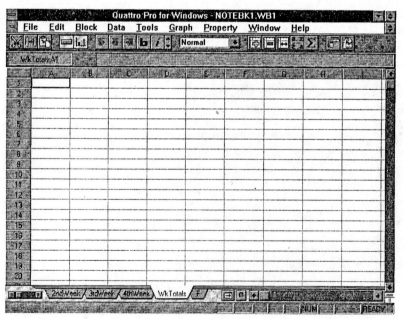

FIGURE 8.2:

The notebook
with renamed
pages

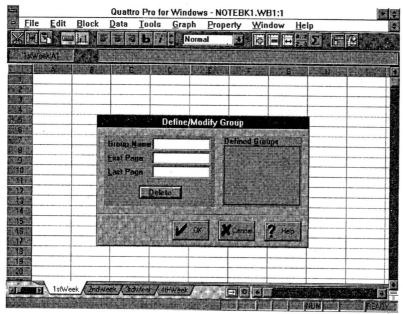

3. Type **JANUARY** in the Group Name field.

4. Click on the First Page field, and type **1stWeek** as the
First Page.

5. Click on the Last Page field and enter **WkTotals** as the
Last Page.

6. Click on OK or press Enter.

Now, when you set the notebook to Group mode, all of the spreadsheet
pages in the group are affected by a formatting change to any one of them.

Next, let's enter the day numbers, using the SpeedFill button.
When Group mode is selected, Quattro Pro for Windows will insert the
day numbers in all four weeks automatically.

1. Click on the **1st Week** tab to make it the active page.

2. Click on the Group button (the button marked with a G to the right of the SpeedTab button) at the bottom of the spreadsheet page. As you can see, Quattro Pro inserts a blue line under the spreadsheet pages contained in the group that you created in the previous exercise.

3. Move the cell selector to cell B3.

4. Type 1 to designate the first day of the month, then click on the left mouse button.

5. Click and drag cells B3..H3.

6. Click on the SpeedFill button (the button to the right of the Sum button).

The numbers one through seven are inserted into the cells. Take a look at spreadsheet page 2ndWeek by clicking on its tab. As you can see, Quattro Pro has filled the cells B3..H3 with the correct numbers. If you look at the other three spreadsheet pages, you will see that the block fill operation has continued all through the group. Although the numbers are incorrect for the WkTotals spreadsheet page, they are easily erased, which we will do in a subsequent exercise.

Turning on Group mode allows you to make a formatting change to one of the spreadsheets in the designated group, which then affects all of the spreadsheets in the group. The salient benefit of this feature is that you can be assured that spreadsheet pages of common design remain consistent.

Adding the Days of the Week

The SpeedFill button is smart. It takes the entry in the first cell in the selected block and increases it by a factor of one. Let's see if it works with labels, too.

1. In cell B2 in the 1stWeek page, enter **Monday**.

2. Click and drag cells B2..H2.

3. Click on the SpeedFill button.

Quattro Pro correctly inserts the names of the days of the week. Notice that the numbers are right-aligned, while the labels are left-aligned. Next, we'll use the SpeedBar to align them more neatly.

Aligning in Group Mode

The SpeedBar includes three buttons for aligning cell entries. Before you can align a cell entry, it must be selected. In this example, we are going to realign the number entries in the block B3..H3 in a single step.

1. Click and drag cells B3..H3.

2. Click on the Center button in the SpeedBar. It is the seventh button from the left.

Instantly, the entries are centered. And because you are in Group mode, the numbers in all of the grouped spreadsheet pages are centered. The block highlighting remains on, in case you decide you want to try a different alignment or use another SpeedBar button. For now, click on any cell outside the selected block to remove the highlighting.

Drilling Entries

Now that the entries unique to 1stWeek have been made, we can focus on the entries that are common to all four weeks' logs:

1. Move the cell pointer to cell A6 in spreadsheet page 1stWeek.

2. Type **INCOME** in cell A6.

3. Hold down the Control key and press Enter.

The INCOME label is inserted into cell A6 in spreadsheet page 1st-Week, and in all of the spreadsheet pages in the Group. The name for this technique is *drilling*. It works only with the combination of being in Group mode and pressing the Control and Enter keys together. If you click the left mouse button, or press Enter by itself, the information is only inserted in the current spreadsheet page.

Finish the Income portion of the spreadsheet by entering the remaining labels. Type each label and press the Control and Enter keys together to drill the label into every spreadsheet page.

Cell A8: **Hardware**

Cell A9: **Ribbons**

Cell A10: **Software**

Cell A11: **Paper**

Cell A13: **Total**

Your spreadsheet page should resemble the one in Figure 8.4.

Now let's add the spreadsheet page title and some special formatting.

1. Move the cell selector to cell D1.

2. Type the heading **January 1993-Daily Log**.

3. Press Control-Enter to drill the heading.

4. Move the mouse pointer to the SpeedBar, and click on the up arrow (next to the italic button) five times. As you can see, the text increases in size with each click of the mouse button.

5. Click on the Bold button in the SpeedBar.

The spreadsheet title is now in bold and is 20 points in size, as shown in Figure 8.5.

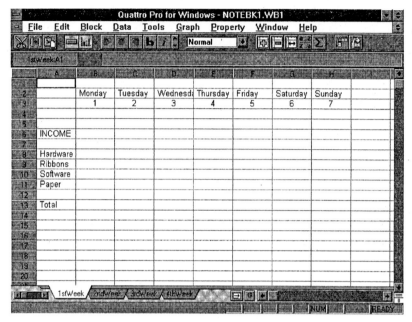

FIGURE 8.4:

The labels added to the company daily log

Let's drill some numbers into the Monday column.

1. In cell B8, type **5000**.

2. Press Control-Enter.

3. Enter the following labels, pressing Control-Enter after each entry:

> In cell B9, enter **1000**.
> In cell B10, enter **500**.
> In cell B11, enter **500**.

4. Click on the Group mode button to turn off Group mode.

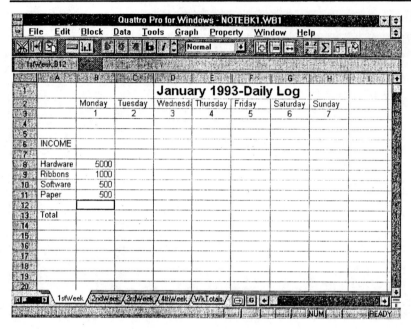

FIGURE 8.5:

The title added

Totaling the Pages

Now we have four spreadsheet pages which have values in the Income portion of the spreadsheet. Let's move to the WkTotals page and edit it by changing some of the labels we drilled earlier and creating formulas to total the daily income from each item.

1. Use the Tab Scroller and the tab to move to the WkTotals spreadsheet page. As you can see, the income numbers have been copied to this page. However, they are incorrect because they do not reflect the totals for each item. To do that, we will create a 3-D formula.

2. Click and drag cells B3..H3.

3. Click on the Cut button to erase the block.

Creating 3-D Formula

1. Move the cell pointer to cell B8.

2. Type **@SUM(**.

3. Click on the Tab Scroller to make spreadsheet page 1stWeek visible.

4. Click on the 1stWeek tab.

5. Click on cell B8. Quattro Pro enters the cell address, **1st-Week:B8** into the formula.

6. Hold down the Shift key and click on the 2ndWeek tab.

7. Click on cell B8.

8. Still holding the Shift key, click on the 3rdWeek tab.

9. Click on cell B8.

10. Still holding the Shift key, click on the 4thWeek tab.

11. Click on cell B8, then finish the formula by typing a close parenthesis,).

12. Click on the check mark, or hit Enter.

Quattro Pro totals the values across the third dimension. Notice that the page names are used in the formula rather than the original tab letters, making it much easier to determine the correctness of the formula, as shown in Figure 8.6.

Copying a 3-D Formula Copying a 3-D formula is no different than copying a 2-D formula. Quattro Pro adjusts the cell address relative to the new position on the spreadsheet page.

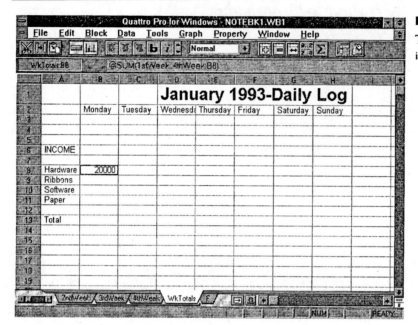

FIGURE 8.6:

The 3-D formula in cell B8

1. Click on cell B8 in WkTotals.

2. Click on the Copy button.

3. Click and drag cells B9..B11.

4. Click on the Paste button.

The WkTotals page now shows the overall totals for each income category for Mondays. But one formula is not finished. Although we know how much of each item was sold on Monday, we do not have a total for the month.

Splitting the Window to See Two Spreadsheet Pages An easier way to see if the formula you are entering is correct, especially if it is across several pages, is to split the window and view both pages at the same time.

1. Move the mouse pointer to the vertical pane splitter button (the vertical split symbol in the lower-right corner of the window).

2. When the mouse pointer changes shape, click and drag the dotted line to the middle of the window, between columns D and E, and release it.

3. Click on the Tab Scroller in the left window, moving it until the 1stWeek page tab appears. Click on the 1st Week tab.

4. Scroll the spreadsheet page so that you can see cell B13.

5. Click on the right window.

6. Scroll the spreadsheet page so that cell B13 is visible, as shown in Figure 8.7.

7. Click on the left window.

8. Click on cell B13. Type **@SUM(**. (You cannot use the Speed-Sum button to enter the formula because B13 is not adjacent to cells with entries.)

9. Click and drag cells B8..B11.

10. Type a close parenthesis, then press Control-Enter.

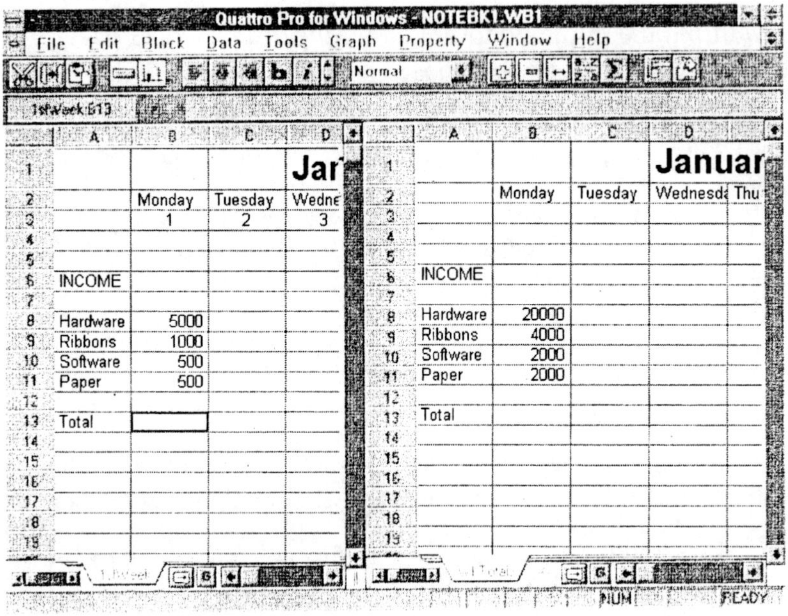

FIGURE 8.7:

Both spreadsheet pages visible

The formula is drilled all the way through to the WkTotals page. The formula is correct in each week's spreadsheet page but is incorrect in the WkTotals page. Change it with the following steps:

1. Make sure Group mode is off. If necessary, turn it off by clicking on the G button.

2. Click on cell B13 in WkTotals.

3. Click on the Cut button.

4. Click on cell B11.

5. Click on the Copy button.

6. Click on cell B13.

7. Click on the Paste button. The correct total, 28,000, is displayed.

In this simple example you have seen some of the power of using window splits to create formulas. As your notebooks become more and more interlaced with formulas, you can use this power to assure yourself that the correct cells are being referenced and calculated.

Absolute or Relative Page References   When you create a 3-D formula, Quattro Pro for Windows assumes that the references should be relative. If, however, you need to make a page portion of the formula absolute, you can do so by pressing the F4 key while in Edit mode, or by adding a dollar sign ($) to the page part of the formula.

The Window Menu

The Window Menu (shown in Figure 8.8) lists the different ways you can arrange spreadsheet windows on the screen. To call it up, click on the menu name.

The different formats are as follows:

New View	The New View command displays a duplicate copy of the active notebook in a new window. This is a quick way to see two parts of the same spreadsheet page or to see different pages of the same notebook.
Tile	The Tile command displays all the open windows, including other notebooks, without overlapping them. If possible, Quattro Pro displays all of the windows in equal size. Figure 8.9 shows a series of tiled windows.

FIGURE 8.8:

The Window menu

Cascade	The Cascade command displays all the open windows stacked on top of each other, with the title bar of each window visible. Figure 8.10 shows an example of cascaded Windows
Arrange Icons	When you minimize windows, you can rearrange the icons into a neat row with this command.
Hide	The Hide command hides the active window. It is still available, but it is not displayed when you use the other Window menu commands such as Tile or Cascade.

Show	The Show command displays a dialog box which lists the Windows that have been concealed using the Hide command. To reopen the hidden window, click on the window name and on OK.
Panes	The Panes command presents a dialog box with the choice of horizontal or vertical window splits. You can also clear a window split.
Locked Titles	The Locked Titles command opens the Locked Titles dialog box. The Locked Titles options were discussed in Chapter 7.

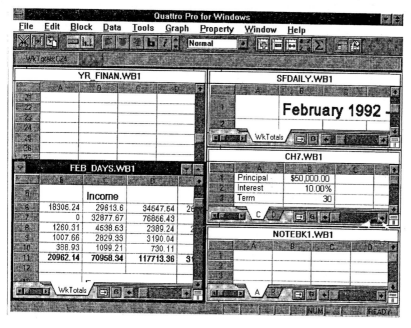

FIGURE 8.9:

An example of tiled windows

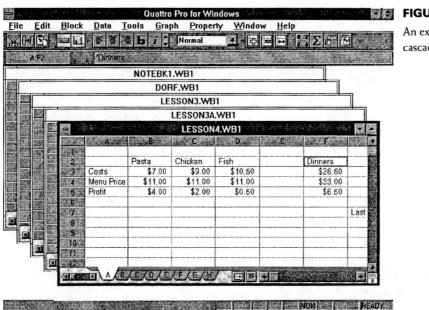

FIGURE 8.10:

An example of cascaded windows

TILING SEVERAL WINDOWS

Now let's open a third spreadsheet page and display the windows in a tiled format.

1. Click and drag the split symbol from the lower left corner of the active window to any location in the middle of the right window and release it. Immediately you have three windows to choose from instead of two.

2. Click on the Maximize button in any of the windows. Whichever window you choose expands to cover the entire window.

3. Click on the Window menu name. Notice in Figure 8.11 that the menu contains a list of available windows, with a check mark indicating which window is active.

4. Click on Tile.

As you can see, the three windows each take a third of the application window. Now you can move or change the position or size of a particular window. Before doing so, however, you have to be able to designate which window you want to change.

CHANGING THE SIZE OF A WINDOW

Because of the flexibilty of a graphic interface, you can reshape any of the windows using the mouse. For example, if you want to see only a small portion of a window, you can resize it using the mouse.

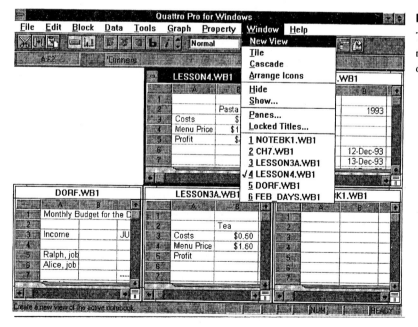

FIGURE 8.11:

The Window menu with a list of open windows

1. Move the mouse pointer to the bottom border of the far left window.

2. The mouse pointer will change in shape to a two-headed arrow, one head pointing up and the other pointing down.

3. Click and drag the pointer toward the top of the screen. As you do, a gray line is displayed, marking the point where the new border will be drawn when the mouse button is released.

4. Release the mouse button when the border is on the middle of the window.

5. Move the mouse pointer to the right border of the same window.

6. When the two-headed arrow appears, now pointing left and right, click and drag the gray line until it is about half-way over the middle window.

7. Release the mouse button. Figure 8.12 shows the result of resizing the window.

ANOTHER WAY TO RESIZE A WINDOW

You can also resize a window by moving two borders at the same time. Clicking on the lower-right corner of any window changes the mouse pointer into a two-headed arrow, pointing diagonally. You can then click and drag the arrow towards the upper-left corner of the window, making the window smaller, or towards the lower-right, making the window bigger. As you move the arrow, the gray lines appear, allowing you to see the magnitude of the change before you actually execute it. (Clicking on the other three corners works in a similar way.)

MOVING A WINDOW

To move a window, click on the document control button in the upper-left corner of the border. The document control window appears. Click

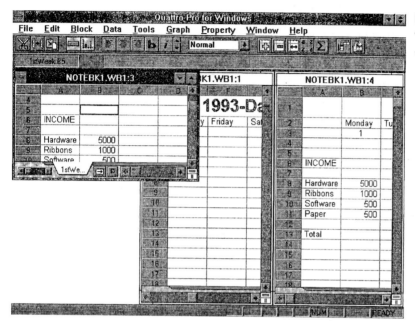

FIGURE 8.12:

The resized window

on Move. When you do, the mouse pointer becomes a four headed arrow. Press any of the arrow keys in the direction you want to move the window. After you have pressed an arrow key, the mouse pointer resumes its normal arrow shape, allowing you to finish the move with the mouse.

MINIMIZING A WINDOW

The fastest way to minimize a window is to click on the down arrow in the upper-right corner of the document window border. Quattro Pro reduces the window to an icon. It is still active and accessible, just no longer open.

MAXIMIZING A WINDOW

After you have minimized a window, opening it again may take a couple of steps. For example, if the active window is maximized in the application window, the document icon will not be visible, because it is underneath the current document.

1. Click on the Window menu and click on Tile. The currently open document window(s) are rearranged so that any minimized document window icon can be seen. Figure 8.13 shows the active window tiled and the document icons visible at the the bottom of the application window.

2. Click on the icon of the document window you want to open. Quattro Pro displays the document control menu.

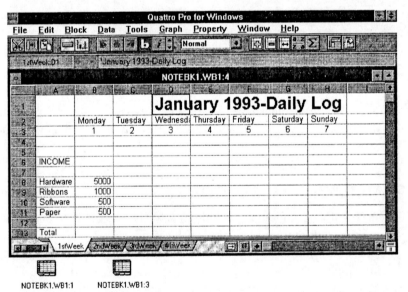

FIGURE 8.13:

The window tiled, revealing minimized document windows

3. Click on either Restore, which redisplays the window in the same size as it was when you minimized it, or Maximize, which displays the document full screen in the application window.

You can also use the Window menu to select the window you want.

SAVING ALL OPEN WINDOWS

The Save All command is found on the File menu. When Save All is selected, Quattro Pro for Windows begins to save all the open notebooks. If any spreadsheet pages of the notebook have been modified during the work session, Quattro Pro asks if you want to Replace or Backup the notebook, or Cancel the Save operation. Selecting Replace copies the new changes to the notebook file. Selecting Backup saves the file with the changes with the new extension .BAK. Save this notebook as CH8 for your reference.

The next chapter introduces you to printing spreadsheet pages, or printing all the information in a notebook.

9 CHAPTER

Printing
Your Spreadsheet

FEATURING

Setting the page layout

Adjusting the printer

Printing to a disk file

Previewing a spreadsheet

Special print features

In this chapter, we discuss printing spreadsheets. You'll learn how to change their orientation and layout, and how to use options such as headings. We discuss using the Print Preview feature to see how the work will appear. Finally, we will take a look at exporting your work for use in word-processed documents.

Overview of Printing Options

All of the options for printing a spreadsheet are accessed via the File menu: Print, Print Preview, Page Setup, Named Settings, and Printer Setup. When you select the Print option, the Spreadsheet Print dialog box appears. Figure 9.1 shows how the Spreadsheet Print dialog box looks on the screen. Clicking on the Options button displays the Spreadsheet Print Options dialog box, as shown in Figure 9.2.

The various settings in both dialog boxes are summarized briefly below (we will discuss them in more detail throughout this chapter).

Print Block	Specifies a block of cells for printing.
Print Pages	Determines which pages of the notebook you want to print.

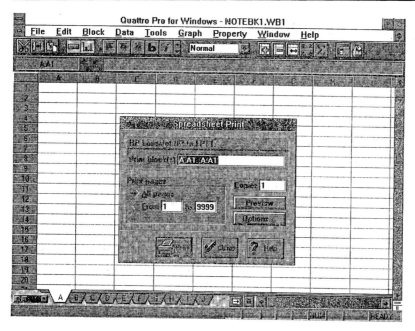

FIGURE 9.1:

The Spreadsheet Print dialog box

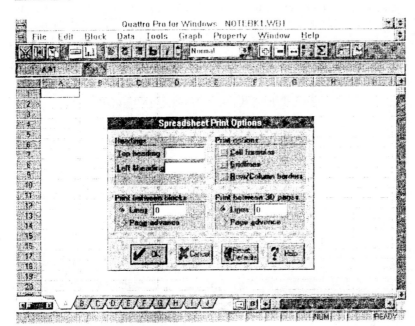

FIGURE 9.2:

The Spreadsheet Print Options dialog box

Copies	Specifies the number of copies you want to print.
Preview	Displays the spreadsheet pages as they will appear when printed, a page at a time.
Headings	Specifies the row and/or column heading that will be printed on each page.
Print between blocks	Determines if Quattro Pro should print a line between noncontiguous blocks, or advance a full page between blocks.
Print Options	Cell Formulas prints the formulas, not the values; Gridlines prints gridlines; and Row/Column borders prints the column letters and the row numbers.

Print between 3-D Pages	Determines if Quattro Pro should print a line between blocks from different pages or print them on separate pages.

If you are printing on a dot-matrix printer, before turning on your printer, make sure that a page perforation appears just above the printer head. That way, Quattro Pro for Windows will know where the top of each page is.

The General Printing Technique

Printing a page from a notebook is easy. Quattro Pro for Windows assumes that you are printing on standard $8\frac{1}{2} \times 11$-inch paper and formats the notebook pages(s) accordingly. If the spreadsheet that you are printing is wider or longer than a single page, Quattro Pro automatically divides it into two or more pages. The Print Options settings to advance a page between blocks or between pages also will print separate pages.

Assuming that you have already installed and set up a printer in Windows, to print any spreadsheet page from a notebook, follow the basic steps below:

1. Select File ➤ Open or File ➤ Retrieve to call up the notebook that you want to print, if it is not already on-screen.

2. Select File ➤ Print. Quattro Pro for Windows assumes that the print block is every cell that contains entries on the current spreadsheet page.

3. Click on Print.

The sections below discuss the various steps and printing options in more detail.

DEFINING THE BLOCK TO PRINT

When you print a notebook for the first time, Quattro Pro for Windows assumes that you want to print all the cells with entries on the current page. After that first printing, if you want to print a block different from the one Quattro Pro selects, you need to specify the cells to be printed. You can use the usual click-and-drag method to highlight the area to print, or you can simply type the block's coordinates (e.g., A1..G27) into the dialog box. Only the cells that you specify will be printed.

If a spreadsheet contains long labels, you need to highlight the *entire* label if you want it printed. For example, if cell A1 contains a long label that spills over into column D, you will want to include columns A, B, C, and D in the block to print. Otherwise, the long label will be cut off to fit within the block you specify. If you want to print a floating object such as a graph, make sure you select it in its entirety, too.

As soon as you've finished highlighting the block, select File ➤ Print to print it. You can also add headings, change margins, and choose other features to create a fancier display. We discuss these options later in the chapter.

Printing Noncontiguous Blocks

To select blocks from different spreadsheet pages, select the first block, then hold down the Control key while you select the remaining blocks. You can then open the Spreadsheet Print dialog box and click on the Print button. Or open the Spreadsheet Print dialog box and double-click on the Print Blocks field. The dialog box is reduced, and you can click and drag the initial block, then hold down the Control key and select the remaining blocks. Click on the up arrow in the title bar to redisplay the dialog box, and click on the Print button to begin printing.

Printing with Headings

If your spreadsheet page is too wide to fit across a single standard page, Quattro Pro for Windows will automatically divide the spreadsheet into two or more pages that you can splice together into one wide spreadsheet (or handle separately). For example, Figure 9.3 shows the campaign spreadsheet divided into two pages.

As you can see in the sample printout, the row headings are not repeated on the second page. Unless you tape the pages together, it will be difficult to determine what the various numbers on the second page refer to. As with frozen titles, discussed in Chapter 8, you can repeat row and/or column headings on consecutive printed pages by defining a left and/or top heading.

DEFINING A LEFT HEADING

The Headings option on the Print Options dialog box allows you to repeat row headings on each printed page of a spreadsheet. To use this option:

1. Click and drag the area to print, *excluding* the columns that you want repeated on each page.

2. Select File ➤ Print.

3. In the Spreadsheet Print dialog box, click on the Options button.

4. Under Headings, double-click on the Left Heading field. The dialog box is reduced in size.

5. Click and drag the column you want to use for the left heading, as shown in Figure 9.4.

6. Click on the up arrow in the title bar.

7. Click on OK.

Figure 9.5 shows the printed copy of the campaign spreadsheet. Notice that the row titles are repeated on the second page and that the gridlines have been turned off.

1992 Campaign Budget (in thousands)

	Jan	Feb	Mar	April	May	June	July	August	Sept	October	Novembe	Decembe
Funds Raised:												
Individuals	7,050	7,550	8,050	8,550	9,050	9,550	10,050	10,550	11,050	11,550	9,000	8,000
PAC'S	15,000	14,700	14,400	14,100	13,800	13,500	13,200	12,900	12,600	12,300	12,000	11,700
Total Income	22,050	22,250	22,450	22,650	22,850	23,050	23,250	23,450	23,650	23,850	21,000	19,700
Cost of Fund Raising	6615	6675	6735	6795	6855	6915	6975	7035	7095	7155	6300	5910
TV	500	500	500	500	500	500	500	500	500	500	500	500
Radio	100	100	100	100	100	100	100	100	100	100	100	100
Print	200	200	200	200	200	200	200	200	200	200	200	200
Direct Mail	250	250	250	250	250	250	250	250	250	250	250	250
Phone Bank	500	500	500	500	500	500	500	500	500	500	500	500
Consultant	50	50	50	50	50	50	50	50	50	50	50	50
Rent for HQ	5	5	5	5	5	5	5	5	5	5	5	5
Phones	5	5	5	5	5	5	5	5	5	5	5	5
Salaries	50	50	50	50	50	50	50	50	50	50	50	50
Travel	20	20	20	20	20	20	20	20	20	20	20	20
Entertainment	1	1	1	1	1	1	1	1	1	1	1	1
Contributions	5	5	5	5	5	5	5	5	5	5	5	5
Other	5	5	5	5	5	5	5	5	5	5	5	5
Total Costs	8306	8366	8426	8486	8546	8606	8666	8726	8786	8846	7991	7601
Net	13744	13884	14024	14164	14304	14444	14584	14724	14864	15004	13009	12099

First printed page

Second printed page

FIGURE 9.3:

The campaign spreadsheet printed on two pages

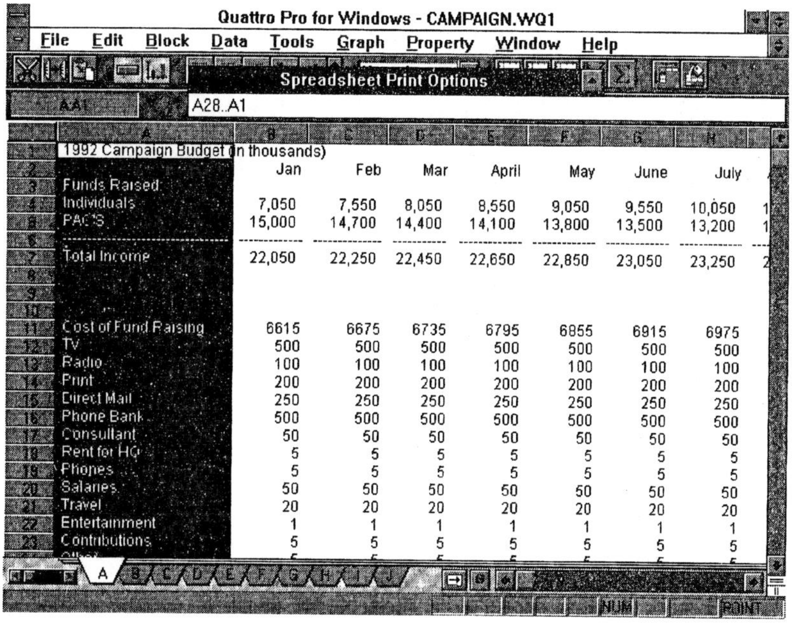

Quattro Pro for Windows - CAMPAIGN.WQ1

FIGURE 9.4:

The left heading
highlighted
for printed
spreadsheet

DEFINING A TOP HEADING

Just as the Left Heading option allows you to specify spreadsheet
columns that you want to repeat on each printed page, the Top Heading
option lets you specify spreadsheet rows to repeat on each page. The
general technique used with top headings is the same as that used with
left headings: click on the Options button in the Spreadsheet Print
dialog box and double-click on the Top Heading field, then click and
drag the block of cells you wish to repeat.

As with the Left Heading option, the block that you specify to
print should exclude the block that you specify as the top heading. For
example, if the spreadsheet that you wish to print has column headings
in the block A1..C4, and data beneath those headings extending to row
90, you would specify A1..C4 as the top heading and A5..C90 as the
block for printing.

First printed page

1992 Campaign Budget (in thousands)	Jan	Feb	Mar	April	May	June
Funds Raised:						
Individuals	7,050	7,550	8,050	8,550	9,050	9,550
PAC'S	15,000	14,700	14,400	14,100	13,800	13,500
Total Income	22,050	22,250	22,450	22,650	22,850	23,050
Cost of Fund Raising						
TV	6615	6675	6735	6795	6855	6915
Radio	500	500	500	500	500	500
Print	100	100	100	100	100	100
Direct Mail	200	200	200	200	200	200
Phone Bank	250	250	250	250	250	250
Consultant	500	500	500	500	500	500
Rent for HQ	50	50	50	50	50	50
Phones	5	5	5	5	5	5
Salaries	50	50	50	50	50	50
Travel	20	20	20	20	20	20
Entertainment	1	1	1	1	1	1
Contributions	5	5	5	5	5	5
Other	5	5	5	5	5	5
Total Costs	8306	8366	8426	8486	8546	8606
Net	13744	13884	14024	14164	14304	14444

Second printed page

1992 Campaign Budget (in thousands)	July	August	Sept	October	Novembe	Decembe
Funds Raised:						
Individuals	10,050	10,550	11,050	11,550	9,000	8,000
PAC'S	13,200	12,900	12,600	12,300	12,000	11,700
Total Income	23,250	23,450	23,650	23,850	21,000	19,700
Cost of Fund Raising						
TV	6975	7035	7095	7155	6300	5910
Radio	500	500	500	500	500	500
Print	100	100	100	100	100	100
Direct Mail	200	200	200	200	200	200
Phone Bank	250	250	250	250	250	250
Consultant	500	500	500	500	500	500
Rent for HQ	50	50	50	50	50	50
Phones	5	5	5	5	5	5
Salaries	50	50	50	50	50	50
Travel	20	20	20	20	20	20
Entertainment	1	1	1	1	1	1
Contributions	5	5	5	5	5	5
Other	5	5	5	5	5	5
Total Costs	8666	8726	8786	8846	7991	7601
Net	14584	14724	14864	15004	13009	12099

FIGURE 9.5:

The campaign spreadsheet printed with left headings

Setting the Page Layout

As mentioned earlier, Quattro Pro automatically assumes that the paper in the printer is the standard 8½ × 11-inch size and formats the printed spreadsheet page accordingly. The Page Setup option under the File menu lets you change the way Quattro Pro formats the printed page. When selected, this option presents the Spreadsheet Page Setup dialog box, as shown in Figure 9.6.

Each of these options is discussed in the following sections.

ADDING HEADERS AND FOOTERS TO YOUR SPREADSHEET

The Header and Footer options in the Spreadsheet Page Setup dialog box let you specify text to be printed above and beneath the spreadsheet on each printed page. Unlike the Top Heading and Left Heading options,

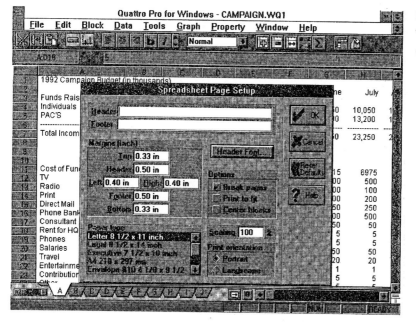

FIGURE 9.6:

The Page Setup dialog box

which repeat spreadsheet rows and columns on each page, the Header and Footer options repeat any text that you enter above and beneath the overall spreadsheet. This text can be up to 254 characters long.

You can use special characters in headers and footers:

@   Displays the current (system) date

Displays the page number

| Centers the header or footer

|| Right-justifies the header or footer

Below are some examples of various headers or footers and the way they would be displayed on the printed page (assuming that the current system date is August 1, 1993, and that this is the fourth page of the printed notebook). If you do not use the vertical bar (|) anywhere—i.e., just type **Monthly Sales**— then the text will be aligned with the left margin:

Monthly Sales

If you precede *Monthly Sales* with a single | symbol—i.e., type |**Monthly Sales**—it will be centered on the page:

Monthly Sales

If you precede the text with two | characters—i.e., type ||**Monthly Sales**—it will be aligned with the right margin of the page:

Monthly Sales

Of course, you can align the other codes as well. Typing |# will center the page number on the page:

4

Typing @||# yields:

1–Aug–93   **4**

And reversing the code gives:

4   **1–Aug93**

Finally, sandwiching *Monthly Sales* between the two—as in @|Monthly
Sales|page #—yields:

1–Aug–93   **Monthly Sales**   **page 4**

To create a header or footer for a printed spreadsheeet, select File
➤ Page Setup, type the header or footer text into the appropriate box,
add any formatting necessary, and click on OK. Note that the header
or footer is not displayed on-screen; it appears only on the *printed*
spreadsheet. You can see it on the spreadsheet in Print Preview, which
we discuss later in the chapter.

Setting the Page Length and Margins

By default, Quattro Pro for Windows leaves a 0.4" margin at the left and
right side of each printed page (for the standard 8½ × 11" page size).
The Margins section in the Page Setup dialog box lets you change these
margins.

SETTING THE LEFT AND RIGHT MARGINS

The Left and Right options in the Margins section in the Page Setup dialog
box let you specify margins for the printed page. Click on the Left field, and
enter a new left-margin setting in inches, if inches are the default measurement. (The default is from Windows. If you have set the Windows default
measurement to centimeters, that will appear in this dialog box. You can
override the default measurement by adding "in" for inches or "cm" for
centimeters as a suffix to the number you enter.)

If you are using a size of paper other than 8 1/2 × 11-inch, you can
select it from the Paper type menu in the dialog box. Simply click on
the size of paper you want.

ADJUSTING TOP AND BOTTOM MARGINS

The Top and Bottom options from the Margins section determine the amount of space to leave at the top and bottom of each printed page.

If you create a header or footer for the printed spreadsheet, it is separated from the notebook data by the amount of space specified in the Header and Footer margin controls, minus the height of the header or footer text. The default alignment is left unless you specify otherwise.

CHANGING THE PERCENT SCALING

The default setting of 100% prints the spreadsheet page the same size as you have selected on the screen. You can set the scale to decrease or increase from 1 to 1000. The margins are not affected by the scale setting.

USING THE PRINT TO FIT OPTION

Selecting the Print to fit option shrinks the entire print output to fit it on as few pages as possible. The margins do not change, except for those in the header and footer, which are reduced. The Print to fit option only reduces the output—it does not increase it to fill unused spaces.

CENTERING BLOCKS

If you are printing multiple blocks, selecting this option centers the printed output on each page, instead of left-aligning it (which is the default).

CHOOSING THE HEADER FONT

Clicking on the Header font button opens the Font dialog box, from which you can select the font and the point size you want. You can also select a special format such as Bold or Underline. Whatever you choose becomes the setting for both the Header and Footer.

CHOOSING THE PRINT ORIENTATION

Quattro Pro for Windows will print your spreadsheets in either of two ways: Portrait mode (text running across width of page) or Landscape mode (text running along length of page). Landscape mode is particularly useful for printing spreadsheets, especially when combined with the Print to fit option, because more columns can be printed on a single page. Click on Portrait or Landscape in the dialog box to choose the Print Orientation.

LEAVING THE PAGE LAYOUT DIALOG BOX

When you finish setting the new page margins and length, click on OK and you will be returned to the spreadsheet page. If you save the notebook after changing margins or page length, these new settings will be saved as well. Unless you change the saved settings, the spreadsheet will always print with these page margins and this length. But they apply only to *this* notebook, not all notebooks.

Adding Page Breaks

Quattro Pro for Windows automatically divides a spreadsheet into separate pages based on the length of the page and the top and bottom margins. You can also insert hard page breaks into a spreadsheet to force Quattro Pro to start printing on a new page at a particular row in the spreadsheet. Select Block ➤ Insert Break. Quattro Pro inserts a page break symbol above the active cell. You can also insert a hard page break simply by typing |:: (a vertical line followed by two colons) into the cell.

Whichever technique you use to enter the hard page break, it will be displayed in the cell as two colons; the vertical line will only be displayed in the input line. Furthermore, any data that are in the same row as the hard-page-break symbol will not be printed. Therefore, be sure to place |:: in a row that is completely blank (or one that you do not want to appear on the printed spreadsheet).

Figure 9.7 shows a sample spreadsheet with a hard page break inserted in row 9 (cell A9). When printed, the Income section (rows 1 through 9) will be displayed on one page, and the rest of the spreadsheet, from row 11 onward, will be displayed on the next page. A single spreadsheet can contain any number of hard page breaks, as long as each is stored in its own row.

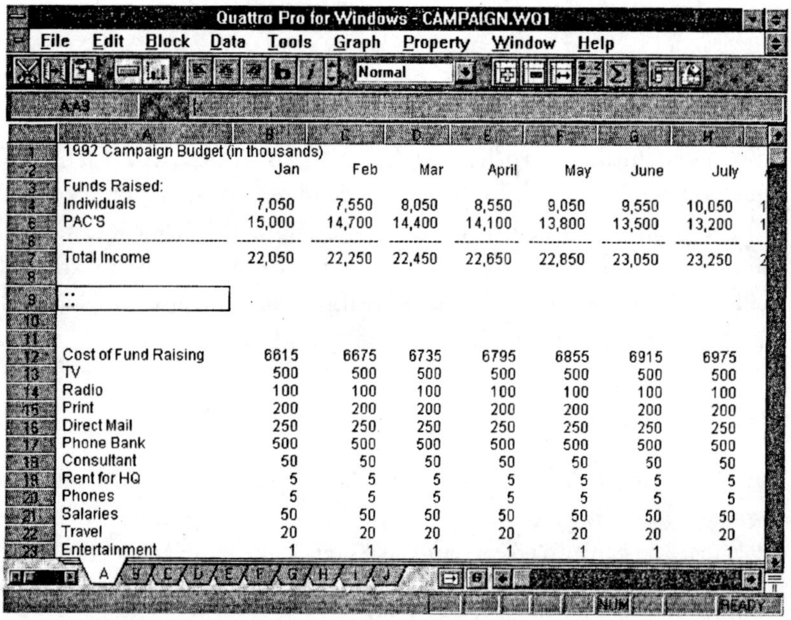

	A	B	C	D	E	F	G	H
1	1992 Campaign Budget (in thousands)							
2		Jan	Feb	Mar	April	May	June	July
3	Funds Raised:							
4	Individuals	7,050	7,550	8,050	8,550	9,050	9,550	10,050
5	PAC'S	15,000	14,700	14,400	14,100	13,800	13,500	13,200
6	------------	------------	------------	------------	------------	------------	------------	------------
7	Total Income	22,050	22,250	22,450	22,650	22,850	23,050	23,250
8								
9	::							
10								
11								
12	Cost of Fund Raising	6615	6675	6735	6795	6855	6915	6975
13	TV	500	500	500	500	500	500	500
14	Radio	100	100	100	100	100	100	100
15	Print	200	200	200	200	200	200	200
16	Direct Mail	250	250	250	250	250	250	250
17	Phone Bank	500	500	500	500	500	500	500
18	Consultant	50	50	50	50	50	50	50
19	Rent for HQ	5	5	5	5	5	5	5
20	Phones	5	5	5	5	5	5	5
21	Salaries	50	50	50	50	50	50	50
22	Travel	20	20	20	20	20	20	20
23	Entertainment	1	1	1	1	1	1	1

FIGURE 9.7:

A sample spreadsheet with a hard page break in row 9

PRINTING WITHOUT PAGE BREAKS

You can also have Quattro Pro for Windows print your spreadsheet as a single, continuous stream of information. This format is often preferred when printing spreadsheets to a disk file (discussed later in this chapter) rather than to a printer, or when you want to print in Landscape mode. To prevent Quattro Pro from inserting page breaks, click on the Break Pages option from the Page Setup dialog box to turn off the check mark.

Note that this technique only prevents natural page breaks from occurring. Hard page breaks inserted as the |:: code will still occur. To prevent these hard page breaks from taking effect, you'll need to delete them from the spreadsheet.

If you save the notebook after turning off the Break Pages option, this setting will be saved as well, and future printouts of this spreadsheet will be printed without page breaks.

Previewing a Spreadsheet

If you want to know how a spreadsheet page will appear on paper without actually printing a hard copy of it, click on Preview in the Spreadsheet Print dialog box. This will tell Quattro Pro for Windows to print to the screen. (You can also select File ➤ Print Preview straight from your document.)

Print Preview will display the spreadsheet, along with its own SpeedBar at the top of the screen, as shown in Figure 9.8.

The right and left arrows, when clicked, cause Quattro Pro to display either the previous or next page of the print job.

The Color button toggles the screen from color to black and white, allowing you to see how the spreadsheet output will appear in either form.

The Margin button overlays dotted lines to illustrate the position of the margins on the printed page, relative to the contents.

The Setup button opens the Spreadsheet Page Setup dialog box. The details of this dialog box are discussed earlier in this chapter.

The Options button opens the Spreadsheet Print Options dialog box. The details of this dialog box are discussed earlier in this chapter.

The Print button sends the file to the Windows Print Manager and begins printing.

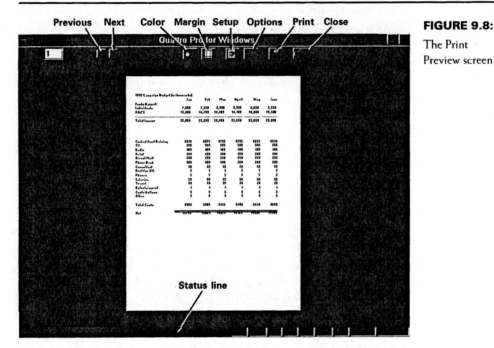

FIGURE 9.8:

The Print Preview screen

The Close button cancels the preview and returns you to the spreadsheet page.

Print Preview offers a mouse zoom feature: click the left mouse button one to four times on an area of the screen to enlarge the text (up to 1600%), and click the right mouse button to reduce it again.

How to Start and Stop Printing

When you are certain that you've selected all the options to define and format the block to print, simply click on the Print button in the Spreadsheet Print dialog box. If you want to print multiple copies of the spreadsheet, click on the Copies field before clicking on Print, and enter the number of copies you want.

Because Quattro Pro is operating in Windows, printing is taken care of by the Windows Print Manager. The Print Manager is a separate application that you can access via the Main window. The Print Manager queues print jobs as they are sent by Windows applications. So you could be working in a word-processing program, and direct the word processor to print a file, and then switch back to Quattro Pro for Windows and begin printing a spreadsheet. The Print Manager accepts the print jobs in order and stores them in a buffer until the printer finishes the current job. If your Quattro Pro spreadsheet contains many different typestyles and/or other special formatting, it may take some time to print. In the meantime, because of the Print Manager, you can go back to work without waiting for the printer to finish printing. If an error occurs—for example, if the printer runs out of paper—the Print Manager will alert you to the problem via a dialog box.

If you start printing and then decide that you want to abort the process, follow these steps:

1. Click on the Minimize button to suspend spreadsheet operations.

2. Click on the Main window. If the Main window is not visible, select Window ➤ Main.

3. Double-click on the Print Manager icon. The Print Manager window appears with a list of print jobs. An example of the Print Manager window is shown in Figure 9.9. In this example, two printers have been installed in Windows, both of which are idle, which means that no print jobs are scheduled.

4. Click on the name of the print job you have sent to the Print Manager.

5. Click on the Delete button. The Print Manager responds with a dialog box asking if you want to quit printing the document.

6. Click on OK. To simply pause the printer, click on the Pause button. The Print Manager will wait until you click on the Resume button before continuing.

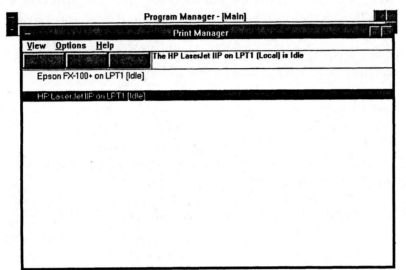

FIGURE 9.9:

Print Manager window

Using the Windows Clipboard

One of the great advantages of Windows is that you can cut and paste information from one application to another. For example, by using the Windows Clipboard, you can select a block of cells from Quattro Pro for Windows, paste it to the Clipboard, and then copy it into a word-processed document. The word processor must be a Windows-based program, too.

Suppose that you are working in Quattro Pro for Windows and have a word-processing program such as Microsoft Word for Windows operating in another application window. The general steps to copy information from Quattro Pro to Word are as follows:

1. Click and drag the block of cells that you want to copy or cut.

2. Click on the Copy or Cut button as appropriate.

3. Click on the application control menu box in the upper left corner of the Quattro Pro for Windows application window.

4. Click on Switch To. The Windows Task List dialog box appears with a list of all the currently open applications.

5. Double-click on Word for Windows. The application window containing Word opens.

6. Move the mouse pointer to the place in the document where you want the information pasted.

7. Select Edit ➤ Paste.

The information you have selected is inserted into the word-processed document. Once inserted, it is treated as text. It is not linked to the spreadsheet: if you change the information in the spreadsheet, it will not be changed automatically in the word-processed document.

A note about the Windows Clipboard: when you have copied or cut information to the Clipboard, you can open the Clipboard Viewer (accessible from the Main window of Windows) to see the block of cells being transferred. Just the block coordinates appear at first—the actual cell information does not appear in the viewer until you select Display ➤ Text.

Printing a Spreadsheet to a Disk File

If you would like to incorporate a printed spreadsheet into a document you've prepared with your word processor, or would prefer to use a word-processing program to print your spreadsheet, you can tell Quattro Pro for Windows to store the printed spreadsheet in a binary file on a disk rather than sending it directly to a printer. This file can be easily imported into most other types of programs, including word processors, and can also be accessed by the DOS commands TYPE, SORT, and FIND. (The file in which Quattro Pro for Windows stores the spreadsheet, with the .WB1 file name extension, can only be accessed by Quattro Pro.)

Sending a printed spreadsheet to a binary file is easy. To begin with, specify the block to print and any other printing options in the usual manner.

If you plan to incorporate the printed spreadsheet into a word-processed document, or want to use your word processor to format the printed spreadsheet, you might want to ensure that no page break characters are inserted into the disk file. You should also set the left margin to zero if your word processor already puts the appropriate left margin into its printouts.

After you've defined the spreadsheet block to print and the format for the printed spreadsheet, select File ➤ Printer Setup from the menu. The Printer Setup dialog box appears, as shown in Figure 9.10.

Click on the box to the left of the Redirect To File field. Quattro Pro for Windows inserts a file name, "OUTPUT.PRN". Click on the field itself and type in a new file name, leaving the extension intact. Choose OK, and Quattro Pro saves the file to your hard disk. Quattro Pro sends the spreadsheet to disk formatted to take advantage of the graphics printer you have installed (for example, if you have installed a PostScript-capable printer, a PostScript file will be created).

If you want to save the file to a different drive and/or directory, click on the Browse button after entering the name. The Browser dialog box appears, which is identical to the File Save or File Retrieve dialog box, except that here Quattro Pro lists files with the .PRN extension. From here, you can select the drive and directory to which you want the file saved. You can even select a different spreadsheet format, such as a Lotus 1-2-3, Excel, or dBase file, by selecting the format from the File Types field.

IMPORTING AN ASCII FILE INTO A NON-WINDOWS WORD-PROCESSED DOCUMENT

Suppose you have a spreadsheet that you would like to insert in a word-processed report, but the word processor is not a Windows application. The ideal situation would be to have the numbers appear beside the relevant text in the report—i.e., to make them *part* of the document. You can do this by printing the numbers in Quattro Pro for Windows to a binary file (as mentioned above) and then inserting that file into your text at any point.

To import (insert) a binary file into a word-processed document, exit Quattro Pro and Windows to return to the DOS prompt, then run your word-processing program in the usual manner. Position the cursor where you want the imported spreadsheet to appear. Use the appropriate

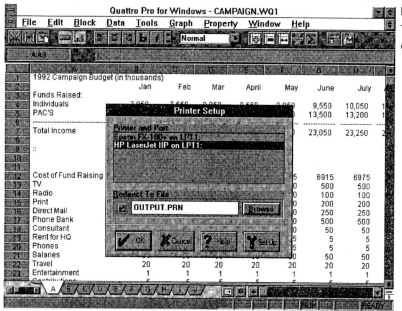

FIGURE 9.10:

The Printer Setup dialog box

command for your word processor to merge or read-in an external file. When prompted, enter the full name of the file to import, including the .PRN extension or any other extension you gave the spreadsheet's file name. (Make sure it's the binary file, not a proper Quattro Pro file!)

If the binary file is not in the same directory as your word processor, be sure to provide the appropriate directory path in the file name. For example, to import a binary file named PROJECT and stored in the \QPW directory of drive C, you would specify C:\QPW\PROJECT.PRN as the name of the file to import. (Remember to save your word-processed document after importing the spreadsheet file.)

Updating and Saving Print Preferences

After you have made the adjustments you want to the print layout of your spreadsheet page(s), you can save the new settings so that you can specify them each time you print. For example, if you have a notebook that has several different reports, you can use File ➤ Named Settings to define the current print settings. This frees you from redefining the print settings manually each time you want a different report.

1. Define your print preferences and test your report to check its accuracy.

2. Select File ➤ Named Settings. The Named Print Settings dialog box appears.

3. Click on Create. The Create Printer Settings dialog box appears. Enter a name for the print settings, such as Quarterly Report, in the field.

4. Click on OK in each dialog box. Repeat the steps above for each set of print options that you want to save. When you next use the notebook, select the Named Setting and then open the Print dialog box to begin the printing process.

Now that we have discussed printing, we will move on to examine the many types of graph that you can create in Quattro Pro for Windows.

10 CHAPTER

FEATURING

Creating and
customizing
different types
of graphs

Inserting
a graph in a
spreadsheet

Combining
graph types

Creating Quality Graphs

uattro Pro for Windows offers many different types of graphs as well as combinations of graphs to help you present data visually. It also offers sophisticated techniques for customizing graphs to help you present information in exactly the format you wish. You can create both "floating graphs," which appear anywhere you wish on the spreadsheet page, and regular graphs, which you create in the graph window. A floating graph (see Figure 10.1) overlies the spreadsheet page but does not erase the information in underlying cells.

Even if you create a graph in the graph window, you can insert it as a floating graph on a spreadsheet page. Figure 10.2 shows the graph window.

Before getting into the specific how-tos of graphs, let's take a moment to discuss the different types of graphs available and the situations for which each is most suitable.

Types of Graphs

The Graph Type option is accessible either from the spreadsheet page (if you have already created a floating graph) or from the graph window. Graph ➤ Type displays a dialog box of the various types of graphs available: line, bar, X–Y, stacked bar, pie, area, rotated bar, column, high-low, text, and three-dimensional (3-D). Keep in mind that you can change a graph's type at any time. For example, if you design a complete bar

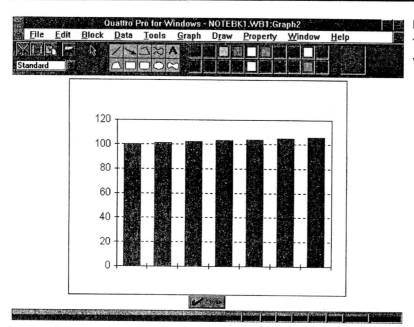

graph and then decide it's not right, you can easily change it to some other type of graph—provided, of course, that the new format is suitable for graphing the same data. You don't have to redefine the plotted data, the titles, or any other customization feature. This means that you can experiment to discover the graph type that best illustrates the information you want to convey.

You can also combine several graph types on a single graph—for instance, to highlight particular areas of interest. In the sections below, we'll discuss the various types of graphs and the most suitable use for each one.

THE GRAPHS PAGE

Along with the 256 spreadsheet pages, Quattro Pro for Windows includes a separate page just for graphs. When you create a graph, either floating or full-screen, a corresponding icon is created on the graphs page. You can jump back and forth between the graphs page and the spreadsheet page from which the graph derives by clicking on the SpeedTab button at the bottom middle of the spreadsheet page window. Figure 10.3 shows the graphs page with two graph icons.

FIGURE 10.3:

The graphs page

THE LINE GRAPH

The most common graph used in business is the line graph. It lends itself well to the linear environment of business because it reflects trends over time. Sales, price movements, and shipping volumes are only a few of the kinds of data that are suitable for line graphs. Figure 10.4 shows a sample line graph that plots sales raised over a 6-month period.

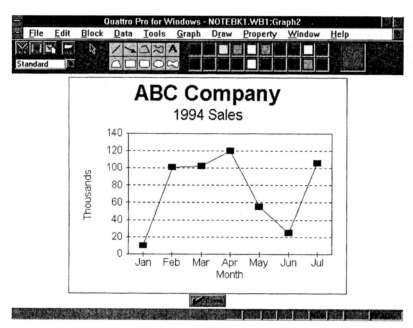

FIGURE 10.4:

A sample line
graph

THE BAR GRAPH

Bar graphs are useful for comparing values at a particular point in time
rather than for reflecting trends. For example, a marketing department
might design a bar graph that compares the market shares of competi-
tive products from one year to the next as a guide for planning marketing strategy, as in Figure 10.5. You can also display information in a
rotated bar graph, as in Figure 10.6.

THE X–Y GRAPH

An X–Y graph shows the relationship between two values, which should be
related so that as one goes up, the other goes up or down proportionally.
For example, an X–Y graph could represent the relationship between

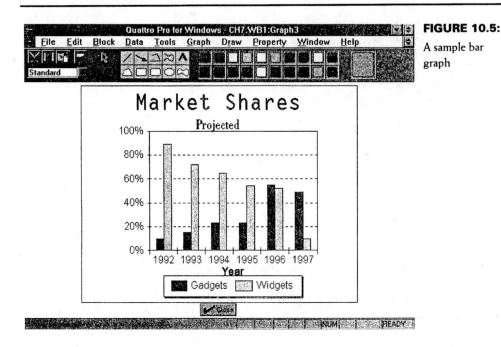

FIGURE 10.5:

A sample bar graph

educational level and annual income or between advertising investment and sales. Figure 10.7 shows a sample X–Y graph that shows sales increasing in proportion to the money spent on advertising.

THE STACKED BAR GRAPH

A stacked bar graph shows the relative value of a series of numbers as they contribute to the whole. For example, a college might want to distinguish the breakdown of where its funds are raised. Figure 10.8 shows a sample stacked-bar graph that reflects the relative contributions of various sources of funds: business, foundation, individual, and grant contributions.

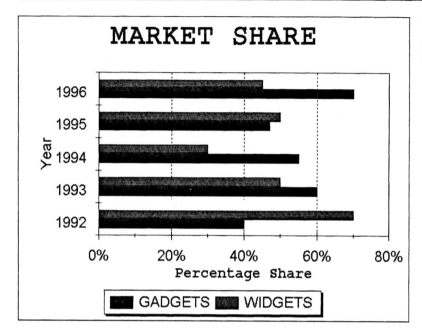

FIGURE 10.6:

A sample rotated bar graph

THE PIE CHART

A pie chart is different from the rest of the graphs because it displays only one series of values at a time. For instance, graphing the total sales of five products in a pie chart will show the relative contribution of each in a way that is much different than a bar graph. This graph is excellent for showing market shares and numeric components. Figure 10.9 shows a sample pie chart that exhibits the relative costs for campaign expenses for a political race.

THE AREA GRAPH

An extension of the line graph, the area graph combines the best features of a stacked-bar graph and a line graph by making a continuum of the values from period to period. Each series is graphed separately and placed, like blocks, alongside the others. The interior of the graph

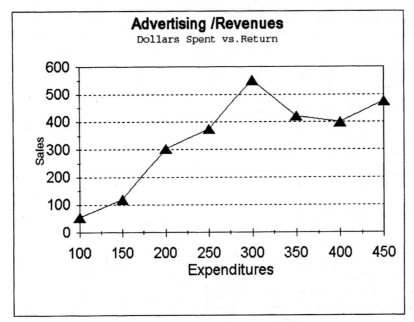

FIGURE 10.7:

A sample X–Y graph

shows the relative contributions of various products by averaging the values in each series.

Figure 10.10 shows a sample area graph that plots market shares over time, along with the names of the chip manufacturers. As the graph shows, market shares as a group have increased over time. However, the relative position of each manufacturer has changed.

THE COLUMN GRAPH

The column graph displays information from a single series in much the same way that a pie chart does. The information is stacked vertically on a rectangular column, as in Figure 10.11.

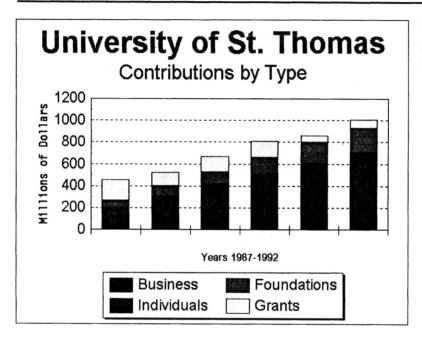

FIGURE 10.8:

A sample stacked bar graph

THE HIGH-LOW GRAPH

The high-low (open-close) graph is most often used for graphing the movement of stock prices. It can be also used for plotting experimental data, such as the concentrations of fluids at different times. Figure 10.12 shows a typical example of using the high-low graph for stock prices.

THE TEXT GRAPH

The text graph is not a defined graphical type. It is a drawing pad for you to create any type of graph you choose. Because of all the many shapes, fonts, and text styles available to you in the Annotate option, you can create a multitude of graphical effects. Figure 10.13 shows an example of what can be produced.

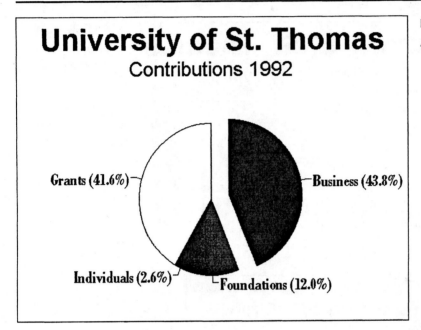

FIGURE 10.9:

A sample pie chart

THE 3-D GRAPHS

There are nine types of two-dimensional (2-D) graphs, twelve types of three-dimensional (3-D) graphs, and eight different two-dimensional combination graphs.

Whenever you are viewing a graph, you can click the right mouse button on open space in the graph to open the Graph Setup and Background dialog box. From the dialog box, you can select the graph type you want to use for the data already selected. Or select Graph ➤ Types to reach the Graph Types dialog box (see Figure 10.14).

Creating and Viewing a Graph

Before you can plot data on a graph, you need some data to work with (except for the text graph). The first few sample graphs you develop in this chapter will use the spreadsheet shown in Figure 10.15. This

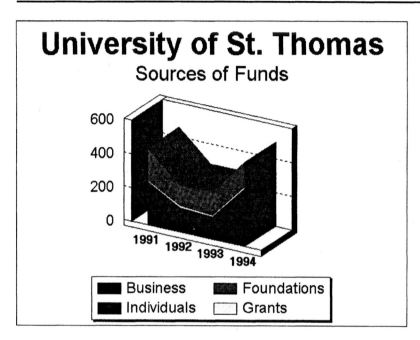

FIGURE 10.10:

A sample area graph

spreadsheet shows the sales, in arbitrary units, of four car manufacturers from 1993 to 1998. The totals at the bottom of the spreadsheet are calculated with the @SUM function, so that any changes in the sales figures above will be immediately reflected in the totals.

To define the data you want to plot, click and drag the cells, then click on the Graph Tool button. In this first graph, we'll plot only one block of data. Create the spreadsheet shown in Figure 10.15, then follow the steps below.

1. Click and drag the block B9..G9.

2. Click on the Graph tool (the fifth button from the left, with a small bar graph icon on it). The mouse pointer changes to a small graph icon.

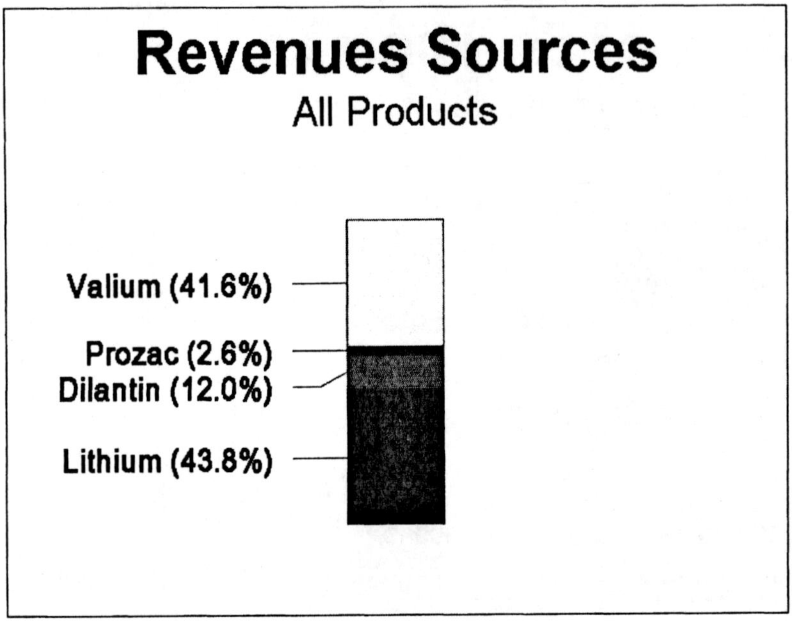

Revenues Sources
All Products

Valium (41.6%)
Prozac (2.6%)
Dilantin (12.0%)
Lithium (43.8%)

FIGURE 10.11:

A sample column graph

3. Position the mouse pointer in cell B11, and click the left mouse button. Quattro Pro draws a border, followed by the graphed data in bar form (see Figure 10.16).

Before going on, save the notebook as **CARSALES** using File ➤ Save. If you would like to experiment with other graph types at this point, select Graph➤Type, then pick another type of graph from the Graph Types dialog box, or click the right mouse button on the graph as described above. Of course, not all types of graph are suitable for these data. Select High-Low, X–Y, or Text, and you'll see why.

Opening the Graph Window

After you have attached a graph to (not inserted into, because it floats above the page) a spreadsheet page, you can make some changes using

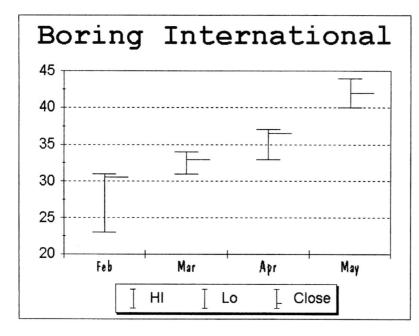

FIGURE 10.12:

A sample high-low graph

the Graph menu, or open the graph window to access all of the graph options.

Double-click on the graph you have just created. The graph window appears, as shown in Figure 10.17.

Notice that the menu names have not changed. You now have access to the graph SpeedBar. (If you are a former user of Quattro Pro for DOS, the graph window is similar to the Annotator.)

Adding Titles to a Graph

A graph alone, without some descriptive information, is not very informative. Quattro Pro lets you add several types of titles to a graph, including a main title (first line), a subtitle (second line), x-axis titles that describe the points along the bottom axis, and y-axis titles to describe the vertical axis.

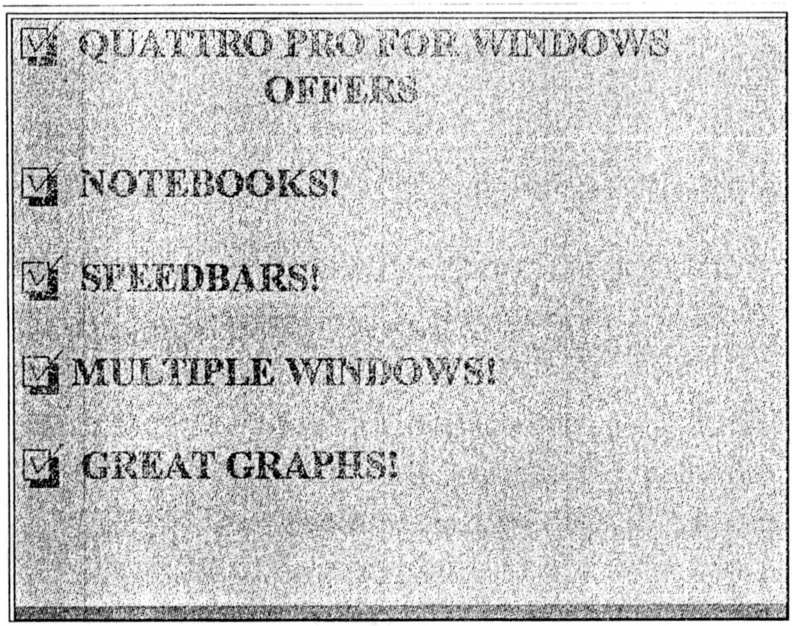

FIGURE 10.13:

A sample text graph

HOW TO ADD A MAIN TITLE AND A SUBTITLE

Select Graph ➤ Titles to choose options for adding a main title and sub-title to a graph. Add a main title to your sample bar graph.

1. Select Graph ➤ Titles. The Graph Titles dialog box appears, as shown in Figure 10.18. The insertion point is placed in the Main Title field.

2. Enter **CAR SALES** in the Main Title field.

3. Click on the Subtitle field and enter **By Company**.

4. Click on the X-Axis Title field and enter **YEARS**.

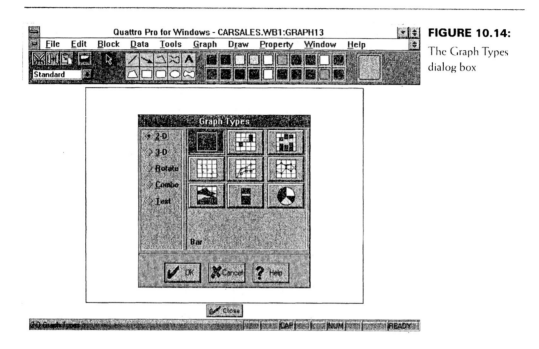

FIGURE 10.14:

The Graph Types dialog box

5. Click on the Y-1 Axis Title field and enter **UNITS**.

6. Click on OK.

The graph with the added titles appears in Figure 10.19.

HOW TO ADD X-AXIS VALUES

The x-axis values appear along the x axis (bottom line) of the graph. These values come from column or row cells already on the spreadsheet, rather than from labels you enter as text. In your sample spreadsheet, you can use the column labels in row 2 as the *x-axis titles*.

Let's return to the spreadsheet page to determine the block to use for the X-Axis.

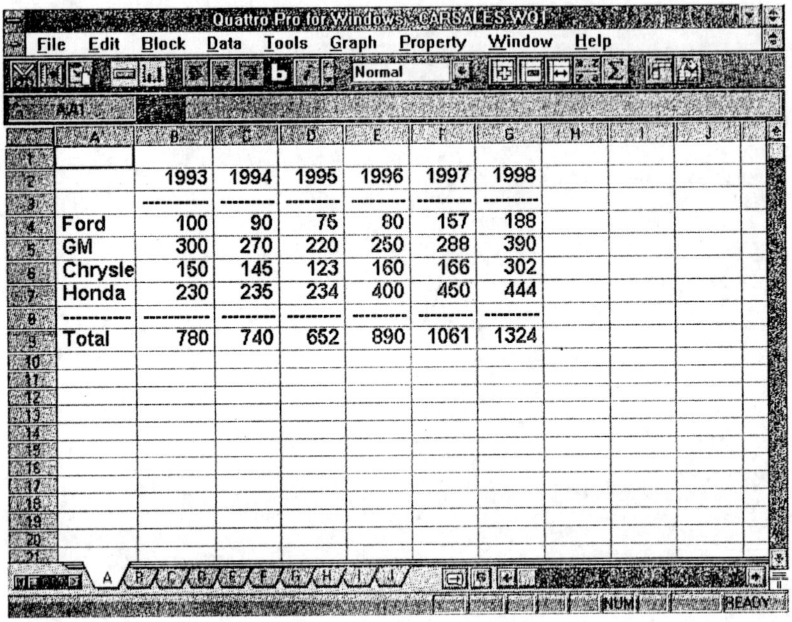
Quattro Pro for Windows - CARSALES.WQ1
File Edit Block Data Tools Graph Property Window Help
Normal
A:A1
A B C D E F G H I J
1993 1994 1995 1996 1997 1998
Ford 100 90 75 80 157 188
GM 300 270 220 250 288 390
Chrysle 150 145 123 160 166 302
Honda 230 235 234 400 450 444
Total 780 740 652 890 1061 1324
NUM
READY

FIGURE 10.15:
The sample spreadsheet for developing graphs

1. Click on the Close button at the bottom of the graph window. Quattro Pro takes you directly to the spreadsheet page from which the graph was derived. Notice that the titles we added in the previous exercise are now a part of this graph, too. No matter whether you edit the graph in the spreadsheet page or in the graph window, the edits are reflected correctly. The X-Axis block is the series of year numbers in block B2..G2.

2. Select Graph ➤ Series. The Graph Series dialog box appears, as shown in Figure 10.20. This dialog box operates the same way as any other dialog box in which you can enter a block of cells.

3. Double-click on the X-Axis field. The dialog box is reduced to the title bar, and displayed above the input line.

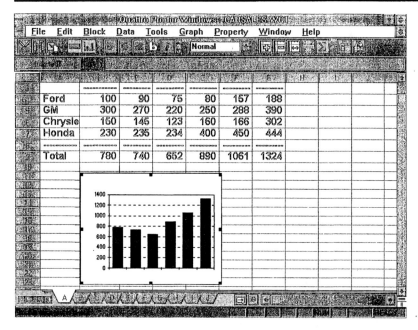

FIGURE 10.16:

A bar graph created with car-sales data

4. Click and drag the block B2..G2.

5. Click on the up arrow in the Graph Series title bar. The dialog box is enlarged, with the block B2..G2 inserted in the X-Axis field.

6. Click on OK. The X-Axis numbers are added to the graph.

CHANGING THE GRAPH SIZE OR POSITION

Because Quattro Pro for Windows automatically calculates graph boundaries, at times the text inside the graph may be difficult to read. So let's make the graph larger.

1. Click on the graph to make it the active object in the spreadsheet page. When active, the graph has eight object

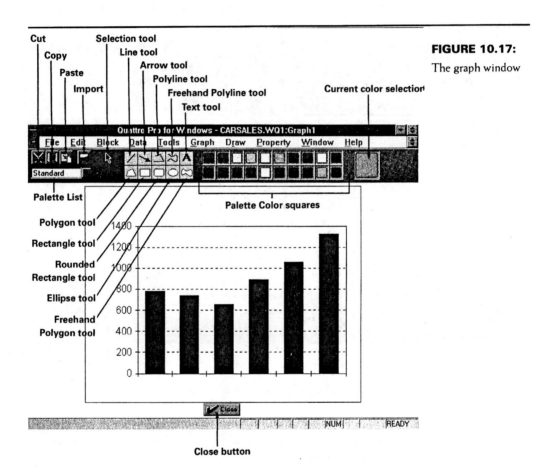

FIGURE 10.17:

The graph window

handles along the border. These handles are used to move the graph or change its size.

2. Move the mouse pointer onto the handle in the lower-right corner of the graph border. The pointer changes to crosshairs.

3. Click and hold the left mouse button, then drag the mouse down and to the right, until the crosshairs are in the bottom right corner of cell G28. Release the button.

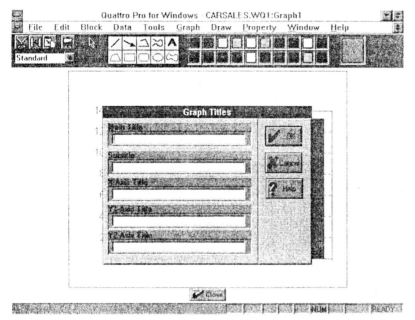

FIGURE 10.18:

The Graph Titles
dialog box

Quattro Pro redraws the graph. By adding size to the graph, you have
made it much easier to read, as shown in Figure 10.21.

Moving a Graph

Because the graph floats on the spreadsheet page, it can be moved in-
discriminately without harming the data entered into the cells.

1. Click on the graph to make it the active object.

2. Move the mouse pointer to the middle of the graph.

3. Click and hold the left mouse button so that the mouse
pointer changes to a hand. Drag the graph until the top border is between rows 4 and 5, then release the mouse button.
The graph is overlaid on the cell data, but does not disturb it.

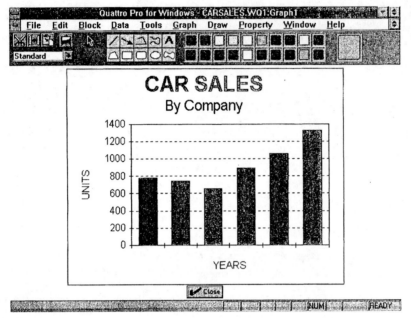

FIGURE 10.19:

The Car Sales
graph with titles

4. Click the left mouse button in the middle of the graph so that
the hand appears.

5. Drag the graph down, so that the top border of the graph is
between rows 10 and 11.

As you can see, the data is undisturbed.

INTERACTION BETWEEN DATA AND GRAPHS

As you might expect, if you make a change in the data from which the
graph is derived, the graph changes to reflect the new data. Try entering
700 in cell D7 of the CARSALES spreadsheet. As you can see, the bar
representing the total sales for 1995 increases in size to reflect the increased total.

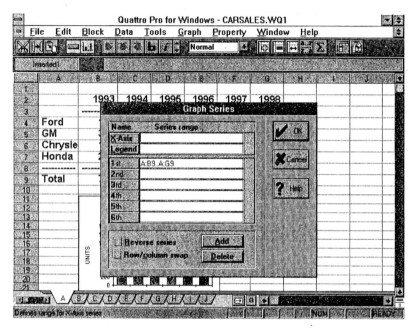

FIGURE 10.20:

The Graph Series dialog box

Naming a Graph

In many situations, you'll want to create several graphs from a single notebook. In order to do so, you must assign a name to each graph associated with the notebook. Quattro Pro assigns a default name to each floating graph as it is created (Graph1, Graph2, Graph3). Graphs created in the graph window can be named immediately, or you can accept the default name Quattro Pro assigns.

To assign the name TOTALS to your sample CAR SALES totals bar graph, follow these steps:

1. Click on the SpeedTab button at the bottom middle of the spreadsheet window. Quattro Pro displays the graph page of the notebook (see Figure 10.22). As you can see, the graph you created in the notebook is named Graph1.

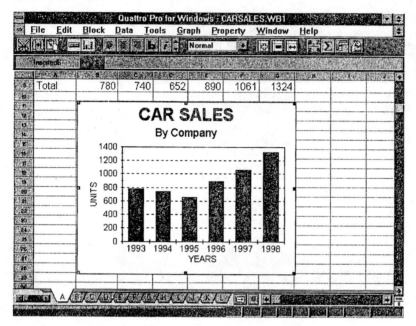

FIGURE 10.21:

The sample bar
graph with titles
and resized

2. Click the right mouse button on the Graph1 icon. The Name
dialog box appears.

3. In the Enter text field, type **TOTALS**.

4. Click on OK.

5. To move back to the spreadsheet page, click on the SpeedTab
button again.

SAVING A GRAPH

No special steps are necessary to save a graph. Quattro Pro treats each
graph as part of the spreadsheet page to which it is attached. So, when
you save the notebook, the graphs are saved, too.

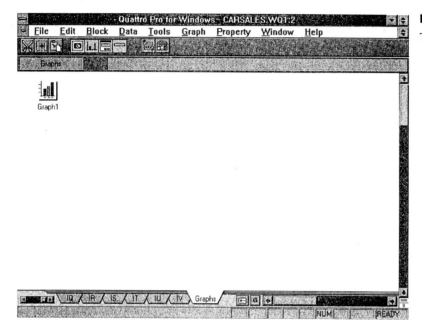

FIGURE 10.22:

The graphs page

RETRIEVING A GRAPH

Whenever you want to retrieve a previously saved graph, choose Graph ➤ Edit. A dialog box of graph names will appear. Click on the graph you want to open, then click on OK. It will then appear on-screen in the graph window. When you return to the spreadsheet, that graph's layout settings will become the new default settings for any new graphs you create.

VIEWING A GRAPH FULL-SCREEN

If you want to see what the graph will look like printed on paper (except for the colors) or as a slide, select the graph and click on Graph ➤ View. Click the mouse button to return to either the graph window or the spreadsheet page.

Erasing a Graph

You can delete any graph by selecting Graph ➤ Delete, choosing the graph you want to delete from the list in the dialog box, and clicking on OK. After you have erased a graph, you will not be able to recall it unless you use Edit ➤ Undo. (Note that this won't work if you've already saved the notebook after erasing the graph.)

Plotting Multiple Data Groups

The first graph you created displays only a single block of data, the total car sales for the years 1993-1998. But you can also combine several blocks of data into a single graph (except a pie chart or a column graph), as we'll demonstrate in this section.

Plot four blocks of data, each representing the sales for a single car manufacturer. Here are the steps:

1. Click and drag cells A4..G7.

2. Select Graph ➤ New. The Graph New dialog box appears, containing the series blocks for the X-Axis and the six years' annual sales for each company (see Figure 10.23).

3. Click on OK.

Your graph should now appear as shown in Figure 10.24. Note that Quattro Pro for Windows still remembers the graph type (bar), titles, and x-axis settings from the previous graph.

Next, let's look at the options available in the Graph Setup dialog box (see Figure 10.25).

Graph Type The graph type option allows you to pick from all the graph types that are available in Quattro Pro. In Figure 10.25, the 2-D graphs are visible; in Figure 10.26, the 3-D graphs; in Figure 10.27, the Rotated graphs; and in Figure 10.28, the Combination graphs.

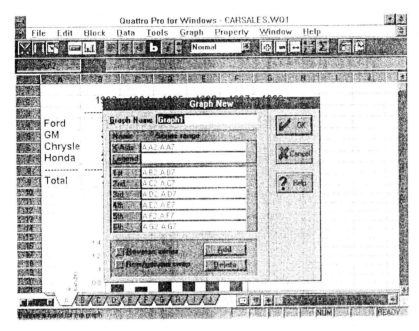

FIGURE 10.23:

The Graph New dialog box

Legend Position   This option gives you three choices for placement of the graph legends.

3-D View   This option can only be used when you have selected a 3-D graph to display. The 3-D View options are discussed in the next list.

3-D Options   This setting offers you the opportunity to remove portions of the graph such as the left wall, the back wall, or the base, or change the thickness of the walls.

Box Type   This option changes the border around the graph.

Fill Color   If you have a color printer or are creating a slide show, this option allows you to select the color that is used to fill the graph area outside the plotted values.

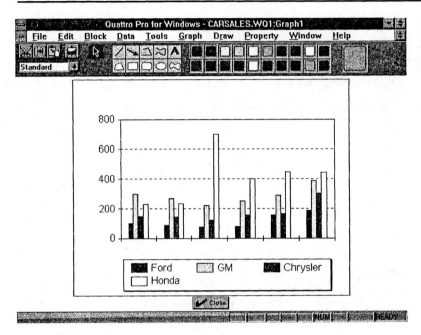

FIGURE 10.24:

Sample bar graph plotted from four blocks of data

Bkg Color   If you have a color printer or are creating a slide show, this option allows you to select the color of the background of the plotted values.

Fill Style   This option allows you to select a fill pattern for the solid objects in the graph, such as the bars.

Border Color   This option changes the color of the border around the outside of the graph.

Graph Button   This option is used to create a button in the graph, that, when selected, runs a macro or causes Quattro Pro to display a different graph. A graph button only works when the graph is displayed using the Graph ➤ View command or during a slide show. A graph button is a text box that you have added to the graph, and then connected to either a macro or a graph.

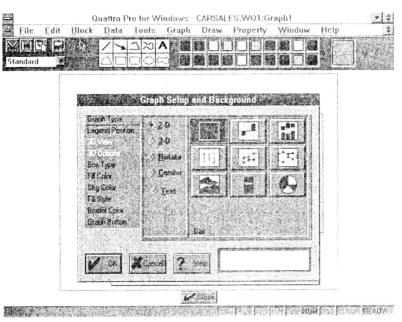

FIGURE 10.25:

The Graph Setup and Background dialog box

Figure 10.29 shows the 3-D View options:

Rotation   3-D graphs are positioned in space at a 30° angle off level. If you wish, you can rotate the graph in either direction. Click on the arrow that points to the rotation you want. As you do so, Quattro Pro rotates the example graph in the dialog box.

Elevation   3-D graphs are also tilted 30° in space. Clicking on the right arrow increases the elevation. You can elevate the graph so that the perspective is from the top down.

Perspective   The perspective setting is used to make the plotted values in the distance appear smaller than those nearer. By clicking this to on, you can adjust the graph to distort the perspective.

Depth   The depth setting is calculated by Quattro Pro to give the best possible view of the graph in conjunction with the

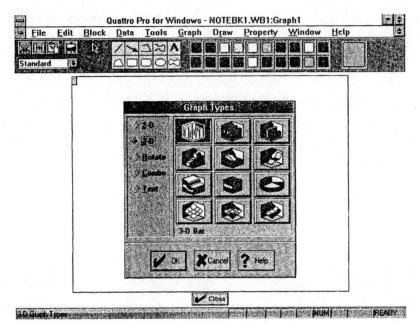

height setting. You can either increase the distance from the front of the graph to the back or decrease it. If you increase the depth, the graph will look more three-dimensional.

Height The height setting is drawn in proportion to the width setting. When the depth is set to 166, the height is 100. To increase the proportion of height to width, click on the right arrow; to decrease it, click on the left arrow.

Click on the Apply button before clicking on OK to change the settings in the graph. The Reset button returns the settings to the defaults.

Perhaps the data in Figure 10.24 would actually be better displayed in a stacked bar graph, which would show the relative contributions of

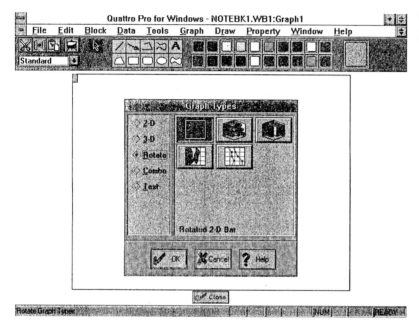

FIGURE 10.27:

Rotated graphs

various manufacturers to the total sales for each year. To change the bar graph to a stacked bar graph, follow these steps:

1. With the mouse pointer on empty space in the graph, click the right mouse button. The Graph Setup and Background dialog box appears.

2. Click on the 3-D option.

3. Click on the 3-D Stacked Bar icon, which is the middle graph in the top row.

4. Click on OK.

You'll see these same data plotted on stacked bars, as shown in Figure 10.30. The relationship of one company's sales to the entire market is much more distinct with this graph than with a standard bar graph.

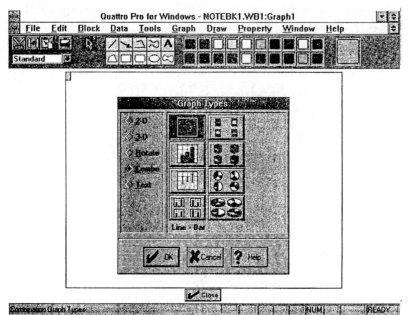

FIGURE 10.28:

Combination graphs

NAMING THE NEW GRAPH

Take a moment now to name this new graph by going to the graphs page, clicking the right mouse button, and entering **STACKED** in the Name dialog box.

HOW TO REMOVE A GRAPH OBJECT

When you created the stacked bar graph, included in the block were the names of the car companies. Quattro Pro for Windows correctly assumed that those labels were the legends for each of the bars. In the Graph Type and Background dialog box, you learned how to position the legends. Suppose that you wanted to delete the legend, or any object in the graph. Because Quattro Pro treats each object as a separate element, you can click on the object you want to remove, so that the

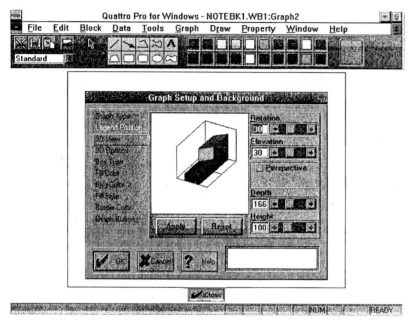

graph handles appear around the outside of the object. In this example, let's remove the legend.

1. Display the STACKED graph by selecting Graph ➤ Edit.

2. In the dialog box, double-click on STACKED. The graph is displayed in the graph window.

3. Click on the legend. Quattro Pro places the object handles on the perimeter of the legend, indicating that it is the active object.

4. Click on the Cut button.

Quattro Pro removes the legend from the graph. You can easily restore the legend by using Edit ➤ Undo.

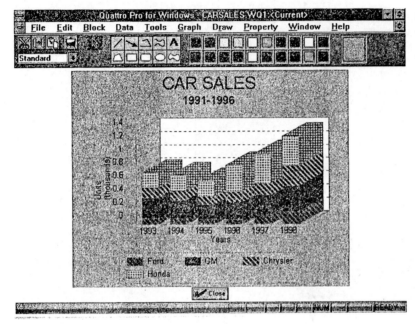

FIGURE 10.30:

The stacked bar graph of car sales

CREATING A PIE CHART

A pie chart is by definition 100% of some series of numbers. To this point, we have charted the total number of cars sold and the totals by manufacturer by year in a stacked-bar. To create a pie chart, you'll need to graph a new set of numbers. It would also be a good idea to explode a segment for emphasis.

1. Return to the spreadsheet page by clicking on the Window menu and selecting CARSALES.WB1.

2. Click and drag the block A4..B7.

3. Select Graph ➤ New and click on OK. Quattro Pro displays the newly selected block as a bar chart in the graph window.

4. Select Graph ➤ Type.

5. In the Graph Types dialog box, click on the Pie Graph.

6. Click on OK. The pie chart appears, as shown in Figure 10.31.

Exploding a Piece of the Pie

Each piece of the pie can be modified in terms of its color, fill pattern or position. To emphasize the car maker with the largest share of the market, let's explode the GM portion of the pie.

1. Click the right mouse button on the GM piece of the pie. Quattro Pro adds the object handles, and the Pie Graph Properties dialog box appears, as shown in Figure 10.32.

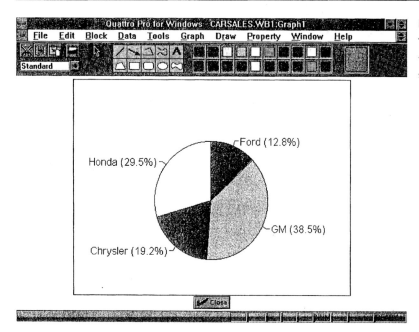

FIGURE 10.31:

The pie chart with distinct pie slices

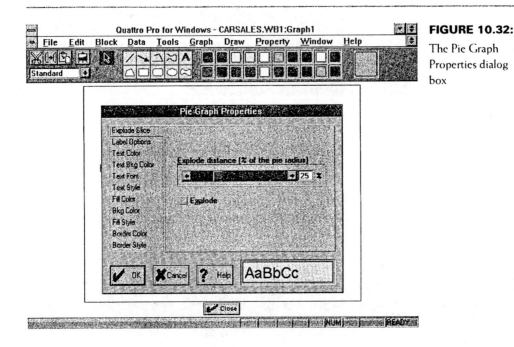

FIGURE 10.32:

The Pie Graph Properties dialog box

2. The default setting is to move the piece of pie out by 25% of the pie radius. You can adjust the distance by clicking on the scroll buttons.

3. Click on Explode.

4. Click on OK. The GM piece of pie is moved away from the remaining pieces, as shown in Figure 10.33.

INSERTING A GRAPH ON ITS SPREADSHEET PAGE

After you have created a graph in the graph window, you may wish to insert it on the spreadsheet page whence it was derived.

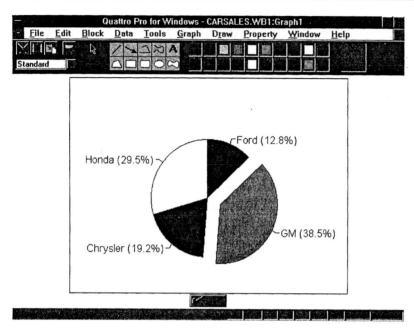

FIGURE 10.33:

The exploded piece

1. Click on the spreadsheet tab that contains the data that created the graph.

2. Select Graph ➤ Insert. The Graph Insert dialog box appears with a list of all the graphs in the notebook.

3. Click on the graph you want to insert.

4. Click on OK. The mouse pointer changes to resemble a small bar graph.

5. Position the mouse pointer in the cell where you want the graph to be overlaid.

6. Click the left mouse button.

If you decide not to overlay the graph, or have selected the wrong graph, click on the Graph Tool button. The mouse pointer resumes its normal shape, allowing you to follow the steps to select another graph or other tasks.

Customizing Titles

Quattro Pro offers several options for customizing titles on a graph, which mainly involve changing the title's font. By default, Quattro Pro displays titles above the graph in a plain block font. If you don't like it, you can select from among a number of fonts for these titles, or use fonts that you have installed via Windows.

To change a font while viewing the graph in the graph window, position the mouse pointer on the title. Click the right mouse button to open the Graph Title Properties dialog box. You can change the color of the text, the background color of the text box (in which all titles are enclosed), the text font, and the text style.

The text font options include the fonts that come with Quattro Pro, and any fonts you have installed via Windows. You may also choose to have the text displayed in bold, underline, or italics, or with a strikeout.

Changing Line or Fill Properties

When you create a line graph, Quattro Pro automatically selects a marker symbol for each block of plotted data. Similarly, when you create a bar, stacked bar, or area graph, Quattro Pro automatically selects a fill pattern for each plotted series. You can change the markers or fill patterns with the Line Series Properties dialog box.

To change marker symbols, click the right mouse button on the line in the graph you want to change. The Line Series Properties dialog box appears, as shown in Figure 10.34.

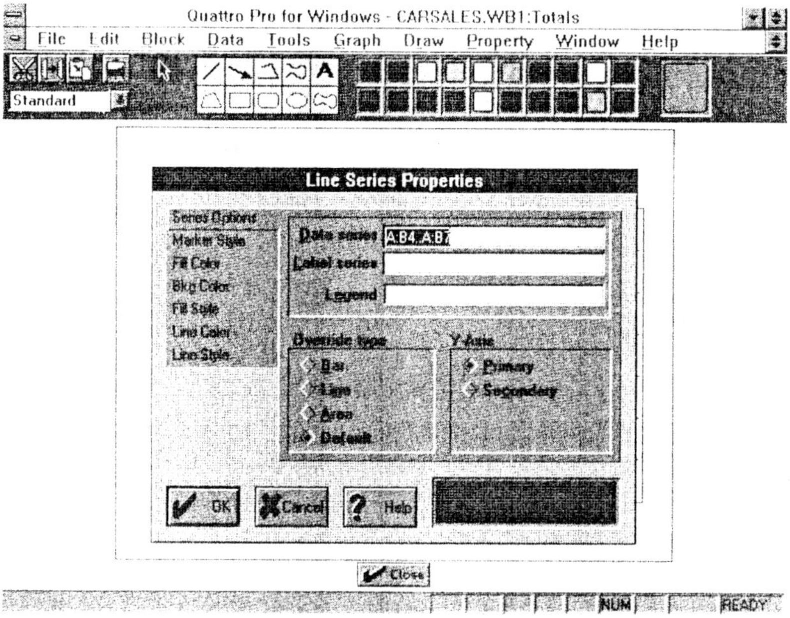

FIGURE 10.34:

The Line Series Properties dialog box

Click on the Marker Style option. Quattro Pro responds by filling the dialog box with 16 different marker patterns. Click on the one you wish to use, then click on OK. The Line Style can also be modified in this dialog box.

In a bar graph, click the right mouse button on a bar. The Bar Series Properties dialog box opens. The Bar options on this dialog box let you determine the bar width, the amount of extra space between the bars, and even whether the bars overlap. The Fill Color option gives you a dialog box with a broad range of colors and textures from which to choose. Click on the color you want, followed by OK.

Both the Line Series Properties and the Bar Series Properties dialog boxes allow you to select the background colors, border colors and border styles of the graph.

Combining Graph Types

To call attention to one particular series in a graph—say, Honda's sales—you may want to choose a different graph type in which to display it. First, you have to override the graph type in which that series is currently graphed and change it to something else. Only line, bar, and X–Y graphs can be overridden in this manner. To do that, click the right mouse button on the line or bar. The Line Series Properties or Bar Series Properties dialog box appears. In the Override Type section of the dialog box, click on the new type you want for that series. For example, if you have a bar chart with several series, you may want the selected series to be displayed as a line. Or if you have a line chart, you may want the selected series to be displayed as an area.

If you like it, save the graph under a new name and save the spreadsheet with the changes. If you don't, select the particular series again, then choose Default from Override Type to reset the series to how it was in the first place.

Enhancing a Graph

The Quattro Pro window is a powerful means of producing graphs with features that could only be produced previously by specialized graphics programs. Figure 10.17 detailed the position of the elements of the Graph SpeedBar.

Figure 10.35 shows the STACKED graph with an arrow and a text box added. The arrow emphasizes the direction of growth for the auto industry and the text box indicates the increasing sales of Japanese-built cars.

There are a few steps involved in adding these elements to the STACKED graph you saved earlier. They're easy, too.

1. Make STACKED the active graph in the graph window.

2. Click on the arrow tool in the Line Drawing tool box.

3. Position the pointer in the middle of the 1995 stacked bar and click and hold the left mouse button.

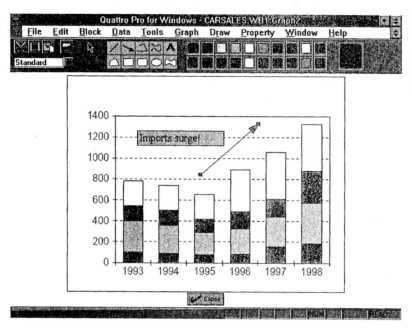

FIGURE 10.35:
The STACKED graph with an arrow and a text box

4. Drag the pointer up and to the right. As you do, a dotted line is drawn in the direction you are moving the pointer.

5. Release the mouse button above the 1998 bar. The arrow is drawn.

Using the Text Box Tool
Adding text to a graph is just as easy as adding the arrow. You draw a box, then type in the text.

1. Click on the Text tool. (It is identified by the letter A in the tool box.)

2. Position the pointer above the 1993 bar and click. This is the upper-left corner of the text box.

3. Drag the pointer down and to the right, finishing above the middle of the 1995 bar. (It does not matter if your box drawing is exact. You can always click on an object and stretch, shrink, or move it as you please.)

4. Release the mouse button. The insertion point begins blinking inside the text box.

5. Type **Imports Surge!**

6. Click on the Selection tool, the button with the shaded arrow next to the Tool Box. The familiar mouse pointer returns.

MOVING AN ELEMENT

To move any graph object:

1. Click anywhere on the object. The object handles appear.

2. Click and hold down the left mouse button on the middle of the object. The mouse pointer is transformed into a hand.

3. Drag the object to where you want it, and release the mouse button.

Note that you cannot drag an object outside the boundaries of the graph border, and that the moved object may overlie another object. To see the underlying object, select it and use the appropriate command from the Draw menu (shown in Figure 10.36).

As you layer objects, you can click on any of them and move it up a layer, all the way to the front, down a layer, or all the way to the back. You can also click on multiple objects and move them as a group. To select multiple objects, click on the first object, then hold down the Control key while you click on the other objects.

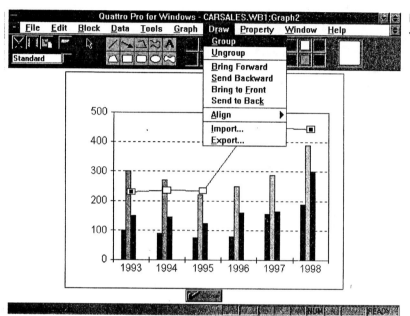

FIGURE 10.36:

The Draw menu

ALIGNING ELEMENTS

When you have selected multiple objects in the graph, you may wish to align them along the sides, centers, tops, or bottoms. Use the Draw ➤ Align options, as shown in Figure 10.37.

To select multiple objects, click on the first object, then hold down the Control key while you click on the other objects. It may be easier to first create a group of objects and then use the alignment options.

RESIZING AN ELEMENT

To resize an element, click on it with the mouse pointer and drag the corner in the direction you want. Release the mouse button.

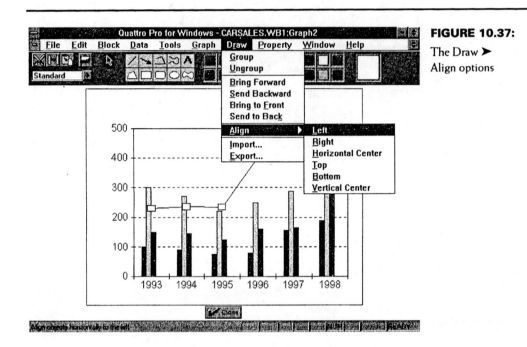

FIGURE 10.37:

The Draw ➤
Align options

As a precaution, before making any drastic changes to any part of the graph, save it and the spreadsheet. That way, if you make a severe mistake, you can retrieve the graph as part of the saved spreadsheet.

Creating a Slide Show

Quattro Pro will display your graphs in order, using the full screen, for a slide-show effect. The slide show can be used to preview actual slides, or as the presentation itself. The slide show is created in the graphs page of the notebook. Figure 10.38 shows the graphs page SpeedBar.

First, you create a slide-show icon, then place the graph icons on top of it.

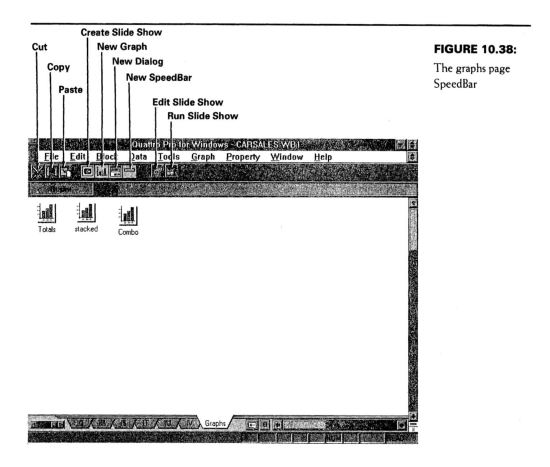

FIGURE 10.38:

The graphs page SpeedBar

1. Click on the Create Slide Show button, which is the fourth from the right in the SpeedBar. When the dialog box appears, type in **TEST** as the name for the slide show.

2. Click on OK. The TEST icon is added to the graphs page, as shown in Figure 10.39.

3. Suppose that you want to display the three graphs on the page in this order: Totals, Stacked, and Combo. Click on the Totals icon and drag it so that it is positioned on top of the

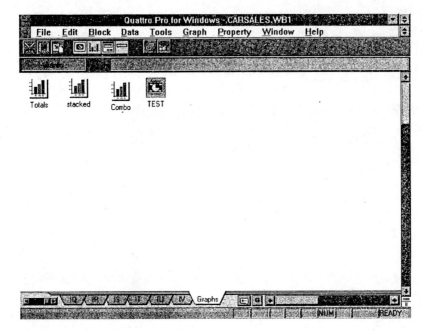

FIGURE 10.39:

The TEST icon in the graphs page

TEST icon. When the graph icon is correctly positioned, it changes to reverse video.

4. Release the mouse button. The graph icon will move back to its original place on the page.

5. Repeat the above steps with the remaining graph icons.

RUNNING THE SLIDE SHOW

1. Click the Run Slide Show button, which is the right-most button on the SpeedBar. The Select Slide Show dialog box appears.

2. Click on the Slide Show name you want—TEST—then click on OK.

In a moment, Quattro Pro displays the first graph. Click the left mouse button to see the next graph in the show. To see the previous slide, click the right mouse button.

EDITING A SLIDE SHOW

Quattro Pro includes a light table for editing the slide show! To access the light table, follow these steps:

1. Click on the slide show icon you want to edit.

2. Click on the Edit Slide Show button (the eighth from the left in the SpeedBar). The Light Table appears, as shown in Figure 10.40.

The graphs are arranged from left to right in the order that you have set. In the bottom-left corner of the screen are the effects that you can

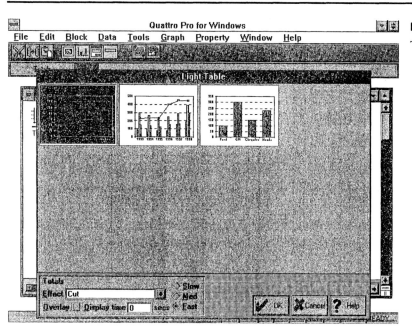

FIGURE 10.40:

The Light Table

add, and the current graph name.

To change the order of presentation, click on the graph you want to move and move it on top of the graph you want to displace. For example, if you want a graph to become the last graph displayed, click on the graph and drag it on top of the last graph. The moved graph becomes the last graph and the rest of the graphs move up one spot toward the beginning of the sequence.

The default segue from one graph to another is a Cut. If you tried the example slide show, you saw that effect. Click on the down arrow in the Effect field to see the wide variety of segues you can select. The Display time is set to zero, which means that the slide remains on the screen until you click a button or press a key. You can enter a value up to 3600 as the number of seconds to display the graph. Last, you can determine the length of time for each segue effect to take place.

The last effect option is the Overlay option. This effect is used in conjunction with several text graphs. For example, the first text graph could be the first line of a bulleted list. By overlaying the next and the remaining text graphs, you could unveil each bulleted line to complete the list.

Creating Text Graphs

Text graphs start out as blank graph windows, into which you insert text boxes and the concomitant text. In this next example, we will create a text graph that uses the entire graph window.

1. Select Graph ➤ New.

2. In the dialog box, give the text graph a name and click on OK.

3. In the Graph types dialog box, click on Text. An empty graph window appears.

4. Click on the text tool.

5. Position the pointer in the upper-left corner of the graph window border, and drag to the lower-right corner, thereby making the entire window a text box.

6. Release the mouse button.

7. Type **This is an example text graph!**.

8. Move the insertion point into the line of text, and click the right mouse button. The Text Properties dialog box appears.

9. Click on Text Font.

10. Click on Point size, and from the pull-down menu, click on 72.

11. Under options, click on Bold.

12. Click on OK. The text graph is shown in Figure 10.41.

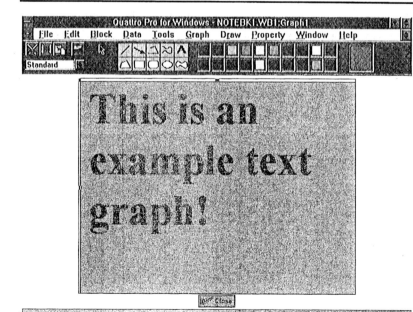

FIGURE 10.41:

An example text graph

The text graph is limited only by your creativity. You can add special formatting to the text graph, such as bullets, as you need it.

Text graphs can be used in many ways. For example, you can create a text graph that acts as the cover to your notebook, and a second text graph to act as the table of contents page. The text graph you just created, if inserted into the spreadsheet page, takes up the entire spreadsheet window, thereby making it appear as a page of text.

PRINTING AN INSERTED GRAPH

To print a spreadsheet with an inserted graph, simply include the entire block coordinates as part of the block to print. Select File ➤ Print. Use Print Preview to check that the block includes all of the graph. (Printing graphs alone is discussed in the next chapter.)

Summary

Quattro Pro's extensive graphing capabilities give you great flexibility. By creating a floating graph, you can immediately see the effect that changes to the spreadsheet numbers make on the graph. In the next chapter, we'll discuss how to print the graphs you've just learned how to create.

11 C H A P T E R

Printing Your Graphs

Printing graphs is fun and easy with Quattro Pro for Windows. Simply make sure you've selected a printer; then select the graph, format it, and print it. You can print a graph as a stand-alone item, or as part of a spreadsheet; you can even create a slide show.

Printing a graph by itself is accomplished from the graphs page at the end of the notebook. To print a floating graph as a part of a notebook, select all the cells that the graph overlies and print the spreadsheet page; the graph is printed as part of it.

Here are the general steps for printing a graph:

1. Click on the SpeedTab to go to the graphs page.

2. Click on the graph icon which represents the graph you want to print.

3. Select File ➤ Print. The Graph Print dialog box appears, listing the name of the default printer. To print multiple copies, click on the Copies field and enter the number. To see how the graph will appear before printing, click on the Preview button.

4. Click on Print.

The graph file is first sent to the Windows Print Manager, and then to the printer. Control of Quattro Pro returns to you almost immediately: you do not have to wait for the printer to finish before resuming work.

Selecting a Printer

When you installed Windows, you were asked to designate the printer connected to your computer. If you have not installed a printer using Windows, you must do so before you can print. Use the Windows Control Panel to install the printer. Quattro Pro for Windows checks the installed printer and assumes that it is the printer you want to use. If you have installed multiple printers via Windows, those selections are available from the Printer Setup dialog box (reached by File ➤ Printer Setup). You can click on the Set Up button in this dialog box to change the default settings for that particular printer. Any changes you make to the defaults apply only to Quattro Pro and will not affect any other Windows application.

You can access the Printer Setup dialog box from either the spreadsheet window or the graphs page of the notebook. You cannot use this dialog box to install an entirely new printer—that must be done in Windows. If you are ready to use the installed default printer, go to the section on Printing a Graph. Figure 11.1 shows the Printer Setup dialog box, accessed from the graphs page.

As you can see, two printers have been installed via Windows: a laser printer and a dot-matrix printer. Each of these printers has options that can be adjusted by clicking on the printer name, then clicking on Options. For example, to select a special font cartridge for the HP LaserJet in the example dialog box:

1. Click on the printer name, HP LaserJet IIP.

2. Click on the Set Up button. Quattro Pro responds with a dialog box specific to the HP printer (see Figure 11.2). Most

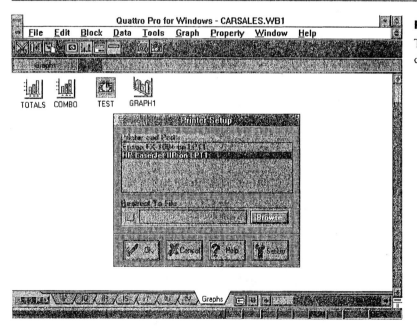

FIGURE 11.1:

The Printer Setup dialog box

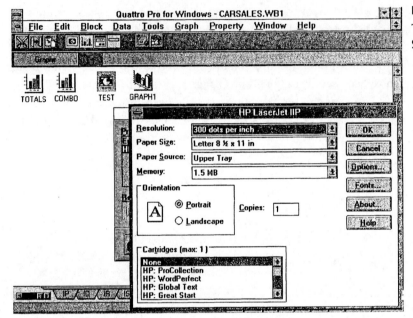

FIGURE 11.2:

The HP LaserJet Setup dialog box

of the options were selected when you installed the printer using Windows.

3. Click on the name of the cartridge you have installed in the printer.

4. Click on OK.

Quattro Pro is now aware that you have new capabilities for printing.

In the dialog box you can also change Orientation from Portrait to Landscape, set the number of copies to print, or add more fonts.

If you had selected the Epson printer and then clicked on SetUp, a different dialog box would have appeared. Even though this is a dot-matrix printer, Quattro Pro still allows for Landscape printing. But you

cannot enter a number of copies to print. Clicking on the Options button allows you to select the dithering and intensity of the printing.

Graph Page Setup

After selecting the printer to print the graph on, you can use File ➤ Page
Setup to open the Graph Page Setup dialog box (see Figure 11.3).

This dialog box allows you to enter a header and/or footer, select
the specific font for the header/footer, and adjust the page margins. You
can select a Paper type other than standard $8\frac{1}{2} \times 11$-inch by clicking
on it. Under Print orientation, you can select Portrait or Landscape; this
will override the setting in the Printer Setup dialog box.

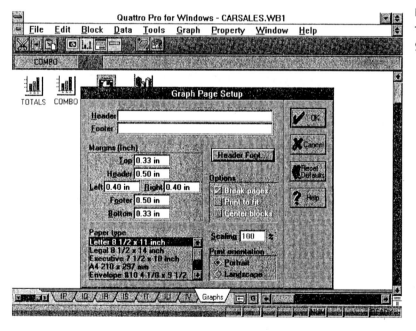

FIGURE 11.3:

The Graph Page
Setup dialog box

FORMATTING A GRAPH

When you print a graph, Quattro Pro automatically uses dimensions that best fill an 8½ × 11-inch page. You can, however, alter these dimensions to control the margins on the page by using the Graph Page Setup dialog box. The options are summarized below:

Top	Designates the number of inches or centimeters to leave blank between the top of the page and the header (if any)
Header	Specifies how much space to leave blank between the top margin and the top of the graph
Left	Designates the number of inches or centimeters from the left edge of the paper to the graph
Right	Designates the number of inches or centimeters from the right edge of the paper to the graph
Print Orientation	Designates whether the graph is to be printed along the width of the page (portrait) or along the length of the page (landscape)
Reset	Resets all printing options to their default settings

Figure 11.4 shows how some of the layout options are affected by the orientation of a graph. The top half shows a graph printed in landscape mode. The bottom half shows the same graph in portrait mode. Note that the top-edge measurement in the top graph is different than the top-edge measurement in the bottom graph. The same applies to the left-edge, height, and width measurements. Make sure you know how you want to orient the graph on the page *before* you set the page-spacing dimensions!

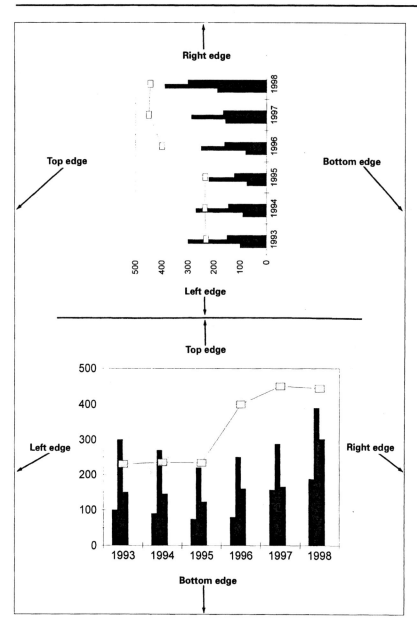

FIGURE 11.4:

Vertical and horizontal orientation of a graph

After changing the various layout settings, click on OK. Note that Quattro Pro may not expand the graph dimensions to fill the entire page. It will size the graph as best fits the page. If you make the margins larger, Quattro Pro will reduce the graph to fit the new margins.

PREVIEWING A GRAPH

After making your margin adjustments and designating the orientation you want, you can preview the graph to see how the adjustments will affect the printed output.

1. Select File ➤ Print. The Graph Print dialog box appears.

2. Click on the Preview button. Figure 11.5 shows a sample preview.

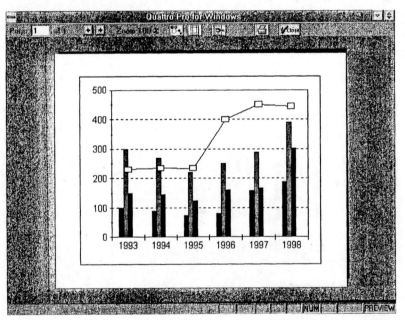

FIGURE 11.5:

Graph Preview window

The mouse pointer, when moved into the graph, appears as a magnifying glass. As with the spreadsheet print preview, you can left click one to four times on a portion of the graph to magnify the view by up to 1600%. To reduce the magnification, click the right mouse button.

Several new SpeedBar buttons appear, too. The first button from the left changes the graph from color to black and white to better show you how the graph will print. The second button from the left is the Margins button. Clicking on it displays the margins using dotted lines, as seen in Figure 11.6. In this figure, the right margin has been set to 3 inches, forcing Quattro Pro to resize the graph to fit. The third button from the left opens the Graph Page Setup dialog box, described earlier in this chapter.

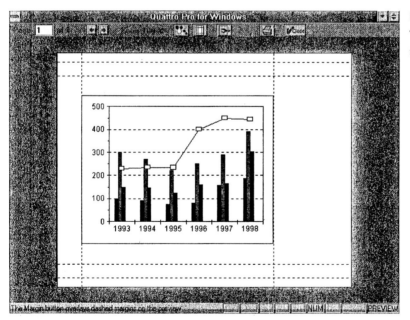

FIGURE 11.6:

The margins revealed

PRINTING A GRAPH TO A FILE

Just as you can print a spreadsheet to a file, you can print a graph to a file. When you do, Quattro Pro for Windows sends all of the printer-formatting attributes with the file. So if the graph is formatted to be printed on a PostScript-compatible printer, the formatting is included.

Here's how to print to a file:

1. Select File ➤ Printer Setup.

2. Click on the box under the Redirect to File section.

3. Type in a file name.

4. Click on OK.

STORING A GRAPH IN AN EPS, PIC, OR PCX FILE

You can store your graph in three other formats. The EPS format creates a PostScript-compatible file, which can be used to import graphs into some desktop publishing and word-processing systems such as PageMaker (Aldus Corp.). The PIC format creates a file that is compatible with Lotus 1-2-3, Lotus Symphony, and WordPerfect. The PCX format creates a file that is compatible with PC Paintbrush (Z-Soft Corp.), a graphics program. The Slide EPS format creates a file that later can be made into a 35-mm slide. This format is similar to EPS, except that it correctly translates the on-screen colors and ensures proper proportions for the slide.

To store a graph in a file using one of these formats, select the Browse option in the Printer Setup dialog box. Enter a file name, and click on File Types to send the file to one of the listed formats.

12 C H A P T E R

Exploring the Quattro Pro for Windows Database

So far you have learned much about Quattro Pro for Windows' considerable spreadsheet and graphing capabilities, and how the two are interconnected. This chapter deals with a third powerful component: database management.

What Is a Database?

A database is an organized collection of information. Even without the aid of a computer, you work with databases quite often. For example, your noncomputerized database might be a stack of receipts or invoices; a checkbook; a list of employees, customers, or prospective clients; a Rolodex; a phone book; a file cabinet; or even a shoe box full of index cards.

Many tasks are involved in managing these databases. You may need to add, update, delete, and rearrange the information. You may also want to locate and perhaps extract specific information, such as the names of all California residents with invoices that are past due. Quattro Pro's database capabilities let you perform all these tasks quickly and easily.

Structuring a Database

Most of your noncomputerized databases consist of individual pieces of paper, each with the same kind of information on it. For example, each Rolodex card might contain one person's name and address, as in Figure 12.1. A computerized database has a similar structure.

SETTING UP RECORDS AND FIELDS

In a Quattro Pro database, the information on a Rolodex card is stored as one record (row) of information. The individual items on the card—the name, address, city, and so forth—are each stored in a field (column) of information. Figure 12.2 shows how information from several Rolodex cards might be stored in a Quattro Pro database. There are eight records in this database, each consisting of six fields. Row 3 contains column labels (field names) that Quattro Pro considers part of the database.

Because Quattro Pro can only perform sorts and searches on specific fields within a database, the manner in which you separate information into the individual fields is vitally important. The basic rule

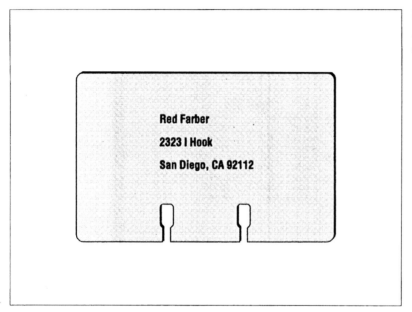

FIGURE 12.1:

A sample Rolodex card

of thumb is to break down each record into as many meaningful fields as possible.

Notice that the names in the sample database are actually divided into two fields, FName and LName. Intuitively, you might want to store people's names in a single field called Name, as below:

Name

Red Farber

Erick Hibertsen

Jackie You

PQ Kelly

Billy Cookie

Todd Simpsen

Rich Budenholzer

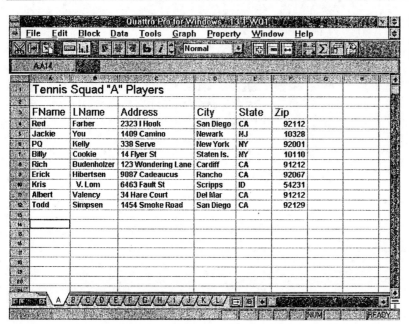

FIGURE 12.2:

A sample Quattro Pro Database

Kris V. Lom

Albert Valency

However, if both the last name and first name were combined in a single field, Quattro Pro would not be able to sort the names into alphabetical order by last name; an alphabetical sort on the Name field above would place Albert Valency above Billy Cookie. This is because Quattro Pro cannot operate upon information that is embedded within a field.

Notice also that the city, state, and zip codes are each stored in a separate field. Once again, you might be tempted to store this information in a single address field, as below:

City, State Zip

San Diego, CA 92122-1101

Newark, NJ 10328-1010

New York, NY 92001

Staten Is., NY 01010-2232

Cardiff, CA 91212

Rancho, CA 92067

Boise, ID 54321

Del Mar, CA 91212

If you combined these items into a single field, Quattro Pro would not be able to perform such tasks as sorting the database into zip-code order for bulk mailing or extracting all the records of people who live in the state of New York.

GUIDELINES FOR CREATING A DATABASE

When you store information in a Quattro Pro database, there are a few basic rules that you must follow:

- The database must be stored in an even, rectangular block of cells, and it cannot contain any blank rows or columns (a given record does not have to contain data in all fields, but at least one field must contain data).

- The first row must consist of field names (which are like spreadsheet column headings).

- An individual field name cannot be longer than 15 characters.

- Field names cannot contain any of the operators +, −, *, /, or ^.

- Avoid embedding blank spaces in field names. You can substitute an underline character (but not a hyphen!) for a blank space; for example, use *First_Name* rather than *First Name* as a field name.

- A field cannot have the same name as another field or block on the spreadsheet.

- All the data within a field must be of the same data type. For example, a field of zip codes cannot contain both numbers, such as 92122, and labels, such as '92J ZZL or '00112. If some of the zip codes need to be stored as labels, then all the zip codes must be stored as labels (e.g., '92122 rather than 92122).

- There can be no blank, or decorative, rows between field names and the first record (row) of data (for example, you cannot place underlines between the field names and the records).

- A field can contain a formula or function that refers to other fields in its own record. For example, a function that calculates an extended price based on the quantity and unit price in the same record as itself is okay. However, a function that calculates values based on information outside its own record will most likely lead to problems when you sort the database.

- All records of the database must be on the same spreadsheet page.

The sample database shown in Figure 12.2 follows all these rules, and is indeed a valid Quattro Pro database.

Note that the size of your Quattro Pro database is limited by the number of rows and columns in a spreadsheet page, which is 256 fields and 8191 records.

Creating a Sample Database

Let's develop a sample database now to use in examples and exercises in this chapter. Rather than enter simple names and addresses, however, you'll set up one that includes some numbers so that you can experiment with techniques for performing calculations on a database. Open a clean spreadsheet page or a new notebook and read on.

Suppose that, as the owner of a used-car lot, you want to set up a database that lets you help customers locate cars that suit their needs. You need to be able to find quickly all cars of a particular type, or within a particular price range, or with a specific number of doors. So you decide to divide the information about each car into the following distinct fields: year, make, model, number of doors, selling price, mileage, lot number, and date sold (leaving the date-sold field blank until the car is sold).

Figure 12.3 shows how you could set up the initial structure of the database. The field names are stored across row 3, and the Column Width command was used to set a reasonable width for each field. The main title above the field names is just a descriptive title; it is not an actual part of the database.

Enter the title and field names for the sample database, and use the Font Size arrows to enlarge the text. Then adjust the column widths using the Fit button or the mouse.

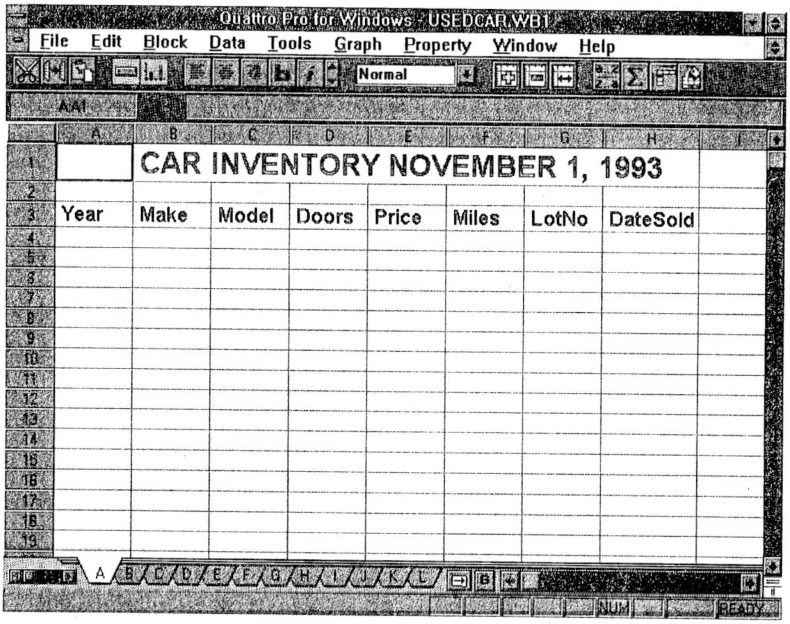

FIGURE 12.3:

Sample database structure for information about used cars

ENTERING RECORDS IN A DATABASE

You enter information into database records the same way that you type data into spreadsheet cells—by positioning the cell selector, typing in your entry, and pressing Enter (or clicking the mouse button). Just be sure to use the correct data type for the field. For example, enter all dates with either the Ctrl-Shift-D command or the @DATE function.

Figure 12.4 shows the used-car database with some sample records. Enter the records shown in the figure.

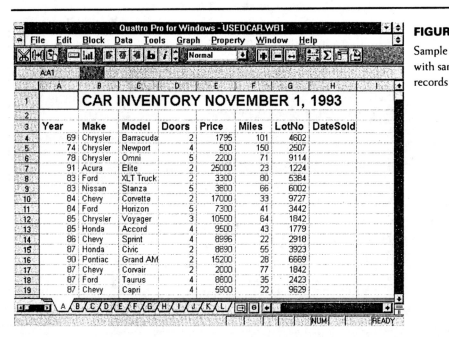

FIGURE 12.4:

Sample database with sample records

Sorting the Database

Typically, you enter information into a database as the information becomes available. But eventually you'll need to sort the information into some more useful order, such as alphabetical order by name, by zip-code order for bulk mailing, by part number, or perhaps by manufacturer. To sort a database, you would follow the steps below. (There's an example for you in a moment.)

1. Click and drag the cells that contain the records you want to sort. Be certain that you have included all of the fields. *Do not include the field names.*

2. Select Data ➤ Sort to open the Data Sort dialog box.

3. Select the 1st Key field and specify the column on which you want to base the sorting order by entering the column address including a record.

4. The default sort is Ascending (smallest to largest). Clicking on the check mark changes the order to Descending. With label fields, ascending order is *A* to *Z*, and descending order is *Z* to *A*. With dates and times, ascending order is earliest to latest, and descending order is latest to earliest. If the data in the field is mixed, you can designate labels or numbers to be placed at the beginning of the sort.

5. If you want the sort based on more than one field (we discuss this later), select 2nd Key and specify the column for the secondary sort order. You can repeat this process for a maximum of five fields.

6. Click on OK after specifying all the fields for the sort.

The records will be sorted immediately.

Sort the records in your sample database now into ascending order by price. Here are the steps:

1. Click and drag the block of fields and records, A4..H19.

2. Select Data ➤ Sort.

3. Select 1st Key by typing in a cell address in the Price field, or by double-clicking the dialog box field to reduce the dialog

box, then clicking on a cell in that field, and clicking the up arrow to restore the dialog box. Figure 12.5 shows the dialog box with the sort entries in place.

4. Click on OK.

Immediately, the records are sorted by the price, with the least expensive vehicle listed first and the most expensive last. This order makes it easy to locate vehicles within a customer's price range. Figure 12.6 shows the database after the sort.

Note that you must *never* include the field names (row 3 in this example) when specifying the block to sort, and always specify *all* the fields in the database. Failure to specify all the fields in a sort will cause the records to go out of alignment, rendering the database useless. However, if the Undo option is enabled before you make the sort, you can use Edit ➤ Undo Sort to return the database to how it was before

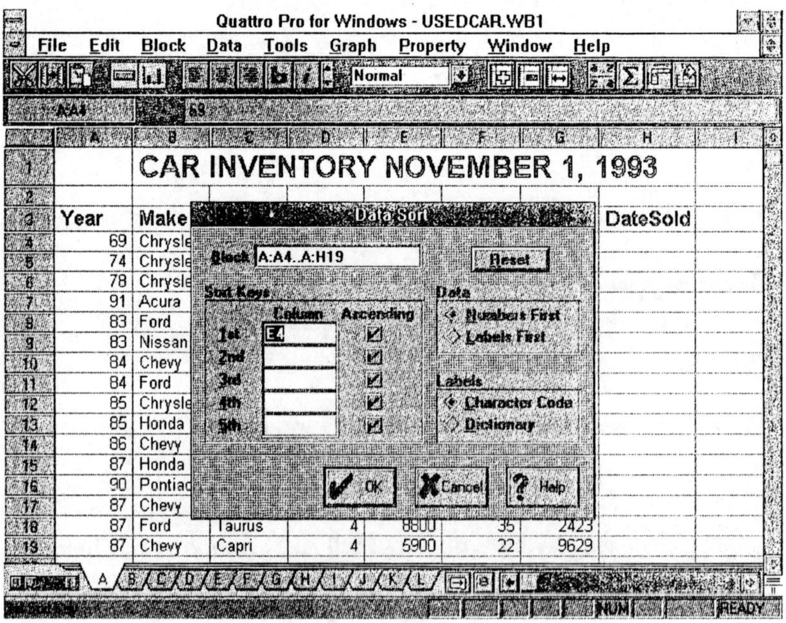

FIGURE 12.5:

The Data Sort dialog box

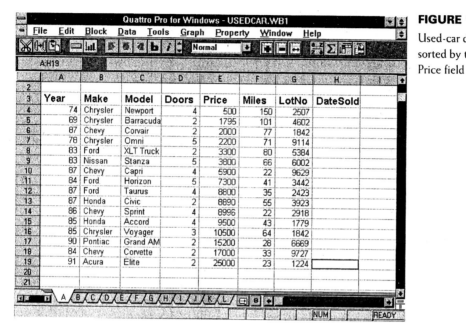

FIGURE 12.6:

Used-car database sorted by the Price field

the sort. (To be safe, always save a database before performing a sort so that you can call it back on-screen should you make a mistake.)

SORTING WITHIN A SORT

In some situations, sorting on a single field is simply not adequate. For example, if you had a database with 5000 names and sorted it by last name only, then all the Smiths would be clumped together—as expected—but they would be in random order by first name. Imagine looking for Joe Smith in the telephone directory for a large city that sorted names in this fashion. You would have to read every Smith entry until you happened to come across Joe Smith.

To have Quattro Pro perform a sort within a sort, you use multiple sort keys. The first key you define is the primary sort order, which specifies the main order for the records. Then you define a second key to specify the secondary, or within-sort, order. For example, if you sort a database with *last* name as the first key and *first* name as the second key, the names will be sorted in alphabetical order by last name, then in alphabetical order by first name within a list of identical last names, as below:

Smidle	Zachary
Smith	Albert
Smith	Millie
Smith	Wilma
Smyth	Joan

You can specify up to five sort keys, each one arranged within the order specified by the previous key. For example, if you sorted a database of invoice records with date as the first key, customer number as the second key, and invoice amount as the third key, the database would be sorted overall by date; within each identical date, invoices would be sorted by customer number; and within each identical date and customer number, records would be sorted by the amount of the invoice.

Sort the used-car database by three keys: the number of doors, make, and model. Unless you have clicked on a different cell, Quattro Pro keeps the highlighting on the selected block.

1. Select Data ➤ Sort. The dialog box opens. Quattro Pro retains the same block of cells to sort.

2. Click on the 1st Key field. Specify the Doors field (cell D4), and select Ascending order.

3. Click on the 2nd Key field. Specify the Make field (cell B4), and select Ascending order.

4. Click on the 3rd Key field. Specify Model as the field (cell C4), and select Ascending order.

5. Click on OK.

Figure 12.7 shows the database after it has been sorted. The records are sorted first by the number of doors, from two to five. Within each group of cars with the same number of doors, the records are sorted alphabetically by make (e.g., Chevy, Chrysler, Ford, Honda). The records for cars of the same make with the same number of doors are sorted alphabetically by model (e.g., Chevy Corvair comes before Chevy Corvette among the two-door cars).

Each field was sorted in ascending order, but you can combine ascending and descending orders in any sort. For example, sorting a database of invoices into ascending order by date and descending order by charge would produce a file of records listed from earliest to latest

FIGURE 12.7:

The used-car database sorted by number of doors, make, and model

Year	Make	Model	Doors	Price	Miles	LotNo	DateSold
91	Acura	Elite	2	25000	23	1224	
87	Chevy	Corvair	2	2000	77	1842	
84	Chevy	Corvette	2	17000	33	9727	
69	Chrysler	Barracuda	2	1795	101	4602	
83	Ford	XLT Truck	2	3300	80	5384	
87	Honda	Civic	2	8890	55	3923	
90	Pontiac	Grand AM	2	15200	28	6669	
85	Chrysler	Voyager	3	10500	64	1842	
87	Chevy	Capri	4	5900	22	9629	
86	Chevy	Sprint	4	8996	22	2918	
74	Chrysler	Newport	4	500	150	2507	
87	Ford	Taurus	4	8800	35	2423	
85	Honda	Accord	4	9500	43	1779	
78	Chrysler	Omni	5	2200	71	9114	
84	Ford	Horizon	5	7300	41	3442	
83	Nissan	Stanza	5	3800	66	6002	

date; within each identical date, records would be listed from the highest charge to the smallest.

Note that if you sort a database that has a field containing a function or formula that makes reference to values outside its own record, the sort will wreak havoc on its result. However, a field in a database *can* refer to an unsorted value outside the database, as long as the reference is absolute. For example, if the sort block is A5..Z109 and a percentage figure is stored in cell A1, a formula that refers to $A$1 will still do so after the block is sorted.

Because the sort order will not pertain to any records entered *after* the database has been sorted, you must sort the entire database again to reorder the new records. Be sure to include the new records in the block to sort.

Searching a Database for Specific Data

Sorting a database can put records into a useful order, but it will not necessarily help you to locate a specific item of information, such as a person's address. Nor will it necessarily help you pull out all records that meet some criterion, such as accounts receivable that are over 90 days past due. To perform these kinds of tasks, you need to use Quattro Pro's searching, or *querying*, capabilities. First, we'll explain how things work, then run you through some examples.

To perform a database query, you must first access the Data Query dialog box by selecting Data ➤ Query. The Data Query dialog box appears, as shown in Figure 12.8, containing the options listed below.

Database Block	Specifies the entire database, including all field names, before querying a database
Criteria Table	Specifies a block of cells on the spreadsheet that contains query criteria
Output Block	Determines where to store extracted records on the spreadsheet page

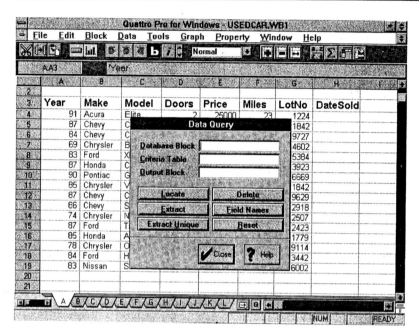

FIGURE 12.8:

The Data Query dialog box

Field Names	Lets you use a field name, rather than a cell address, when entering a query formula
Locate	Locates the first record in the database that matches the specified query criteria
Extract	Extracts all records that meet a query criterion and places them in another part of the database
Extract Unique	Extracts only unique values that match a query criterion—does not extract duplicate records
Delete	Deletes all records in a database that match a specified query criterion
Reset	Undoes all previous query criteria settings

Close	Leaves the Data Query dialog box and returns to the spreadsheet in Ready mode

DEFINING A QUERY BLOCK

Before performing a database query, you must select the entire database as the block to query. This time, the block you specify *must* include the field names at the top of the database. Use the click and drag method to specify the block to search or just enter the cell coordinates of the block (A3..H19).

Any time that you add new records to a database, be sure to select the Query option from the Data menu and redefine the block so that it includes those new records.

ASSIGNING FIELD NAMES

Before you enter the query criteria, you should click on the Field Names button in the Data Query dialog box so that you can use field names in your query formula. They make the formula easier to understand later on. For example, to search for all Fords in the used-car database without first assigning field names, you would need to enter a formula like +B4=Ford (where B4 refers to the first cell under the Make field name). However, if you gave this field the name Make, you could enter the formula as +Make=Ford.

When you click on Field Names, you don't really have to do any assigning; you won't see any prompts on the screen. Quattro Pro assumes that the first row of the query block contains field names and automatically assigns these names to the fields. But watch out: problems may arise if any names have more than one word or are more than 15 characters long.

If you add new fields to a database structure or change any field names, you should remember to click on the Field Names button again to reassign the names to the fields.

SETTING UP A DATABASE-CRITERIA TABLE

A criteria table consists of field names in the top row and values to search for in the row(s) beneath. The field names in the table must match the field names in the database exactly. (You can use the Copy and Paste buttons to copy the field names from the top of a database to a criteria table.)

After you set up your criteria table with field names, values to search for, and/or query formulas, select Data ➤ Query to display the Data Query dialog box. Use the click and drag method to highlight the appropriate field names, search values, and formulas, and then click on OK. To actually perform the search, click on Locate, Extract, or Extract Unique in the Data Query dialog box, as discussed later in this chapter. (Before choosing Extract or Extract Unique, of course, you must select Output Block to tell Quattro Pro where to place the data found by the search.)

If you want to isolate records that meet one specific criterion, place the value to search for directly under the appropriate field name. For example, Figure 12.9 shows a criteria table that will search for records that have Ford in the field named Make.

If you wish to search for records that are less than or greater than some value, you must enter a formula that begins with a plus sign, followed by a field name, a logical operator, and a comparison value. For example, Figure 12.10 shows a highlighted criteria table that is set up to isolate records of Fords with prices of $5,000 or less.

Note that you can only use field names in these formulas if you clicked on the Field Names button in the Data Query dialog box. When you enter such a formula, the cell will display either 1 or 0, for a true or false condition in the first record. To view the actual formula instead (as in Figure 12.10), format the cell as Text.

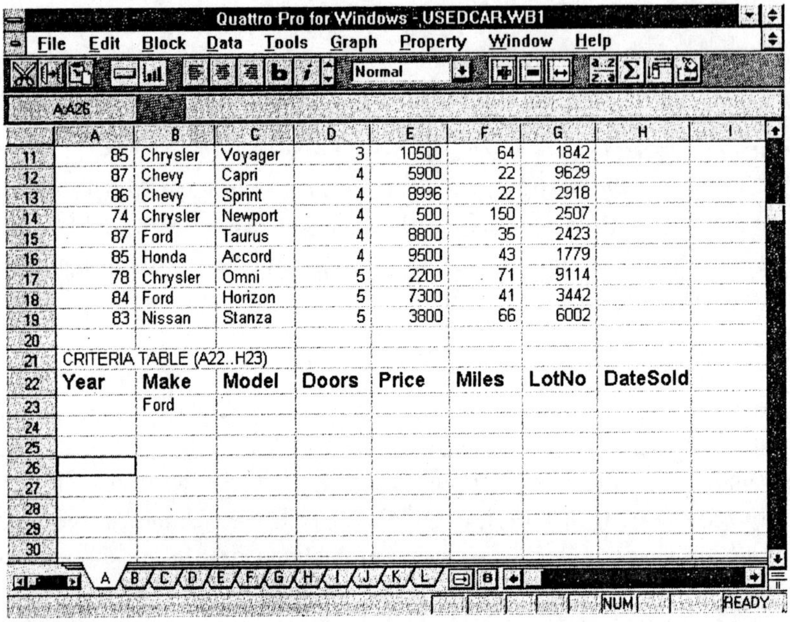

FIGURE 12.9:

Criteria table to search for Fords in the used-car database

	A	B	C	D	E	F	G	H	I
11	85	Chrysler	Voyager	3	10500	64	1842		
12	87	Chevy	Capri	4	5900	22	9629		
13	86	Chevy	Sprint	4	8996	22	2918		
14	74	Chrysler	Newport	4	500	150	2507		
15	87	Ford	Taurus	4	8800	35	2423		
16	85	Honda	Accord	4	9500	43	1779		
17	78	Chrysler	Omni	5	2200	71	9114		
18	84	Ford	Horizon	5	7300	41	3442		
19	83	Nissan	Stanza	5	3800	66	6002		
20									
21	CRITERIA TABLE (A22..H23)								
22	Year	Make	Model	Doors	Price	Miles	LotNo	DateSold	
23		Ford							
24									
25									
26									
27									
28									
29									
30									

Locating and Changing Records

Regardless of whether you use a criteria table or enter a formula to specify your search criteria, the Locate option on the Query submenu will allow you to pinpoint and edit the records that meet those criteria.

When you select Locate, the cell selector highlights the first record in the database that matches your search criteria. For example, Figure 12.11 shows the result of selecting Locate after specifying the block A22..H23 to search in the criteria table. The cell selector is on the first (and only, in this example) record that matches the two criteria: a Ford, and costing less than $5000.

If you change some data in the database or information in the criteria table without adding or deleting rows from either, you can quickly repeat your database query by pressing the Query key (F7).

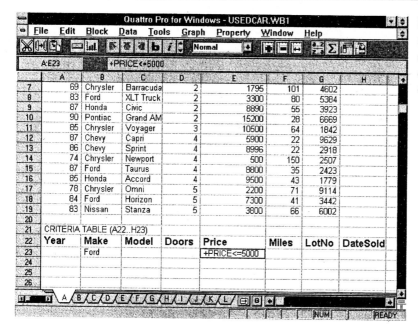

FIGURE 12.10:
Criteria table set up to isolate Fords costing $5,000 or less

While the entire record is highlighted during a Locate operation, you can use any of the keys listed below to work with the database (e.g., to type new values in a particular cell):

↓   Highlights the next record in the database that matches the search criteria (if none of the records below matches the search criteria, Quattro Pro beeps instead)

↑   Highlights the previous record in the database that matches the search criteria (if none of the records above matches the search criteria, Quattro Pro beeps instead)

→   Moves the cell selector one field to the right in the current record

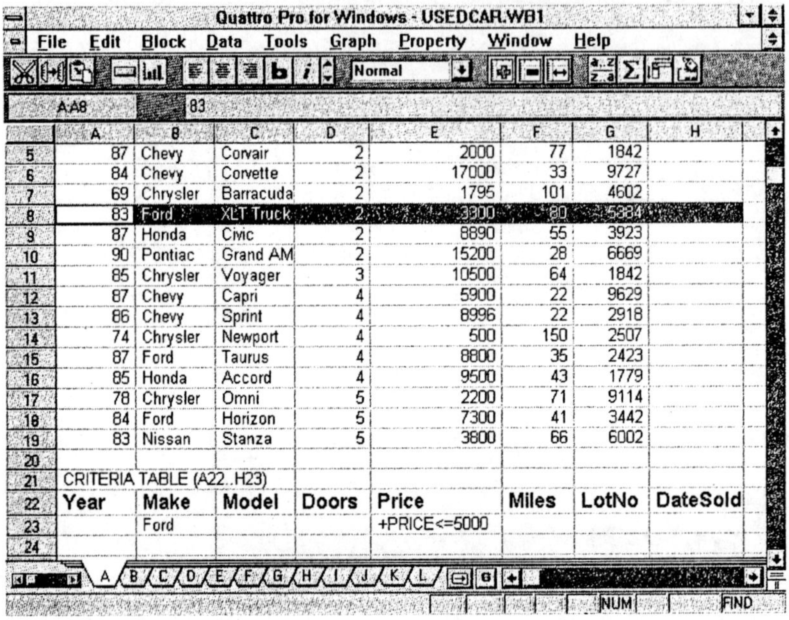

FIGURE 12.11:
The result of selecting Locate after setting up a criteria table

	←	Moves the cell selector one field to the left in the current record
	Home	Moves the cell selector to the first record in the database (whether it matches the search criteria or not)
	End	Moves the cell selector to the last record in the database (whether it matches the search criteria or not)
	F2	Lets you edit the currently selected cell (press Enter when done editing)
	Escape	Quits the Locate operation and returns you to the Data Query dialog box—or takes you back to the spreadsheet in Ready mode if you did a search with the Query (F7) key

Extracting Database Records

You can also use criteria formulas and tables to extract (or pull out) a copy of database records that meet some search criteria. The extracted records will be stored in an *output block* elsewhere on the database, which can contain all or some of the fields from the original database.

Now we'll pull out from the sample database a copy of all records that have Ford in the Make field. To do so, follow these steps:

1. Create the criteria table shown in the block A22..H23 in Figure 12.12. Copy the field names: select cells A3..H3, click on the Copy button, then move the cell selector to cell A22 and click on the Paste button.

2. Enter **Ford** in cell B23.

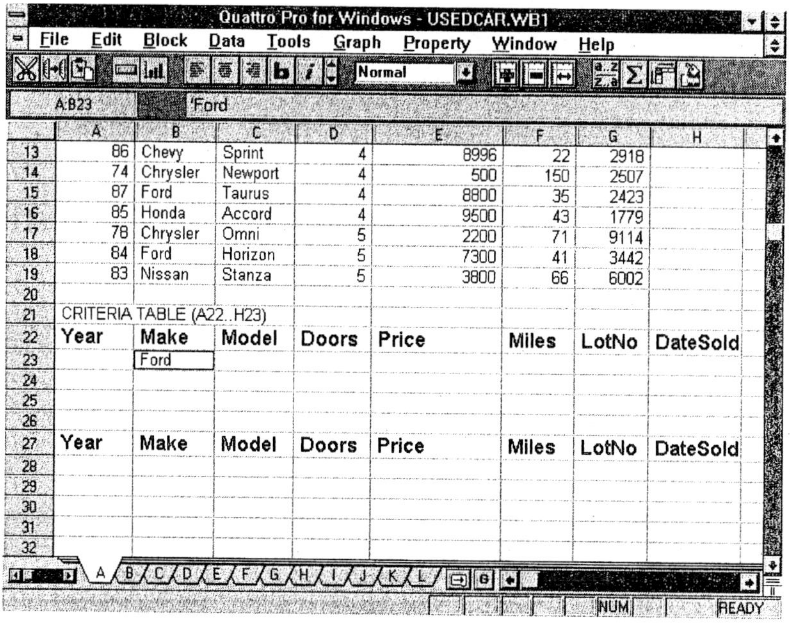

FIGURE 12.12:

The criteria table and output block on the spreadsheet

3. Create an output block for the extracted records below the database. Click on cell A27, then click on the Paste button again to enter the field names.

4. Select Data ➤ Query to open the Data Query dialog box.

5. Double-click on the Database Block field to reduce the dialog box. Select the whole database as the block to query by clicking and dragging cells A3..H19. Click on the up arrow to restore the dialog box.

6. Double-click on the Criteria Table field to reduce the dialog box again. Highlight the criteria table in cells A22..H23, then click on the up arrow to restore the dialog box.

7. Double-click on the Output Block field. Highlight the field names in the output block in cells A27..H27, then restore the dialog box.

8. Select Extract in the dialog box.

Copies of records that meet the search criteria are copied into the output block, as shown in Figure 12.13.

EXTRACTING UNIQUE VALUES

In a large database, you might want to extract certain entries from a database without having them repeated if they occur more than once. For example, suppose you want to see a list of all the makes of car in the used-car database. Follow these steps:

1. Set up a criterion formula that will not exclude any records in a given field. The simplest way to do this is to highlight a field name and the blank cell beneath it when you define the criteria block. Here, highlight cells B22..B23.

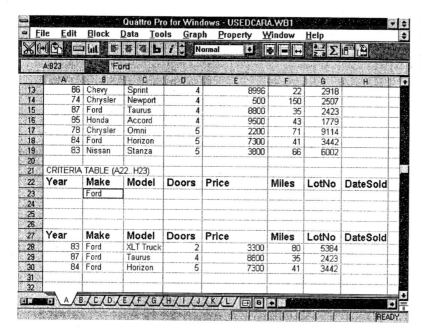

FIGURE 12.13:

Copies of extracted records in the output block

2. Create an output block that consists of only the field name you are interested in—the Make field. Figure 12.14 shows what you want: B27..B40 is the output block and B22..B23 is the criteria block.

3. Click on Extract Unique in the Data Query dialog box.

A list of unique values in the Make field will appear in the output block, as shown in Figure 12.14.

Deleting Database Records

You can use the SpeedBar Delete button as usual to delete any single record from a database. But you can also use the Delete option on the Data Query dialog box to delete all records that match a specific search criterion. To play it safe, always save your database before deleting any

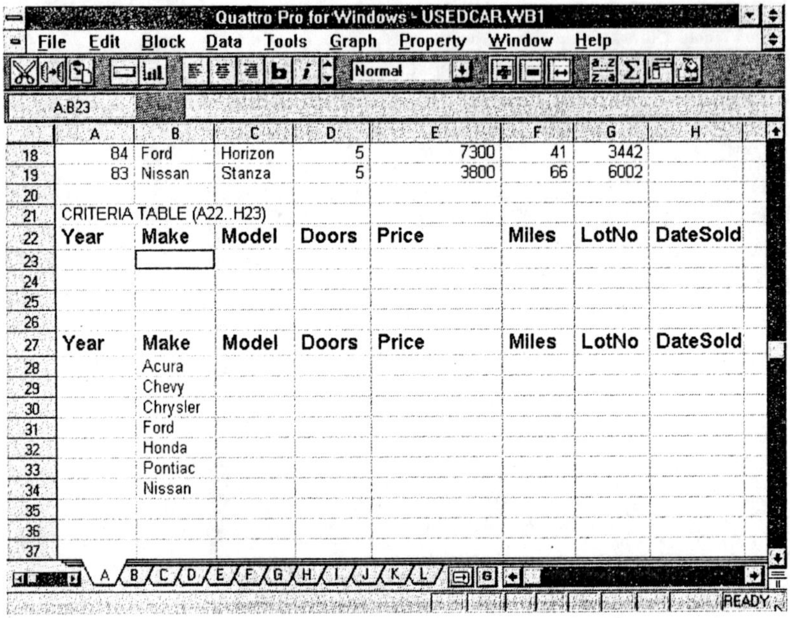

FIGURE 12.14:

The unique output

data, so that you can retrieve them if you make a mistake. You can also use Undo, provided it has been enabled.

Don't forget that the Delete option deletes the *entire* row from a spreadsheet, all the way over to column IV. The Delete command on the Data Query dialog box, however, has no effect on cells outside the database block.

The technique for using Delete is basically the same as the one for using Locate: specify the entire database block, specify a query formula or criteria table, then select Delete and choose Yes in the Delete Record dialog box. For example, Figure 12.15 shows the results of a delete operation: because the criteria table specified records with Make values equal to Chevy, all cars that are Chevy were erased.

Delete is a drastic operation to perform on a database, so if you used Delete, use Edit ➤ Undo to restore the data.

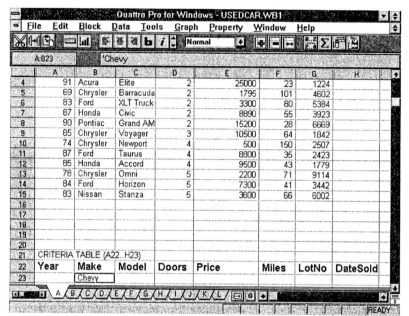

FIGURE 12.15:

The result of a database delete operation

Using Database Statistical Functions

Quattro Pro's database statistical functions allow you to perform basic statistical operations, including sums and averages, on databases. Unlike Quattro Pro's regular statistical functions, these functions let you perform operations only on database records that meet a search criterion, such as the average selling price of Fords on the lot, the number of cars on the lot per manufacturer, and so forth.

All of the database statistical functions use the basic syntax @DX(*block,column,criteria*), where block is the entire database block, *column* is the column position of the database field on which to perform the calculation (starting with zero as the left-most column), and criteria is a block in the criteria table. For example, the averaging function @DAVG(A3..H17,4,B22..B23) calculates the average price of Fords in the used-car database.

The database statistical functions are summarized below:

@DAVG(*block, column,criteria*)	Averages the entries in a numeric field, including only records that meet the specified search criteria
@DCOUNT (*block,column, criteria*)	Counts how many records in the database meet the specified search criteria
@DMAX(*block, column,criteria*)	Calculates the largest value (or latest date or time) in a numeric field, including only records that match the specified search criteria
@DMIN(*block, column,criteria*)	Calculates the smallest value (or earliest date or time) in a numeric field, including only records that match the specified search criteria
@DSTD(*block, column,criteria*)	Calculates the standard deviation of a numeric field, including only records that meet the specified search criteria
@DSUM(*block, column,criteria*)	Sums the entries in a numeric field, including only records that meet the specified search criteria
@DVAR(*block, column,criteria*)	Calculates the variance of a numeric field, including only records that meet the specified search criteria

Figure 12.16 shows the used-car database set up with a criteria table in the block B22..B23 that limits calculations to Fords on the car lot. The database statistical functions calculate all statistics on prices of

those cars, including a count of the number of Fords on the lot. Note that each formula specifies the entire database block (A3..H17), Price field (column 4), and criteria table (B22..B23).

1. Set up your criteria table to look like that in Figure 12.16 by deleting all the field names except Make.

2. Enter **Sum** in cell B25, and in cell C25 the function @DSUM(A3..H19,4,B22..B23).

3. Enter **Average** in cell B26, and in cell C26 the function @DAVG(A3..H19,4,B22..B23).

4. Enter **Count** in cell B27, and in cell C27 the function @DCOUNT(A3..H19,4,B22..B23).

	A	B	C	D	E	F	G	H
14	74	Chrysler	Newport	4	500	150	2507	
15	87	Ford	Taurus	4	8800	35	2423	
16	85	Honda	Accord	4	9500	43	1779	
17	78	Chrysler	Omni	5	2200	71	9114	
18	84	Ford	Horizon	5	7300	41	3442	
19	83	Nissan	Stanza	5	3800	66	6002	
20								
21	CRITERIA TABLE (B22..B23)							
22		**Make**						
23		Ford						
24								
25		Sum	19400					
26		Average	6466.667					
27		Count	3					
28		Highest	8800					
29		Lowest	3300					
30		St. Dev.	2321.398					
31		Variance	5388889					
32								
33								

FIGURE 12.16:

Database statistical functions in the used-car database

5. Enter **Highest** in cell B28, and in cell C28 the function @DMAX(A3..H19,4,B22..B23).

6. Enter **Lowest** in cell B29, and in cell C29 the function @DMIN(A3..H19,4,B22..B23).

7. Enter **St. Dev.** in cell B30, and in cell C30 the function @DSTD(A3..H19,4,B22..B23).

8. Enter **Variance** in cell B31, and in cell C31 the function @DVAR(A3..H19,4,B22..B23).

9. Select Data ➤ Query to open the Data Query dialog box.

10. Enter the Database Block as A3..H19 using the mouse or by typing the cell address into the field.

11. Enter the Criteria Table as B22..B23 using the mouse or by typing the cell address into the field.

12. Click on Extract to extract the information.

Changing the label in cell B23 from *Ford* to *Chevy* would instantly recalculate all the formulas to display the price statistics of Chevys on the lot.

The more you become familiar with the workings of the Quattro Pro database, the more you'll find that it provides an excellent means of recording and manipulating information, analyzing data, and discerning trends.

13 C H A P T E R

Customizing Quattro Pro for Windows

This chapter shows you how to modify Quattro Pro for Windows to suit your needs and tastes. For instance, you might need to show dates in a non-American format—25/12/93 rather than 25-DEC-93. You might also like to change the color scheme of spreadsheet data to alert you to numbers out of the normal range. Whatever your reasons, you need not feel stuck with the various default styles that came with the software. Customizing Quattro Pro for Windows is surprisingly easy—and fun.

There are several levels of customization, starting with the Quattro Pro for Windows application itself. Modifying options at this level changes the options for every notebook you use, old or new. The next level down is the specific notebook in which you are working. Last, you can customize a particular page in the notebook. In this chapter we will discuss all three levels.

Changing the Application Options

Quattro Pro for Windows is fully customizable. You have already seen how you can change the fonts, typestyles and colors of information in cells. You have also changed the width of columns and the height of rows. There are many other options that you can explore to customize Quattro Pro to your desires. Let's begin by looking at the Application options. Click the right mouse button on the application title bar, or select Property ➤ Application, to open the Application dialog box (shown in Figure 13.1).

DISPLAY

The first option is Display. Quattro Pro does not show a clock as the default. However, you may want to be able to see what time it is as you are working. If you click on Standard as the clock display, Quattro Pro displays the date and time in the following format: DD-MMM-YY HH:MM AM/PM. So, for December 31, 1993 at 11 PM, the display reads 31-Dec-93 11:00 PM. The International option displays date and time as: DD/MM/YY HH:MM in 24-hour format. So that same December date and time is displayed 31/12/93 23:00.

If you want to see more of the spreadsheet window, you can do so by removing the SpeedBar, input line, and status line, or a combination of the three. Figure 13.2 shows the spreadsheet window without the SpeedBar, Input line, or Status line.

The last option in this dialog box is the 3-D Syntax. This is most significant when you are working in multiple spreadsheet pages. The default is to list the page and then the first cell address, followed by the

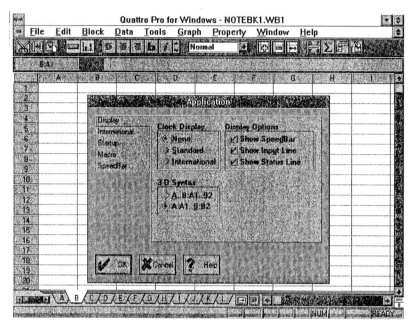

last page in the block followed by the cell address. So if the block is cells B12..B13 on spreadsheets A through D, the syntax is A:B12..D:B13. The other syntax is to have the spreadsheet pages listed first: A..D:B12..B13.

INTERNATIONAL OPTIONS

Every country has its own way of dealing with numbers, dates and currency formats. (In fact, Windows has its own specific format for currency, perhaps for simplicity.) Clicking on International displays the options, as shown in Figure 13.3.

Currency

Normally, Quattro Pro displays currencies with a leading dollar sign: $1,234.56. The Currency Symbol field appears for you to replace the $

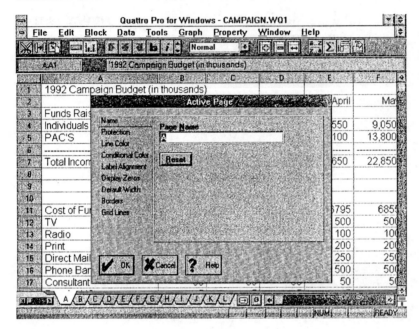

FIGURE 13.2:

The spreadsheet window with no SpeedBar, status line, or input line

with something else—such as **DM** for German marks, **Skr** for Swedish kronor, and the like.

If the currency symbol you want is not available on your keyboard, you'll need to hold down the Alt key and enter the appropriate ASCII code for that currency sign on the numeric keypad (not the numbers at the top of the keyboard). You must first enter a zero, followed by the ASCII keystrokes. These symbols and their ASCII codes are summarized below.

CURRENCY SIGN	KEYSTROKES
¢	0 Alt–155
£	0 Alt–156
¥	0 Alt–157

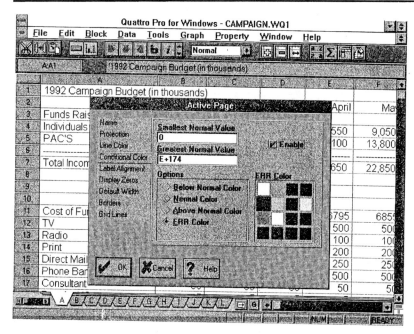

FIGURE 13.3:

The Application: International options.

CURRENCY SIGN	KEYSTROKES
Pt	0 Alt–158
ƒ	0 Alt–159

Click on the appropriate choice for Prefix or Suffix.

Punctuation

Clicking on the Punctuation option causes Quattro Pro to display the list of eight different types of numeric formats and corresponding function-argument separators. The default is International Number Format from Windows. Click on the one you want to change to.

1,234.56 (a1,a2)

1.234,56 (a1.a2)

1,234.56 (a1,a2)

1.234,56 (a1,a2)

1 234.56 (a1,a2)

1 234,56 (a1.a2)

1 234.56 (a1,a2)

1 234,56 (a1,a2)

American punctuation is the default setting, as in 1,234.56. A comma is also used to separate the arguments within a function, as in @PMT(1234.56,7%,30).

After selecting your preferred format, follow it! For example, the fifth option on the list in the dialog box uses the format 1.234,56 to display numbers. If you selected this option and entered a formula such as **@PMT(1.234,56,7%,30)**, the system would beep and return an error message—**Too many arguments**—because the formula contains three commas rather than the two required. Quattro Pro can't distinguish between the decimal separator (,) and the argument separator (,). To avoid confusion, all formats employ different punctuation for each. The correct format for the formula, then, is **@PMT(1.234,56;7%;30)**.

Date Format

Click on the date option to see the list of four alternate formats. Quattro Pro uses the default International Date Format from Windows. When you enter a date, you still must use the Ctrl-Shift-D key combination to format the cell if you want to see the date displayed in your chosen format.

These options, along with each corresponding Short International format, are:

MM/DD/YY (MM/DD)

DD/MM/YY (DD/MM)

DD.MM.YY (DD.MM)

YY–MM–DD (MM–DD)

After you have selected a format, any dates already on the spreadsheet will be reformatted immediately.

Time Format

Click on the Time option to see the list of four formats, in both long and short format. After you enter a time, use the Style List to format the cell. Quattro Pro then displays the time according to the format you have selected.

> HH:MM:SS (HH:MM)
>
> HH.MM.SS (HH.MM)
>
> HH,MM,SS (HH,MM)
>
> HHhMMmSSs (HHhMMm)

After you select a format, all serial times on the spreadsheet will be updated immediately.

Language

If you are sharing notebooks with colleagues in a country other than the U.S. or are using Quattro Pro in a country outside the U.S., you can designate that country as the Quattro Pro language. The sort order for numbers and labels will then be consistent with that country's format. Figure 13.4 lists the country settings in the dialog box.

Startup

When you first open Quattro Pro, it checks the start-up settings: the default directory for files, a notebook file that opens automatically, a Startup Macro, and the default file extension for notebook files.

Before you designate a new directory, you must create it either using the MKDIR command in DOS before entering Quattro Pro, or by using the File Manager in Windows. To access the File Manager, minimize Quattro Pro and click on the Main window. Double-click on the

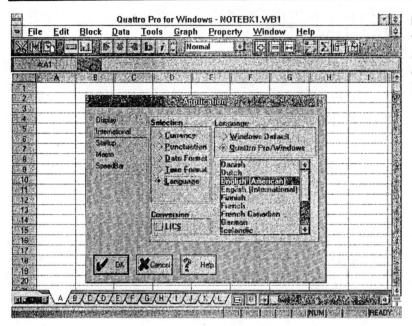

Windows File Manager icon to open it. Then select File ➤ Create
Directory. You can create a new directory, or a subdirectory under
QPW. After creating the directory, use the Task Manager to return to
Quattro Pro.

If you want to have a specific notebook loaded every time you start
the program, type the name of that program in the Autoload File field.
If the notebook file is saved in a directory other than the default (listed
right above this field), then include the path. For example, if the
notebook file is stored on the D drive in the 123 directory, enter
D:\123\FILE.WB1. That way, Quattro Pro can find the file. If you want
to run a macro when you start the program, enter its name in the Startup
Macro field.

The other options here include Undo (discussed in Chapter 2), having the beep enabled, and compatible keys. The beep sounds when you have incorrectly entered an @ function name in a formula. The compatible keys option is for users of the DOS version of Quattro Pro.

Macros

If you use macros, this option allows you to designate what is displayed on screen as the macro executes. The Windows environment is at its weakest when redrawing screens, because it slows down appreciably. You can shut down the redraw function while a macro runs in order to accelerate the process.

If you are a Quattro Pro for DOS user, you can have the forward slash key activate the DOS menu bar .

Quattro Pro allows you to build your own SpeedBars with buttons that execute commands as you program them to. This option allows you to load your SpeedBar automatically every time Quattro Pro is loaded. Check the Borland documentation for the steps to building your own SpeedBar.

Changing the Active Notebook Settings

The Active Notebook options change the settings for the notebook in which you are currently working. Select Property Menu ➤ Active Notebook to open the Active Notebook dialog box (shown in Figure 13.5).

RECALC SETTINGS

The first option on this dialog box instructs Quattro Pro how to recalculate the formulas in the notebook. The default is that all formulas are recalculated as soon as you make a change in the spreadsheet. Quattro Pro only recalculates those formulas that are affected by the change. However, if your notebook gets very complex, you may have to wait

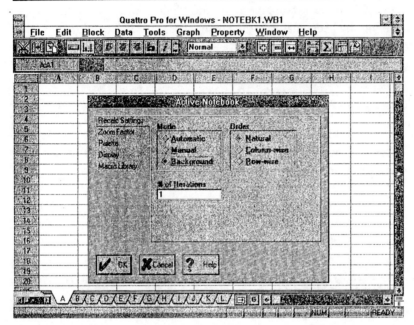

FIGURE 13.5:

The Active Notebook dialog box

after making a change for Quattro Pro to finish recalculating. So two other options are possible.

Automatic	Pauses other operations in Quattro Pro in order to finish the calculations at a faster rate than the Background setting.
Manual	Allows you to decide when to recalculate the spreadsheet. No recalculations are performed until you press the F9 key.

ZOOM FACTOR

This is a fun feature of Quattro Pro. With it you can shrink or expand the display of all of the spreadsheet windows from 25% to 200%. The default setting is 100%. This allows you to see more of, or, if you have not changed your eyeglass prescription lately, less of the spreadsheet, but more clearly. Figure 13.6 shows the spreadsheet zoomed to 200% of normal.

Easy to read, wouldn't you say? Going the other way, Figure 13.7 shows the same spreadsheet at 25% zoom.

Now it's hard to see individual figures, but you can get an idea of where all the information is on the spreadsheet page.

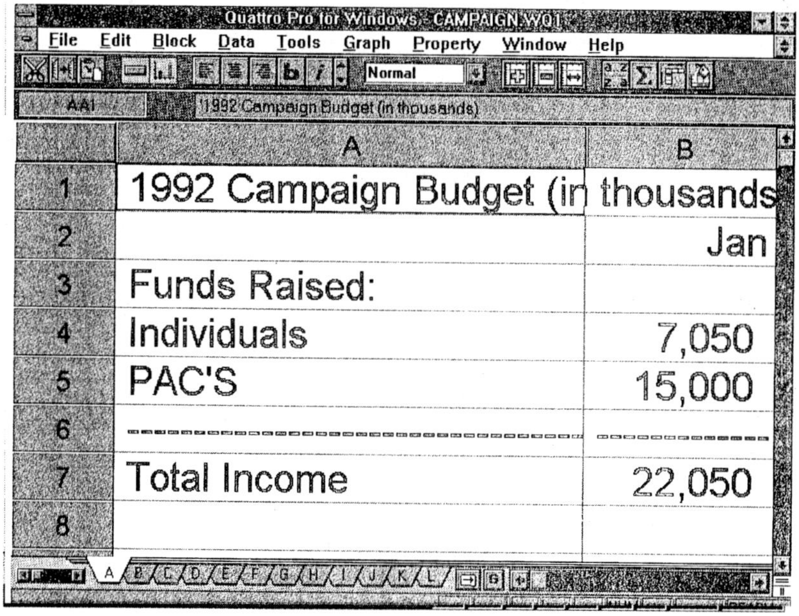

FIGURE 13.6:

The spreadsheet zoomed to 200% of normal

PALETTE

In the preceding chapters, you were exposed to changing colors for different Quattro Pro objects. When you access the Active Block dialog box and select Text Color as the attribute you want to change, a color palette appears offering color choices. The colors in that palette are derived from the colors specified in the Active Notebook Palette. So if you want to have a

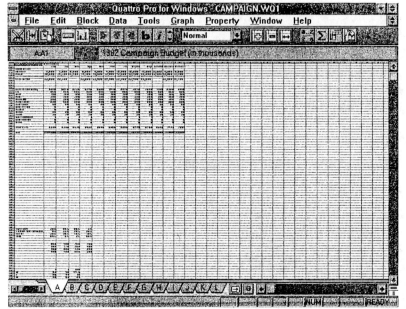

FIGURE 13.7:

The spreadsheet zoomed to 25% of normal

particular color in the individual palettes throughout the notebook, you must modify the colors in this dialog box. Click on the color you want to modify and then click on the Edit Color button. The Edit Palette Color dialog box appears. Click on the color you want, then click on OK. The color you have selected replaces the one in the default palettes.

DISPLAY

Earlier in this chapter, we discussed how you could remove the Speed-Bar and other screen attributes from the display. This option allows you to go further: you can remove the vertical and horizontal scroll bars and the page tabs from the screen display. Figure 13.8 shows the Quattro Pro screen with the scroll bars and page tabs removed.

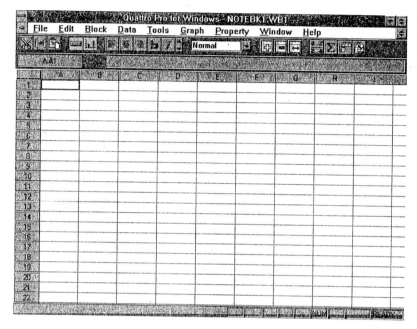

FIGURE 13.8:

Scroll bars and tabs removed from display

MACRO LIBRARY

As you become proficient with the use of macros, you can create a library containing all of your macros. Having a macro library eliminates the need to copy your macros into every notebook you create. When this option is set to Yes, Quattro Pro searches the library for the macro if it does not find it in the current notebook.

CHANGING THE ACTIVE PAGE SETTINGS

You have already used three of the options in the Active Page dialog box. You have named a spreadsheet page, activated the protection scheme, and changed the label alignment using the SpeedBar. Let's look at all the other options available through this dialog box. Figure 13.9 shows the Active Page dialog box, which you can access by clicking the right mouse button on the page tab, or by selecting Property ➤ Active Page.

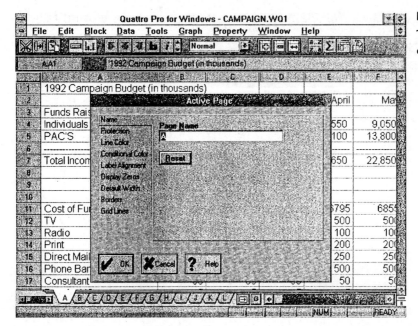

FIGURE 13.9:

The Active Page
dialog box

Line Color

We discussed the line drawing feature in Chapter 7. As well as selecting the position and form of the lines, you can specify their color. The default is black. Click on the color you want in the color palette, and both lines that are already drawn and lines that you now draw will be displayed in that color.

Conditional Color

The Conditional Color option lets you specify colors of cells according to the values displayed in them. This is handy for pointing out values that fall above or below some predefined range of normal (or acceptable) numbers, and for highlighting erroneous calculations (ERR). When you select the Conditional Color option, you'll see the dialog box shown in Figure 13.10.

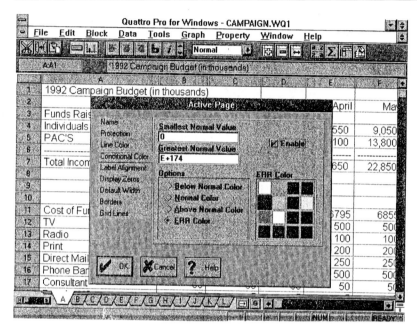

FIGURE 13.10:

The Active Page:
Conditional
Color dialog box

Quattro Pro has preset defaults for each condition: all you have to
do is click on Enable, and the colors will appear as those numbers within
each range are entered or calculated. To see which color is attached to
what value, click on the label. For example, click on Below Normal
Color, and a border appears around the designated color.

By default, the Smallest Normal Value is 0; when a number less
than 0 appears in the spreadsheet, it is colored in red. For the Greatest
Normal Value, if you enter 10000, all numbers greater than 10,000 will
be displayed in the color you specify.

The Normal Color displays in black those cells with numbers between (and including) the values you specified with the Smallest Normal Value and Greatest Normal Value options.

Enter the numbers you want for Smallest and Greatest Normal
Values and then click on Enable and on OK. Of course, the options you
select for conditional colors will not take effect until the spreadsheet

cells actually contain values that are less than, within, or greater than the ranges you have specified. Go ahead and enter some suitably bizarre numbers and watch the results. Similarly, a cell that contains an error will not actually be displayed in your chosen color until that cell reads ERR. (You can easily test this by placing the @ERR function in any cell.)

Display Zeros

When copying a formula down a row or across columns, there may be cells where the formula does not apply because the cell is blank. Quattro Pro will not display the ERR message, but will display a 0 (zero). This option allows you to suppress the display of zeros, rather than having to go to each cell individually and delete the zeros.

Default Cell Width

In previous examples, you have set the column width using the SpeedFit button, or used the mouse pointer to move the horizontal border line. The default width of each column is nine units of Characters in the default font. You can enter a new value and different unit of measure with this option. For example, if you click on Inches as the unit of measurement, the default of 9 changes to .67, which is the equivalent of 9 characters. Clicking on Centimeters yields 1.69 (which equals 9 characters per inch). For building spreadsheets for presentations, you can determine exactly the width of each column, using one of these three measurements.

To set the default width to 10 centimeters:

1. Click on Default Width in the Active Page dialog box.

2. Click on Centimeters.

3. Enter 10 in the Column Width field.

4. Click on OK.

The spreadsheet page is reformatted to reflect the new column width.

Row and Column Borders

You can remove from display the row and column borders with this option. This option is most useful when you have created a notebook with a text graph cover and need the maximum room for displaying the graph.

Showing Gridlines

In the early days of spreadsheets, it was sometimes difficult to tell where the information was located because no gridlines were available. Gridlines add visual reference points to your data entry, and to placing floating graphs. However, if you prefer the old way of working in a spreadsheet, you can turn the gridlines off by clicking on Horizontal and Vertical to remove the check marks. (Printing gridlines is set in the Spreadsheet Print Options dialog box.)

Applying a Named Style

The SpeedFormat button at the far right of the SpeedBar applies named styles. It contains too many formats to describe in detail here; we suggest you try them yourself. To apply a format:

1. Click and drag the cells you want to format.

2. Click on the SpeedFormat button. The dialog box opens, as shown in Figure 13.11. As you can see, the formats are named after composers, so we have format compositions!

3. Click on the name of the format you want to use. Before applying the format, you can see how the cells are affected in the Example window.

4. Click on OK.

Quattro Pro applies the chosen format to the selected cells.

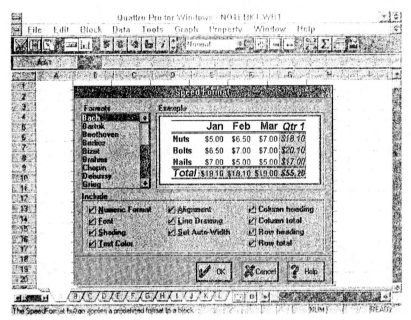

When you select the named style you want to use, you can also
decide which attributes to include. Figure 13.11 shows the Bach format.
Perhaps you want all of the format attributes except the Column heading. Click on the Column heading attribute so that the check mark is
removed, then apply the format.

To remove formatting from a block, click and drag the block and
select Normal from the Style list.

14 CHAPTER

FEATURING

Linking data among notebooks

Building 3-D links

Updating linked notebooks

Saving your workspace

Linking Notebooks

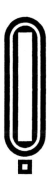

uattro Pro for Windows' notebook-linking feature highlights the program's power and effectiveness. This feature allows you to link the data in several notebooks to a master file or graph, thus extending the scope of Quattro Pro's spreadsheet capability significantly.

Linking Data among Notebooks

In Chapter 8 you learned about Quattro Pro's ability to load multiple spreadsheet pages onto the screen, and how to move from one to the other by clicking on the window. You probably found this to be a helpful feature. But there is more: Quattro Pro can *link* several notebooks together.

Suppose you are responsible for developing sales forecasts for a corporation that has three different geographical regions, each with its own sales figures. You can first create a notebook for each division: the West Coast, the Midwest, and the East Coast. Then you can display all three notebooks on-screen simultaneously and link them to a single operating statement (another notebook) in which you display, say, the total sales of the three regions. The benefit of this is clear: if you revise one number in the West Coast notebook, the master notebook will reflect that change immediately.

CREATING A NOTEBOOK LINK

To link notebooks, you have to add a *link reference* to an entry in a cell. There are three ways to do this:

- Type in the reference and enclose it in square brackets

- Use the point method to establish the link

- Make a 3-D link, in which a link is established among the same cell addresses in every open notebook.

Once you establish a link reference, the notebook to which a cell is linked does not have to be open to be active. Quattro Pro can "refresh" the links from the files on disk.

When you decide to create links, your work will be much easier if all the files are in the same directory. The master notebook must be a Quattro Pro for Windows file, but the supporting files can be in any format that Quattro Pro for Windows can read, such as Quattro, Lotus 1-2-3, or Excel.

TYPING IN A LINK REFERENCE

The format for entering a link reference is +*[filename]block*. For example, if the file you want to reference is in the same directory as the Quattro Pro software (probably C:\QPW\) and is named SALESW.WB1, and the cell you wish to reference is cell B6 on spreadsheet page A, the entry would be +[SALESW.WB1]A:B6. When you type this link reference in a cell, the cell will display whatever is in cell A:B6 in the SALESW.WB1 notebook.

Figure 14.1 shows two notebooks, identical in design, tiled. The left one, which we've called COMPANY, is the master notebook and is concerned with the sales forecast for the entire company. The one on the right is a supporting notebook named SALESW, which lists the sales forecast for the western region.

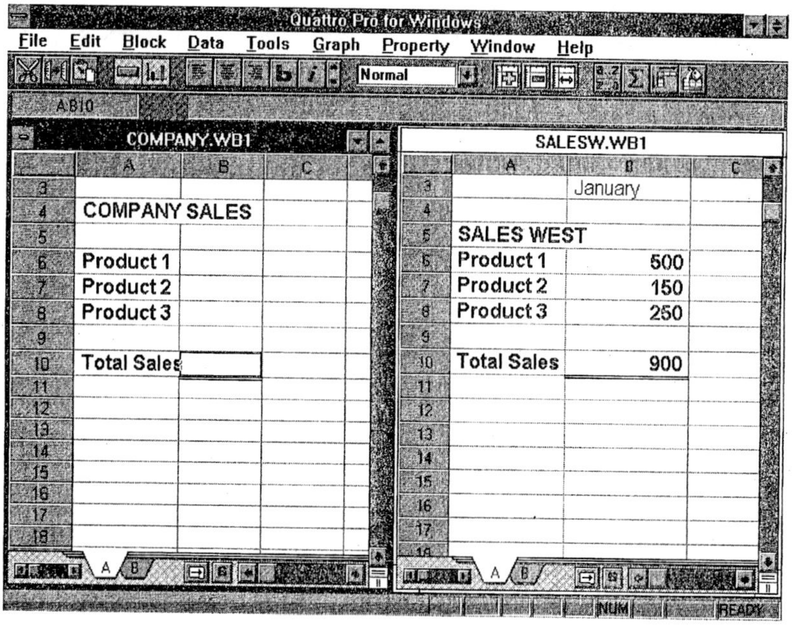

FIGURE 14.1:

The COMPANY and SALESW notebooks

Create and save the notebooks now, then follow these steps to create the link reference:

1. Make COMPANY the active notebook, if it is not so already, by clicking on it.

2. Move the cell selector to cell B6 on the COMPANY notebook.

3. Type +[SALESW.WB1]A:B6.

4. Press Enter.

The link will be established and the value 500 inserted in cell A:B6 in the COMPANY notebook. If the SALESW file had not been opened, the link would still have been created and the value inserted. You can create a link with *just* the master notebook open, as long as you know the names of the supporting notebook(s) and cell(s) you wish to reference.

Note that in order for the link to work, both notebooks must first have been created and saved.

CREATING A LINK REFERENCE WITH THE POINT METHOD

Using the same two notebooks, you can create a link reference with the pointing method:

1. Move the cell selector to cell B6 on the COMPANY notebook.

2. Press the Delete key to erase the existing notebook link.

3. Type + to begin the formula.

4. Click on cell B6 in the SALESW notebook. Notice on the entry line that the link reference is entered for you.

5. Click on the check mark to create the link reference and reposition the cell selector in the COMPANY notebook.

The link is created.

The pointing method is the most accurate way to create a link, since you can see the location of the cell(s) that you are referencing. However, unlike with the previously mentioned method, you must have *all* the supporting notebooks open to make this method work.

MAKING A 3-D LINK

In order to build this 3-D link, create two new notebooks similar to SALESW and save them as **SALESE** and **SALESC**. You can either do this using File ➤ Save As on SALESW, or by copying the information as SALESW onto the Clipboard, opening new notebooks, and pasting it into them.

Since your master notebook and supporting notebooks share the *same layout*, you can create a link reference with a single command:

1. Close any notebooks that do *not* support the master notebook.

2. In the master notebook, move the cell selector to cell B6.

3. Begin your function: @SUM(.

4. Next, type brackets and the *: @SUM([*]. The brackets indicate the use of other open notebooks, and the * indicates that every open notebook should be linked. To finish the linked reference, add the cell reference: @SUM([*]A:B6).

This function will sum all the values in cell B6 of all the open notebooks and insert that total in the master notebook.

Now let's finish the formulas in the master notebook:

1. Copy the contents of cell B6 into cells B7 and B8 using the Copy and Paste buttons.

2. Move to cell B10 and enter a formula to sum the values for the three products: @SUM(B6..B8).

Now COMPANY reflects the sales of all three regions.

Limiting the 3-D Link

In the previous example, the brackets contained the * symbol to indicate to Quattro Pro that *all* open notebooks should be linked to the master notebook and included in the calculation. You can decide which open notebooks to link by substituting other codes for the *, as detailed in Table 14.1.

LINK CODE	EFFECT
[]	Quattro Pro for Windows looks first in the active notebook for a value and then in all open notebooks
[*]	Links all open notebooks to the master
[AB*]	Links to all notebooks that have the letters *AB* (or any letters you choose) at the beginning of their names. For example, a notebook named FIRSTQ would be linked to the master if the entry in the brackets were [FI*], while a notebook named FQRTR would not be linked
[A*B]	Links the master to all open notebooks that have names that begin with the letter *A* and end with the letter *B* (or any letters you choose). For example, a notebook named BREAD would be linked if the entry in the brackets were [B*D], while a notebook named BROKE would not be linked
[A??]	Links the master to all open notebooks that have three-character names beginning with *A*. For example, a notebook named ATE would be included in the link, while a notebook named BED would not

TABLE 14.1:

3-D link codes

LINK CODE	EFFECT
[A?E]	Links the master to open notebooks that have three-character names that begin with the letter A and end with E. You can add question marks as needed. For example, [A???E] would link all open notebooks whose names begin with A, end in E, and have three characters in between

TABLE 14.1:

3-D link codes (continued)

MOVING AND COPYING LINK FORMULAS

If you copy a cell in a master notebook that contains a link reference (as we did in the above example), the cell addresses in the link will be adjusted in a relative fashion.

If you move a cell or block in a supporting notebook to another location, any link references to it in an on-screen master notebook will be adjusted accordingly. The supporting notebook must be loaded in order for the adjustment to happen. If you want to create a link to unloaded notebooks, use block names in the link reference. Then, when you load a master notebook, Quattro Pro will automatically update any block names that have been moved.

UPDATING LINKED NOTEBOOKS

When you load a master notebook that has links in it, Quattro Pro for Windows automatically verifies whether the supporting notebooks are loaded. If they are not, Quattro Pro displays the Link Update menu with the following choices:

Open Supporting	Directs Quattro Pro to load all supporting notebooks
Update References	Directs Quattro Pro to update the references without loading the supporting notebooks
None	Causes Quattro Pro to display **NA** temporarily in the link-referenced cells

If you choose not to open the supporting notebooks or update the references when prompted, you can open or update them later. To do so, choose Tools ➤ Update Links. You'll have the following options:

Open Links	Opens one or more files linked to the master notebook.
Refresh Links	Updates the links to the referenced notebook files. Before the updating occurs, Quattro Pro presents a list of all the referenced files. Select the files from which you want the values by clicking on the file name.
Delete Links	Removes the link references to one or more of the supporting notebooks. When you select this option, Quattro Pro presents a list of the supporting notebooks. Select which link(s) to delete by clicking the notebook name.
Change Link	Unlinks the master notebook from a selected supporting notebook and then creates identical links to another notebook of your choice.

ADDING A GRAPH TO A LINK

Just as you linked a cell from a supporting notebook to a master notebook, you can link a series of data to a master graph. For example, graph the total sales figures by product in the COMPANY notebook with a floating bar graph. If you tile the notebook windows, you'll see how the bars in the graph move as you change the sales figures in any of the supporting, linked notebooks. Figure 14.2 shows an example of such a link.

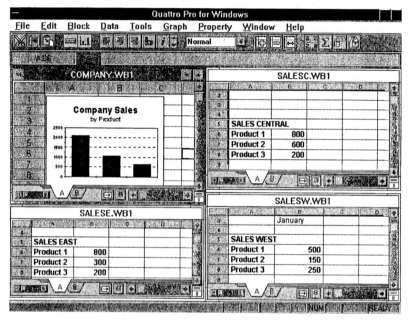

FIGURE 14.2:

A graph linked to three notebooks

SAVING THE WORKSPACE

Saving a workspace involves saving the position of the assortment of notebooks and spreadsheet windows that you have been working in. In the previous example, you could save the four open notebooks in the same positions, as seen in Figure 14.2. If you have made changes to the notebooks, you will have to save them also.

To save a workspace:

1. Select File ➤ Workspace. The Save Workspace dialog box appears.

2. In the dialog box, type a name with the .WSB extension, then click on OK.

To retrieve a Workspace:

1. Select File ➤ Workspace ➤ Restore.

2. In the dialog box, click on the Workspace name, then click on OK.

The notebooks and spreadsheet windows magically appear!

15 CHAPTER

Using Formulas and Functions

In this chapter, we will explore different types of functions and their uses with and within formulas. The key difference between a function and a formula is that a *function* is a condensation of a complex *formula*. Also, a function always begins with an @ symbol. Begin by using File ➤ New to open an empty notebook so you can try out some of the functions and formulas that we describe in this chapter.

Why a Function?

In previous chapters, you saw how we used the @SUM function to total a long column of numbers, because @SUM(C12..C24) was much simpler than entering the longer formula +C12+C13+C14+C15+C16+C17 +C18+C19 +C20+C21+C22+C23+C24. All of Quattro Pro for Windows' many functions are designed similarly to simplify your work.

Suppose you want to calculate the monthly payments on a loan when you know the principal, interest rate, and term. The formula for calculating the payments is fairly complex, so to simplify matters Quattro Pro offers the @PMT function, which calculates the payment directly from the known information. If cell A1 contains the principal amount of the loan, cell A2 the monthly interest rate, and cell A3 the term of the loan (in months), then the function @PMT(A1,A2,A3) will calculate and display the monthly payments on the loan.

Getting Help with Functions

Let's face it—it's hard to remember which arguments go where in functions, especially when you're first learning. But you can use the Quattro Pro Help system to get a quick reminder at any time.

Select Help ➤ Functions. This brings you to the Function Descriptions screen, shown maximized in Figure 15.1. From there, you can select the Function Index to see a list of individual functions that you might need help with. Or you can select Function Arguments to get help with the topic of arguments. Or you can select a specific function category—say, Financial—to find out which functions are of particular interest at the moment.

As usual, you can click on the Minimize button in the document window at any time to leave the Help system and return to your work.

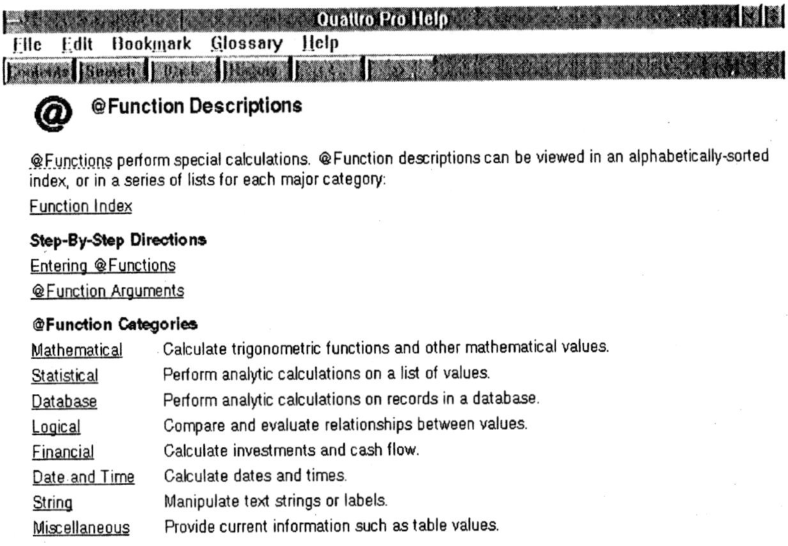
Quattro Pro Help
File Edit Bookmark Glossary Help
@Function Descriptions
@Functions perform special calculations. @Function descriptions can be viewed in an alphabetically-sorted index, or in a series of lists for each major category:
Function Index
Step-By-Step Directions
Entering @Functions
@Function Arguments
@Function Categories
Mathematical Calculate trigonometric functions and other mathematical values.
Statistical Perform analytic calculations on a list of values.
Database Perform analytic calculations on records in a database.
Logical Compare and evaluate relationships between values.
Financial Calculate investments and cash flow.
Date and Time Calculate dates and times.
String Manipulate text strings or labels.
Miscellaneous Provide current information such as table values.

FIGURE 15.1: The Function Topics help screen

Types of Function Arguments

Most functions require at least one *argument*, enclosed in parentheses, to perform their calculations. The arguments needed for the @PMT function are the principal, the monthly interest, and the term of the loan in months. One function can also be another function's argument. There are eight types of function: mathematical, statistical, database, logical, financial, date and time, string, and miscellaneous. For simplicity, we have grouped them as follows:

- Numeric
- String
- Date
- Block

In addition, some functions support *lists* as arguments. These argument types are discussed below.

NUMERIC ARGUMENTS

Many functions work only on numbers and not on any other type of data. A numeric argument must be one of the following:

- A number

- A formula that results in a number

- A reference to a cell that contains a number or a formula or function that results in a number—A1, for example, if A1 contains the formula 200*4 or the function @COS(37).

The @SQRT function *returns* (calculates and displays) the square root of a number. Therefore, @SQRT expects to operate on a number. Entering **@SQRT(Smith)** or **@SQRT(31-DEC-93)** results in an **Invalid reference** message, since trying to find the square root of a name or date is nonsensical.

When Quattro Pro cannot perform a requested calculation because the argument is of the wrong type, you will see the **Invalid Reference** error message. But when the argument is of the right type, yet still mathematically invalid—as in @SQRT(−5)—the function will return **ERR** in its cell. (Quattro Pro does not recognize complex numbers.)

STRING ARGUMENTS

Some functions expect labels (also called *character strings* or just *strings*) as their argument. For example, the @UPPER function converts all lowercase letters in a label to uppercase. A label argument can be one of the following:

- A label enclosed in quotation marks

- A label function

- A reference to a cell that contains a label—or a formula or function that results in a label

For example, the function @UPPER(Hello there) returns **HELLO THERE.** If cell A1 contains the label **Joe Smith**, then the function @UPPER(A1) will return **JOE SMITH**. If cell B7 contains the label **Welcome**, and cell B9 contains the label **Quattro Pro Users**, the function @UPPER(B7&B9) will return **WELCOME QUATTRO PRO USERS**. (The & operator connects labels, so cell B7 will need a blank space after *Welcome* in order for the function to space all the words out properly.) If you like, try this on your spreadsheet and set up a complex message of your own.

Obviously, you cannot convert a number to uppercase; hence, a function such as @UPPER(123.45) would return only ERR. (If the number were enclosed in quotes, however the function would simply echo the number.)

Date and Time Arguments

As we mentioned in Chapter 2, dates entered using Ctrl-Shift-D are displayed on the screen as dates, though they are actually stored by Quattro Pro as serial dates (which are just numbers). Technically speaking, then, any function that operates on numbers will also operate on dates. But practically speaking, some functions are designed to work specifically on dates.

The @DAY function, for example, takes a serial date argument and returns the day of the month as a number between 1 and 31. So @DAY(34090) tells you that serial date 34090 (May 1, 1993) fell on the first of the month.

BLOCK ARGUMENTS

Some Quattro Pro functions operate on entire groups or blocks of cells. For example, the @SUM function calculates the sum of all the numbers in a block of cells.

Figure 15.2 shows a sample spreadsheet with several numbers in the block of cells B3 to D10. The total of all the numbers in that block is calculated in cell D12 with the function @SUM(B3..D10). Of course, changing any number in the block will instantly recalculate the total.

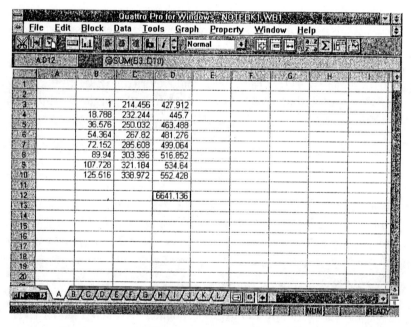

FIGURE 15.2:

The sample spreadsheet with the @SUM formula

LIST ARGUMENTS

Some functions allow lists of items as function arguments. Such a function can have any number of arguments, separated by commas: values, formulas, functions, cell references, and even blocks. The only restrictions are that the entire function size cannot exceed 254 characters, and that all the data types must match.

For example, the @SUM function also accepts lists. Therefore, the function @SUM(100,C99,B3..D10) calculates the sum of the number 100 plus the number stored in cell C99 plus all the numbers in the block of cells from B3 to D10. Note that each of the three arguments is separated by a comma, as required in all functions that work on lists or multiple arguments.

Summary of Quattro Pro for Windows Functions

This section presents a brief description of most functions that Quattro Pro for Windows offers, categorized by the type of task they perform. There is no need for you to memorize the entire list; instead, just note those functions you think will prove useful in your own work with Quattro Pro. (Quattro Pro offers far more functions than most individuals will ever use.)

Later in this chapter, we'll demonstrate techniques for building powerful formulas that employ a variety of Quattro Pro's functions.

COUNTING AND AGGREGATION FUNCTIONS

Counting and aggregation functions perform calculations on groups (blocks) of cells. All these functions accept blocks, lists, numbers, formulas, functions, and cell references as arguments. For example, the function @SUM(A1..Z28) sums all numeric values in the block of spreadsheets cells from A1 to Z28.

The function @SUM(A1,B3..R9,200,J22/2) adds up the number in cell A1, plus the numbers in the block of cells from B3 to R9, plus the number 200, plus one-half the quantity in cell J22. Any nonnumeric entries that these functions come across will be counted as zero.

Here are some of Quattro Pro's counting and aggregation functions:

@AVG(*list*)   Averages the numbers in a *list*

@COUNT(*list*)	Counts the number of nonblank cells in a *list*
@MAX(list)	Select the highest number (or the latest date) from a *list* of numbers (or dates)
@MIN(*list*)	Selects the lowest number (or earliest date) from a *list* of numbers (or dates)
@STD(*list*)	Calculates the standard deviation of a *list* of numbers
@SUM(*list*)	Adds a *list* of numbers together
@VAR(*list*)	Calculates the variance of a *list* of numbers

FINANCIAL FUNCTIONS

Financial functions perform calculations that are commonly used in financial work, such as computing the payment on a loan, future value, present value, and depreciation. When using financial functions, you must make sure that the various arguments have matching units.

For example, to calculate the *monthly* payment on a loan when you know only the *annual* interest rate and the *years* of the term, you must first divide the annual interest rate by 12 (to get the monthly interest rate) and multiply the number of years by 12 (to get the total number of months).

Not that there's anything special about monthly payments. Suppose you're keen to know the *daily* payment on a home loan with a principal of $100,000, an annual interest rate of 9.75 percent and a term of 30 years. You would first need to divide the rate by 365 and multiply the term by 365. With time expressed in the same unit, the function @PMT(100000,9.75%/365,30*365) could then operate successfully.

Here are several of Quattro Pro's financial functions:

@CTERM (*interest,future, present*)	Determines the number of compounding periods required for an investment at a *present* value to reach a *future* value, given a fixed *interest* rate.
@DDB(*cost, salvage, life,period*)	Calculates the depreciation allowance for a given asset at a certain *period* in the investment, given the initial *cost, salvage* value, and *life* of the asset (using the double-declining balance method).
@FV(*payments, interest,term*)	Returns the future value of a series of regular *payments* at a fixed *interest* rate, for a specified *term*. (This function is included in Quattro Pro for compatibility with Quattro and Lotus 1-2-3.)
@FVAL(*rate, nper,pmt,<pv>, <type>*)	Returns the future value of a series of regular payments at a fixed interest *rate*, for a specified term. This is a more accurate version of the future value calculation above. The arguments in <> are optional.
@IRR(*guess, block*)	Returns the internal rate of return for a *block* of cash flows, based on an initial *guess* (estimate).
@PMT(*principal, interest,term*)	Calculates the payment on a loan with a given *principal, interest* rate, and *term*.

MATHEMATICAL FUNCTIONS

These functions perform mathematical operations on numbers—and all expect numeric arguments, except for @PI and @RAND, which do not use any arguments.

Here are a number of Quattro Pro's mathematical functions:

@ABS(x)	Converts the number x to its absolute (positive) value
@COS(x)	Determines the cosine of x
@DEGREES(x)	Converts x radians to degrees
@EXP(x)	Calculates e to the x power
@INT(x)	Lops off the decimal portion of x, leaving an integer value
@LN(x)	Calculates the natural logarithm of x
@LOG(x)	Calculates the base-10 logarithm of x
@PI	Gives the value of &p to as many places as the cell is wide (up to 13)
@RADIANS(x)	Converts x degrees to radians
@RAND	Returns a random decimal number between 0 and 1
@ROUND(x,y)	Rounds the number x to y decimal places of accuracy
@SIN(x)	Determines the sine of x
@SQRT(x)	Calculates the square root of x
@TAN(x)	Determines the tangent of x

DATE AND TIME FUNCTIONS

Date and time functions operate on Quattro Pro *serial date* and *time* values. Serial dates, described in detail in Chapter 2, are calculated based on the number of days elapsed since December 31, 1899. Serial times are calculated as the percentage through the day, from 0 (for midnight) to 0.999999 (11:59:59 PM). For example, 0.50 is noon, exactly halfway through the day. Serial times can be tacked onto serial dates, so 34090.5 tells you that serial date 34090 (May 1, 1993) is noon on May 1, 1993.

Date and time functions accept a variety of arguments, and they can be used to convert numbers or labels to serial dates and times. (In the list, *serial date* means serial date *and* time.)

@DATE(*year, month,day*)	Converts a given *year, month,* and *day* into a serial date
@DATEVALUE (*datestring*)	Returns a serial date from a label or character *string,* in quotes, in an acceptable date format (*dd-mmm-yy, dd-mmm,* or *mmm- yy*)
@DAY(*serialdate*)	Reveals the day of the month (1 to 31) of a given *serial date*
@HOUR (*serialtime*)	Reveals the hour (0 to 24) of a given *serial time*
@MINUTE (*serialtime*)	Reveals the minute (0 to 59) of a given *serial time*
@MONTH (*serialdate*)	Reveals in which month (1 to 12) a given *serial date* lies
@NOW	Prints the current date and time as a serial number (no argument needed)
@SECOND (*serialtime*)	Reveals the second (0 to 59) of a given *serial time*
@TIME(*hour, minute,second*)	Converts an *hour, minute,* and *second* into a serial time
@TIMEVALUE (*timestring*)	Returns the serial time from the time value stored as a label

@TODAY	Gives the current date (no argument needed)
@YEAR (*serialdate*)	Gives the year of a given *serial date* as a value between 0 (for 1900) and 199 (for 2099)

LOGIC FUNCTIONS

Logic functions study the existence of an item, or the relationship between two items, and decide whether it is true or false. Following the universal standard, Quattro Pro signifies true by the number 1 and false by the number 0.

The function @IF is the only logic function that does not directly answer true or false. Instead, @IF returns whatever you want it to, based on the result of a comparison. It uses the basic structure @IF(*this is true, then return this, otherwise return that*). For example, when translated into plain English, the function @IF(A1<10,"Less than","Greater than") says, "If the number in cell A1 is less than 10, then display 'Less than' in the cell; otherwise display 'Greater than.' " Try it now if you like. We will give examples of how you can apply this useful function later in this chapter.

Here are a few of Quattro Pro's logic functions:

@FALSE	Returns the logical decision of false (0) automatically (no argument needed)
@IF(*condition, true false*)	Returns whatever is in the *true* argument if the comparison in *condition* proves true; otherwise returns whatever is in the *false* argument
@TRUE	Returns the logical decision of true (1) automatically (no argument needed)

STRING FUNCTIONS

String functions operate on labels (nonnumeric data). Most use at least one label type of argument, and many also use numeric arguments. For example, the @REPEAT function repeats a character a certain number of times, using the syntax @REPEAT(character,n). Thus, the function @REPEAT(=,80) prints 80 equal signs across the screen. If cell A1 contains the character A, and cell A2 contains the number 20, then the function @REPEAT(A1,A2) will display twenty A's: AAAAAAAAAAAAAAAAAAAA. Try this too if you like.

Here is a partial list of Quattro Pro's string functions:

@CHAR(*x*)	Returns the ASCII character of *x*
@HEXTONUM (*string*)	Converts the hexadecimal number stored as *string* to a decimal value
@LENGTH (*string*)	Returns the length of *string*
@LOWER (*string*)	Prints all letters in *string* as lowercase
@NUMTOHEX (*x*)	Converts the decimal number *x* to a hexadecimal value
@PROPER (*string*)	Prints *string* with the first letter of each word in uppercase, and all other letters in lowercase
@REPEAT (*string*,*n*)	Prints *string* *n* times
@TRIM(*string*)	Removes all blank spaces from *string*
@UPPER(*string*)	Prints all letters in *string* as uppercase

@VALUE(*string*)   Returns numeric characters stored as numeric data in *string*

MISCELLANEOUS FUNCTIONS

These miscellaneous functions perform a variety of advanced tasks. Many are used only in *macros* (stored series of keystrokes that can be invoked with a single key) or extremely sophisticated spreadsheets. However, @VLOOKUP and @HLOOKUP might be useful to you right away.

Here are some of Quattro Pro's miscellaneous functions:

@@(*cell address*)   Prints the contents of the cell at *cell address*

@CHOOSE(*n, list*)   Prints the *n*th item from the *list* of options

@COLS(*block*)   Prints the number of columns in the specified *block*

@HLOOKUP (*x,block,n*)   Looks up the value *x* in *block*, and prints the value from *n* rows down

@MEMAVAIL   Reveals the amount of RAM memory currently available

@MEMEMS-AVAIL   Returns the amount of expanded memory (EMS) available (no argument needed)

@ROWS(*block*)   Counts and displays the number of rows in *block*

@VLOOKUP (*x,block,n*)   Looks up the value *x* in *block*, and prints the value from *n* columns across

DATABASE STATISTICAL FUNCTIONS

The database statistical functions listed below are similar to the counting and aggregation functions listed earlier, but they are used specifically with

Quattro Pro databases. All need three arguments to run: the database *block*, database *field* (or *column* therein), and *criterion* range. (For more information about databases, see Chapter 12.)

Here are some of Quattro Pro's database statistical functions:

@DAVG(*block*, *field,criterion*)	Calculates the average of numbers in *field*, given a *block* and *criterion* range
@DCOUNT (*block,field*, *criterion*)	Counts the number of nonblank cells in a *field*, given a *block* and *criterion* range
@DMAX(*block*, *field,criterion*)	Selects the highest number (or latest date) from a *field*, given a *block* and *criterion* range
@DMIN(*block*, *field,criterion*)	Selects the lowest number (or earliest date) from a *field*, given a *block* and *criterion* range
@DSUM(*block*, *column,criterion*)	Sums the numbers in a *column* of a *field* that meet the *criterion* range

A Shortcut for Entering Functions

A handy technique for entering functions is to use the Functions button. Suppose you wanted to calculate the average of the numbers in cells A1..A13. You would use the @AVG function to calculate the average as follows:

1. Enter the numbers into column A, as per Figure 15.3.

2. Move the cell selector to cell B14.

3. Press F2. The Edit SpeedBar appears.

4. Click on the @ sign in the SpeedBar. The Functions dialog box appears, as shown in Figure 15.3.

5. Click on the @AVG function.

6. Click on OK to select the function. **@AVG(** appears on the input line.

7. Press Home to move the cell selector to cell A1. The function now reads **@AVG(A1.**

8. Click and drag cells A1..A13. The function now reads **@AVG(A1..A13.**

9. Type) (a close parenthesis) to complete the function as **@AVG(A1..A13).**

10. Click on the check mark to insert the function into the cell.

Cell B14 now displays **87.38**, the average of the numbers in the block A1..A13. On the input line, you can still see the actual function, @AVG(A1..A13).

If you want to save this spreadsheet now, go ahead.

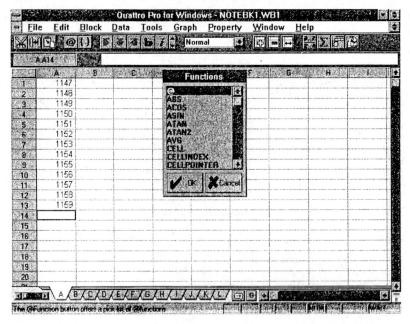

FIGURE 15.3:

The Functions dialog box

Nesting Functions

You can *nest* functions inside other functions, as long as you remember to include a complete pair of parentheses for each function. In fact, most Quattro Pro functions must have an equal number of opening and closing parentheses to be acceptable; if one or more is missing, Quattro Pro returns an error message.

Nested functions can be helpful even in relatively simple calculations. For example, the @SQRT function works only with positive numbers, so @SQRT(A1) would return **ERR** if cell A1 contained a negative number. You can avoid such an error by nesting the @ABS function, which ensures that an argument remains or becomes positive, inside the @SQRT function: @SQRT(@ABS(A1)).

Because Quattro Pro always calculates by starting with the innermost parentheses and working its way out, this function *first* returns the absolute value of the number in cell A1, and *then* the square root of that absolute value. For example, if cell A1 contained −81, the @ABS function would convert it to +81 and the @SQRT function would return 9, which would be displayed in the cell that contained the function.

@ROUND is another function that commonly has other functions nested within it. It rounds a number to a specified number of decimal places. Suppose you want to know the monthly payment on a loan, with the result rounded to two decimal places. The principal for the loan (say, $50,000.00) is stored in cell B1. The annual interest rate (10 percent) is stored in cell B2. The term (30 years) is stored in cell B3. The function @ROUND(@PMT(B1,B2/12,B3*12),2), then, displays monthly payments to two decimal places.

How so? The innermost function, @PMT(B1,B2/12,B3*12), calculates the monthly payment by dividing the annual interest rate by 12 to get the monthly interest rate, and then multiplying the years by 12 to get the number of months. This function returns the value 438.785785 and substitutes it into the function @ROUND(438.785785,2). The actual value returned by the entire function is 438.79—that is, the monthly payment on the loan rounded to the nearest penny is $438.79.

Even though these examples show only two levels of function nesting, you can actually nest functions as deeply as you wish. In fact, a single function can contain any number of nested functions, as long as it does not exceed the 254-character limit and the number of open parentheses matches the number of close parentheses.

Advanced Use of Operators

In our examples so far, you've seen the use of the basic arithmetic operators: + (addition), − (subtraction), * (multiplication), and / (division). Quattro Pro actually offers quite a variety of operators, listed in Table 15.1 in descending order of precedence.

Operators that have the same level of precedence are calculated from left to right as they appear in a formula. Any natural order of precedence can be overridden by the use of parentheses, just as in everyday mathematics: any operator enclosed in parentheses will be

OPERATOR	DESCRIPTION	PRECEDENCE
^	Exponentiation	7
−, +	Negative, positive	6
*, /	Multiplication, division	5
−, +	Subtraction, addition	4
>=	Greater than or equal to	3
<=	Less than or equal to	3
<, >	Less than, greater than	3
=, <>	Equal, not equal	3
#NOT#	Logical NOT	2
#AND#, #OR#	Logical AND, logical OR	1
&	Links two labels (strings)	1

TABLE 15.1:

Quattro Pro for Windows operators and their order of precedence

used first in the calculation. (The logical operators =, <>, <, >, <=, >=, #AND#, #OR#, and #NOT# are special operators used with logical functions.)

The order of precedence of operators can affect the results of a formula dramatically. For instance, the formula 12+2*100 equals 212 because the multiplication (2*100) takes place before the addition, according to the order of precedence. However, using parentheses to group the addition, as in (12+2)*100, forces the addition to take place before the multiplication, so the result is 1400 (i.e., 14*100).

By natural order of precedence, exponentiation takes place before addition, subtraction, multiplication, or division. Therefore, 10^3+17 equals 1017—that is, 10 cubed (1000) plus 17. Using parentheses to group the addition, as in 10^(3+17), yields the much larger number of 10 to the 20th power because now the addition takes place before exponentiation. Similarly, the formula 4096^1/4 first raises 4096 to the power of 1, then divides that result by 4 to yield the result 1024. However, 4096^(1/4) raises 4096 to the power of 1/4, which equals the 4th root of 4096, or 8.

Keep in mind that if you leave out parentheses for grouping, Quattro Pro for Windows will follow the order of precedence specified in Table 15.1. If you are not sure how Quattro Pro will perform a complex calculation, just add parentheses as required to ensure that it performs as you want it to.

For example, the formula 2*(43*(5+10)+(4*7)) will first add the 5 and 10 in the middle, since they are surrounded by parentheses. Then it will multiply the result (15) by 43, add that result (645) to 28 (the product of 4 by 7), and finally multiply *that* result (673) by 2, yielding a total of 1346. Note that the parentheses around 4*7 are redundant; the formula 2*(43*(5+10)+4*7) works as well. Since the * operator between the 4 and the 7 has precedence over the + to the left of the 4, the formula would never have added 43*(5+10) to 4 before multiplying by 7. Still, it doesn't hurt to add too many parentheses if you're not sure; it'll take only a little more time to type the formula out.

Sample Applications of Formulas

In this section, we'll discuss and demonstrate some practical applications of the concepts we've discussed so far. Open an empty spreadsheet page now.

Let's suppose you are responsible for developing some financial scenarios. Your task is to determine the feasibility of expanding the plant and facilities to meet expected increases in sales. The sample formulas and functions below will aid you in making decisions.

CALCULATING THE MORTGAGE PAYMENT

The spreadsheet in Figure 15.4 contains some loan information, including the monthly payback and total payback. The values in cells C1, C2,

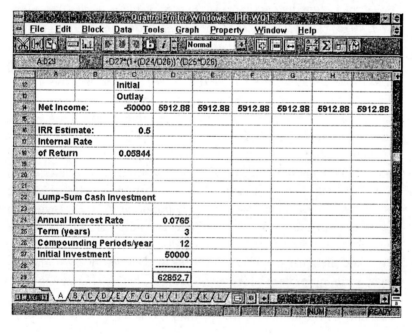

FIGURE 15.4:

Spreadsheet that calculates the payment on a loan

and C3 were typed in simply as numbers. The payment and payback were calculated with a function and formula respectively.

The financial function that calculates the monthly payment, @PMT(C1,C2/12,C3*12), is stored in cell C5. As mentioned before, because the loan parameters are expressed in years (an 11 percent *annual* interest rate and a *5-year* term), the function divides the annual interest rate in cell C2 by 12 to calculate the monthly interest rate and multiplies the term in cell C3 by 12 to calculate the number of months in the loan. The result is the monthly payment on the loan.

The formula that calculates the total payback simply multiplies the monthly payment in cell C5 by the number of months required to pay off the loan (the years in cell C3 multiplied by 12). The formula +C5*(C3*12) in cell C6 calculates this value.

The monthly payment on the mortgage can now be used in some other calculations. Save the spreadsheet now as LOAN (in case you make accidental deletions later) and continue reading.

CALCULATING THE INTERNAL RATE OF RETURN

The next step is to calculate the rate of return on net sales in order to make a viable return on the capital outlay. Cash flows are based on the capacity of the plant and equipment. The initial entry is negative, since it corresponds to the capital outlay. Monthly cash flows are then reduced by monthly carrying costs to determine the net operating income.

To calculate the internal rate of return, input the block of cash flows, including the initial outlay, as arguments of the @IRR function. The rate returned will be somewhere between 0 and 1, with 0 being no return and 1 being 100 percent return. (It is possible to have a rate of return higher than 100 percent.) In Figure 15.5, @IRR(C16,C14..O14) calculates the internal rate of return using the estimate of 50 percent in cell C16 and all the cash flows in the block C14..O14. (The months extend past the right edge of the screen out to December.)

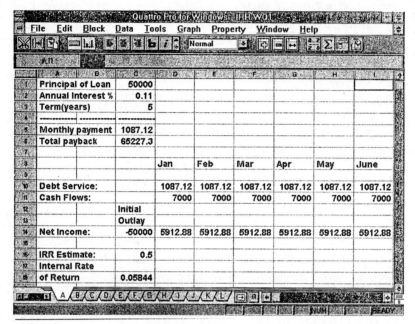

FIGURE 15.5:

The internal rate of return

COMPUTING THE FUTURE VALUE OF A LUMP-SUM INVESTMENT

Suppose that you want to compare the investment of expanding the physical capacities of your firm to the simpler investment of depositing the return in an interest-bearing account.

Quattro Pro for Windows does not have a function that calculates the future value of a lump-sum investment directly, but you do not need such a function if you know which formula to use. The future value of a lump-sum investment can be calculated with the complex formula $Inv*(1+(APR/Per))^{(Term*Per)}$, where Inv is the dollar amount of the lump sum investment, APR is the annual percentage rate, Per is the number of compounding periods per year, and $Term$ is the number of periods in the investment.

Figure 15.6 shows a lump-sum investment calculation, given an interest rate of 7.6 percent compounded monthly and a 3-year term. Cell D24 contains 0.0765 (the annual interest rate), cell D25 contains 3 (the number of years of the investment), cell D26 contains 12 (the number of compounding periods per year), and cell D27 contains 50000 (the single lump-sum investment). The formula in cell D29, +D27*(1+(D24/D26))^(D25*D26), returns **62852.74**—or $62,852.74, the future value of the initial investment after three years.

Save the spreadsheet again, then switch to a clean spreadsheet page in case you want to try some of the following sample spreadsheets.

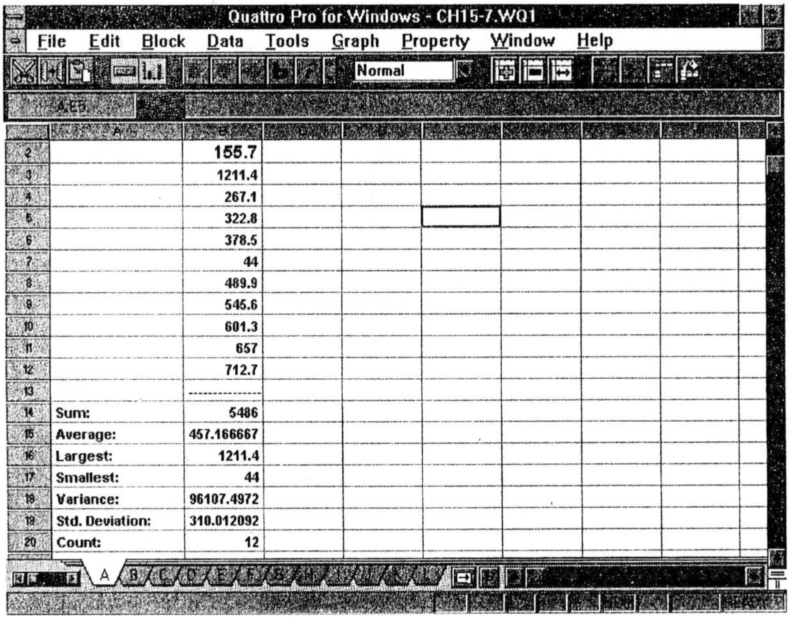

FIGURE 15.6:

The annual return on an investment

SAMPLE COUNTING AND AGGREGATION FUNCTIONS

Figure 15.7 shows a spreadsheet with sample counting and aggregation functions. Cell B14 contains @SUM(B1..B12), which displays the sum of the numbers in the block B1..B12. Cell B15 contains the function @AVG(B1..B12), which displays the average of these numbers. The cells beneath contain @MAX, @MIN, @VAR, @STD, and @COUNT, which display the results of other calculations.

DATE ARITHMETIC AND A LOGIC FUNCTION

Figure 15.8 shows a spreadsheet that demonstrates some date arithmetic and a logic function. Near the top of the spreadsheet are two dates—11/01/92 and 12/15/92—each of which was previously entered by first pressing Ctrl-Shift-D. Cell C4 calculates the number of days between

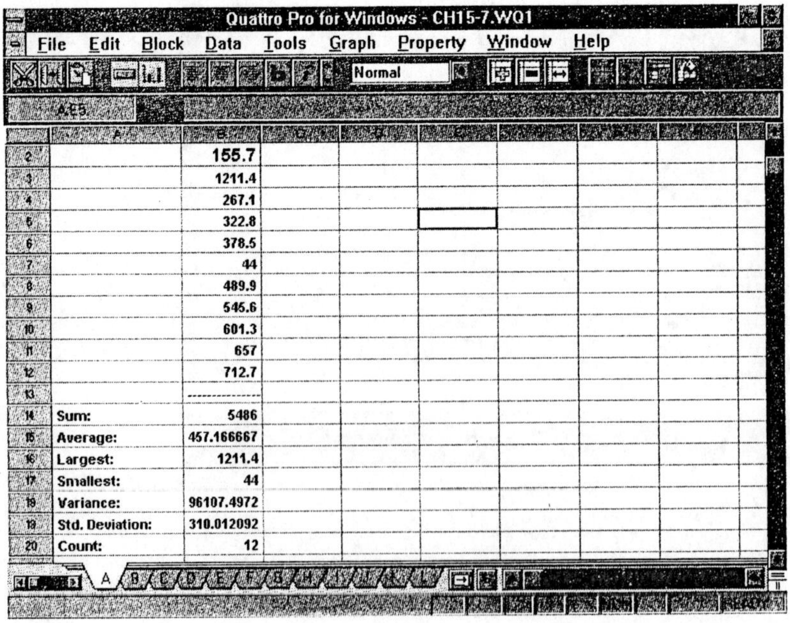

FIGURE 15.7:

Sample counting and aggregation functions

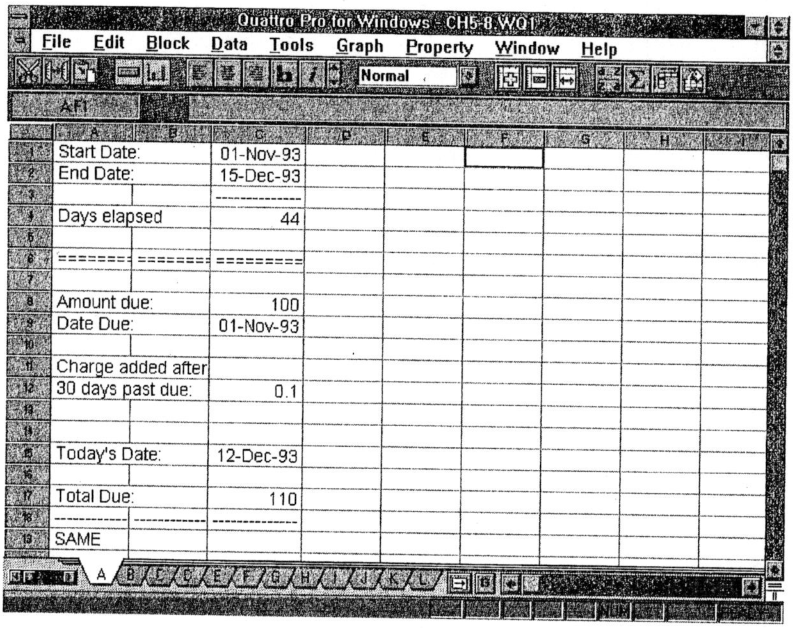

FIGURE 15.8:

Spreadsheet with date arithmetic and a logic function

the two dates by using the formula +C2–C1 to subtract the later date from the earlier date.

The bottom half of the spreadsheet demonstrates the use of the logic function @IF to calculate a payment due, based on whether or not the payment is late. Cell C8 contains 100, the amount due. Cell C9 contains 11/01/92, the due date. Cell C12 contains 0.1, the percent added to the amount due if the payment is not made within 30 days (i.e., a 10 percent late fee). Cell C15 contains the current date, 12/15/92. (Both dates were entered using Ctrl-Shift-D.)

Cell C17 shows 110, the amount due. Note that the spreadsheet has added 10 percent to the amount due because more than 30 days have elapsed. The function @IF(C15–C9<=30,C8,C8*(1+C12)) calculated the amount due. In English, it says, "If the number of days between today and the due date is less than or equal to 30 [C15–C9<=30], then display the amount due [,C8]; otherwise, display the amount due with the appropriate percentage added [,C8*(1+C12)]."

Note that there are equal numbers of open and closed parentheses in the function, as all Quattro Pro formulas and functions require.

If you need to enter a date directly into a function, you cannot use Ctrl-Shift-D. Instead, you must use the @DATE function with the syntax @DATE(*yy,mm,dd*), where *yy* is the year (last two digits), *mm* is the month (1–12), and *dd* is the day.

The function in cell A19, @IF(@DATE(92,12,15)=C2, "Same","Not the same"), shows an example. This formula says: "if @DATE(92,12,15) is equal to the date in cell C2, then display the word 'Same'; otherwise, display 'Not the same.'" As you can see in cell A19, the formula displays **SAME**, indicating that the date 12/15/92, entered into cell C2 with Ctrl-Shift-D, is the same as the date expressed by @DATE(92,12,15).

Solving for X

So far, you've been shown only one way to use a Quattro Pro function: plug in its arguments and let it calculate an answer. There are many times, however, when you'll need to use a function in reverse, to solve for an argument when you know the result.

As you know, the financial function @PMT calculates the monthly payments on a loan, given the principal, interest rate, and time period. But suppose you would rather figure out the *principal*, given a monthly payment plan of your own design. That way, you *know* you'd be able to pay it off. Rather than chance upon the loan amount by trial and error—repeating *what-if* scenarios that haphazardly hit or miss your desired monthly-payment amount—run the @PMT function backwards and solve for it directly.

Figure 15.9 shows a loan-calculation spreadsheet. The function in cell C4 is @PMT(C1,C2/12,C3*12). It says that monthly payments of $438.79 will pay off a loan of $50,000 over 30 years at an interest rate of 10 percent.

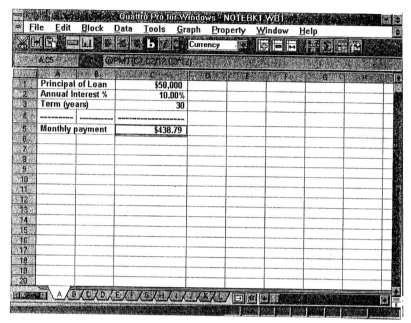

FIGURE 15.9:

A loan-calculation spreadsheet

Now, it so happens that you can afford to part with $700 per month, so you know you are able to take out a larger loan. The question is, how much larger? To calculate the principal of such a loan:

1. Click on Tools to open the menu.

2. From the menu, select the Solve For option. The Solve For dialog box appears, as shown in Figure 15.10.

3. Cell C4 is the formula cell. Enter **C4** into the Formula Cell box.

4. In the Target Value box, enter **700**.

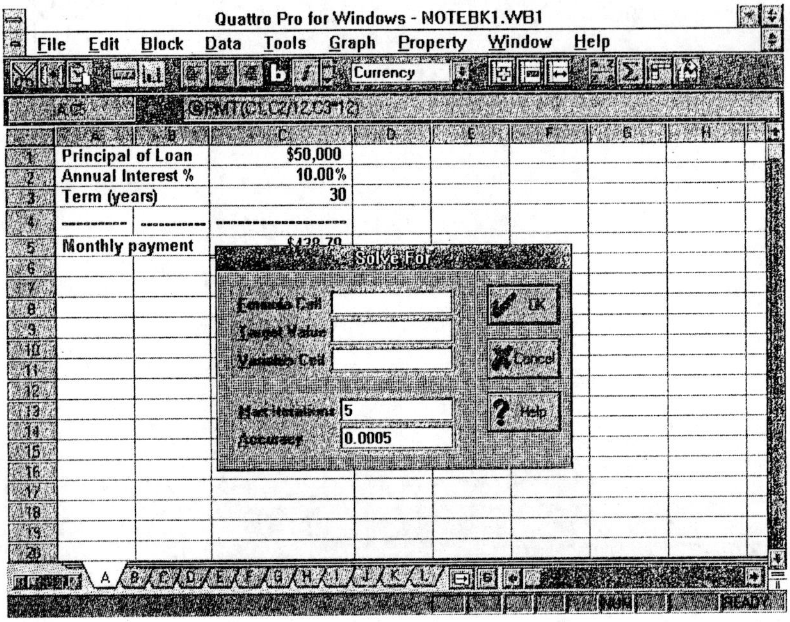

FIGURE 15.10:

The Solve For dialog box

5. The variable cell is the principal, as that is the size of loan that you can comfortably make payments upon. Enter **C1** as the variable cell.

6. Click on OK.

The answer appears immediately in the cell where the principal of $50,000 used to be: the loan you can pay off in monthly installments of $700 over 30 years at 10 percent interest is $79,765.57.

Try another variation of this feature by changing the principal in cell C1 to $100,000, leaving the target value as $700, and solving for the *interest*:

1. Delete the current interest rate in cell C2.

2. Enter 100000 in cell C1. (If the number is too wide to be displayed, click on the Fit button in the SpeedBar.)

3. Select Tools ➤ Solve For.

4. In the Solve For dialog box, enter cell C2 as the variable cell.

The answer appears immediately in cell C2: in order for you to make monthly payments of $700 on a $100,000 loan over 30 years, the rate of interest has to be 7.51 percent.

This Solve For feature can be incorporated into many different situations. You can also refine the calculation if you want. Choose the Max iterations option to specify how many times Quattro Pro should iterate the function it uses to solve for x (1 to 99), and to decide how close to the Target Value it should attempt to get. The default settings should be adequate for most techniques.

The use of functions and formulas to create powerful and flexible spreadsheets is limited only by your creativity and understanding of the functions themselves. Virtually any calculation that can be done in any other manner can be translated into the spreadsheet format.

Installing Quattro
Pro for Windows

To install Quattro Pro for Windows, you must first have installed Windows Version 3.0 or greater. Quattro Pro for Windows needs at least 8 megabytes of free disk space and a minimum of 4 megabytes of RAM.

To install the program:

1. Start Windows on your computer. Usually, this is done by switching to the WINDOWS directory and typing **WIN**.

2. When the Program Manager window appears, click on the Main window.

3. Insert the install disk in drive A.

4. Select File ➤ Run. The Run dialog box appears.

5. In the Command Line field type: **A:\install**. Press Enter or click on OK.

Quattro Pro takes over at this point. You must enter your name and the serial number on the install disk. Follow the messages on the screen to insert the remaining disks. Quattro Pro does give you a choice as to the drive and directory into which you want to install the program. The default is C:\QPW.

Note: If you are using the B drive to install, substitute that letter in the Run dialog box.

Swapping the Mouse Buttons

If you want the right mouse button to be dominant, follow these steps:

1. Go to the Main window and double-click on the Control Panel icon.

2. Double-click on the Mouse icon to open the Mouse dialog box.

3. Click on the Swap Left/Right Buttons box. L and R in the demonstration box change places.

4. Click on OK to close the dialog box.

The buttons are swapped. To make the left button dominant again, repeat the above steps. Happy mousing!

INDEX

Printed in the United States
4342